IMAGINAL POLITICS

New Directions in Critical Theory

NEW DIRECTIONS IN CRITICAL THEORY
Amy Allen, General Editor

New Directions in Critical Theory presents outstanding classic and contemporary texts in the tradition of critical social theory, broadly construed. The series aims to renew and advance the program of critical social theory, with a particular focus on theorizing contemporary struggles around gender, race, sexuality, class, and globalization and their complex interconnections.

Narrating Evil: A Postmetaphysical Theory of Reflective Judgment, María Pía Lara

The Politics of Our Selves: Power, Autonomy, and Gender in Contemporary Critical Theory, Amy Allen

Democracy and the Political Unconscious, Noëlle McAfee

The Force of the Example: Explorations in the Paradigm of Judgment, Alessandro Ferrara

Horrorism: Naming Contemporary Violence, Adriana Cavarero

Scales of Justice: Reimagining Political Space in a Globalizing World, Nancy Fraser

Pathologies of Reason: On the Legacy of Critical Theory, Axel Honneth

States Without Nations: Citizenship for Mortals, Jacqueline Stevens

The Racial Discourses of Life Philosophy: Négritude, Vitalism, and Modernity, Donna V. Jones

Democracy in What State? Giorgio Agamben, Alain Badiou, Daniel Bensaïd, Wendy Brown, Jean-Luc Nancy, Jacques Rancière, Kristin Ross, Slavoj Žižek

Politics of Culture and the Spirit of Critique: Dialogues, edited by Gabriel Rockhill and Alfredo Gomez-Muller

Mute Speech: Literature, Critical Theory, and Politics, Jacques Ranciere

The Right to Justification: Elements of Constructivist Theory of Justice, Rainer Forst

The Scandal of Reason: A Critical Theory of Political Judgment, Albena Azmanova

The Wrath of Capital: Neoliberalism and Climate Change Politics, Adrian Parr

Social Acceleration: A New Theory of Modernity, Hartmut Rosa

The Disclosure of Politics: Struggles Over the Semantics of Secularization, María Pía Lara

Radical Cosmopolitics: The Ethics and Politics of Democratic Universalism, James Ingram

IMAGINAL POLITICS

IMAGES
BEYOND
IMAGINATION
AND THE
IMAGINARY

CHIARA BOTTICI

COLUMBIA UNIVERSITY PRESS   New York

COLUMBIA UNIVERSITY PRESS

PUBLISHERS SINCE 1893

NEW YORK   CHICHESTER, WEST SUSSEX

cup.columbia.edu

Library of Congress Cataloging-in-Publication Data

Bottici, Chiara.

Imaginal politics: images beyond imagination and the imaginary / Chiara Bottici.

pages cm — (New directions in critical theory)

Includes bibliographical references and index.

ISBN 978-0-231-15778-0 (cloth)—ISBN 978-0-231-15779-7 (pbk.)—

ISBN 978-0-231-52781-1 (e-book)

1. Imagination—Political aspects.   2. Imagery (Psychology)—Political aspects.

3. Visualization—Political aspects.   4. Political science—Philosophy.   I. Title.

JA71.B583 2014

320.01'9—dc23

2013030821

COVER IMAGE: © J. R. EYERMAN, TIME & LIFE PICTURES / GETTY IMAGES

BOOK & COVER DESIGN: CHANG JAE LEE

To my parents,
who taught me the power of imagining,
and to my children,
who taught me how to use it.

CONTENTS

ACKNOWLEDGMENTS

It is a hard if not desperate enterprise trying to acknowledge all the intellectual debts that I have acquired in writing this book over more than a decade. Any list would be inevitably incomplete. Instead of a partial list, I will therefore begin by telling an equally partial story of how this book came about. When I was still finishing *A Philosophy of Political Myth*, Benoît Challand, in his usual provocative style, invited me to look beyond myth and try to conceive of politics itself as a "struggle for people's imagination." That seed, planted in the summer of 2003, found fertile terrain, and although it required much longer than he probably would have hoped for, it has now grown into the present work.

An important intermediate step was the workshop entitled "Politics as Struggle for People's Imagination" (25–26 January 2007) that we organized together, thanks to the generous support of Bo Stråth and the History Department of the European University Institute in Florence. I am grateful to all the participants of that event, along with the other contributors to the publication of the volume that followed it, for very lively and stimulating discussions (see our *The Politics of Imagination*, Birkbeck Law Press, Routledge, 2011).

Among the institutions that supported me during this enterprise, I would like to acknowledge the Department of Philosophy of the University of Florence and the Istituto Italiano di Scienze Umane for grating me a five-year fellowship (2004–2009) that assured enough tranquility to embark on an ambitious enterprise. I also thank the Political Philosophy team of the Goethe Universität in Frankfurt and Rainer Forst, who invited me to the city of the "School," where I found an ideal environment to teach and conduct research for this book in 2009–2010.

Finally, I thank my current colleagues at the Philosophy Department of the New School for Social Research, where this book has been completed. I have found here not only an ideal intellectual environment in which to pursue this enterprise but also an atmosphere of friendship and intellectual companionship that is truly unique. In particular, I would like to thank Omri Boehm, for his Kantian insights; Jay Bernstein, for many virtual lectures and for less-virtual philosophical conversations; Zed Adams, for sharing with me his thoughts on the nature of images; James Dodd for his careful phenomenological insights; and Alice Crary for sharing her ideas on feminism and epistemology. Cinzia Arruzza and Dmitri Nikulin must be thanked both for their friendship and for lending me their "ancient" and "modern" erudition. Simon Critchley has been an inspiring colleague and friend on too many occasions to be listed. My deepest thanks to all my colleagues as well as to my students who have also contributed to the development of the ideas presented in this book. For invaluable research assistantship, I wish to thank Veronica Dakota, Ryan Gustafson, Alejandro Quintero, Meghan Robison, Scott Schushan, Elisabeth Suergiu, and Max Tremblay.

Outside of the Philosophy Department, the New School of Social Research has also provided me with an ideal interdisciplinary environment to work out my ideas. Among those with whom I have worked more closely in the past years, I would like to mention Banu Bargu, Andreas Kalyvas, Ross Poole, Janet Roitman, Ann Stoler, Ken Wark, and Jamieson Webster. Nancy Fraser has been an inspirational critical companion, between Philosophy and Political Science.

I am indebted to Laura Bazzicalupo for her commenting on this project along the way and to Elena Pulcini for many philosophical symposia. For reading earlier drafts or parts of the manuscript, my deepest thanks to Amy Allen (editor of this series), Suzi Adams, Omri Boehm, Robin Celikates, Dimitri D'andrea, Furio Cerutti, Costa Douzinas, Roberto Esposito, Alessandro Ferrara, Thomas Hippler, Paul Kottman, Todd May, Cristoph Menke, Rainer Forst, Angela Kühner, Maria Pia Lara, Nicola Marcucci, Alessandro Pizzorno, Elena Pulcini, Armando Salvatore, Camil Ungureanu, Peter Wagner, and Hayden White. Without Dario Squilloni, who guided me through the labyrinth of the imaginal world, this book would not have had its current subject. Simona Forti provided me the generous gift of a careful comment of the entire manuscript along with that, impossible to thank for, of a true friendship. A special thank you to my "critical" colleague and friend Richard Bernstein for his meticulous comments on the first draft of this manuscript as well as for his constant encouragement to continue in this enterprise.

Some chapters of this book have already been published elsewhere. In particular, chapter 7 draws from a joint research project that I conducted with Benoît Challand and whose results have been published in the volume *The Myth of The Clash of Civilizations* (London: Routledge, 2010). I am also indebted to Angela Kühner, with whom I coauthored a paper on the clash of civilizations, which first appeared in a shorter German version under the title "Der Mythos des 'clash of civilizations' zwischen Politischer Philosophie und Psychoanalyse" (published in *Psychoanalyse–interdisziplinär–international–intergenerationell. Festschrift zum 50 Jährigen Bestehen des Sigmund-Freud-Instituts*, edited by Rolf Haubl and Marianne Leuzinger-Bohleber, Vandenhoeck and Ruprecht Verlag, pp. 352–373) and, subsequently, in a longer English version published in *Critical Horizons* (volume 13, no. 1, 2012).

A previous version of chapter 8 has been published with the title "The Politics of Imagination and the Public Role of Religion" in *Philosophy and Social Criticism* (Volume 35, Issue 8, pp. 985–1005, 2009) and in an Italian translation titled "La politica dell'immaginazione ed il nuovo ruolo pubblico della religione" in *Iride* (volume 55, pp. 617-640, 2009). An earlier version of chapter 9 has also appeared elsewhere with the title "Imagining Human Rights: Utopia or Ideology?" in *Law and Critique* (volume 21, no. 2, pp. 111-130). The conclusion contains the development of ideas elaborated in "Black and Red: The Freedom of Equals," published in *The Anarchist Turn*, edited by Jacob Blumenfeld and Simon Critchley, along with me, and forthcoming by Pluto Press. Those thoughts also reflect an ongoing research project with Laura Corradi called Paint It Pink. The publication of this book also benefits of a contribution by the PRIN research project, Biopolitical Governamentality: Inclusion and Happiness, funded by the Italian Ministry of University and Research in 2010-2011 and coordinated by the unit of the Oriental Piedmont University.

Finally, I reserve a special place for Benoît Challand, my companion in life and writing. Without his erudition, this book would have been less rigorous. Without his presence in my life, it would have been much less imaginative. For this, and not only, this book is also dedicated to him.

IMAGINAL POLITICS

Introduction

We often hear that our politicians lack imagination. Indeed, in the current world of global governance, politics seems to have been reduced to simple administration, within a general neoliberal consensus. In such a world there seems to be no space for imagination understood as the radical capacity to envisage things differently and construct alternative political projects. Those who argue that "another world is possible"—to quote a slogan of the new global movements—are easily labeled unrealistic, if not fanatical, and thus are excluded from the spectrum of viable political options.[1]

Deprived of imagination, the political world we live in is, nonetheless, full of images. One only has to think of the role of the media in our political life. If we compare the activity that we described as politics a few centuries ago with the politics of today, we cannot but perceive a fundamental change. Politics was once the activity that concerned a few elites (the rulers), with whom ordinary people had almost no visual contact in the course of their life. By contrast, today's rulers are constantly in front of us: their images dominate our screens, nourishing, soliciting, and perhaps even saturating our imagination. Democratization and mediatization brought about a deep revolution in the nature of politics itself, so much so that it has become inseparable from the flow of images entering the homes of billions of spectators around the globe daily.

This phenomenon is perhaps most observable in the current global resurgence of religion and identity politics. If new social movements pushing for an alternative globalization have been an attempt to rekindle the political imagination, 9/11 has precipitated a veritable explosion. We now live in a globalizing world which, despite having eliminated geographical distances between peoples, has nevertheless also fostered internal divisions in the form of a spectacular separation between "us" and "them" (Bottici and Challand 2010). As the myth of a clash between civilizations unfolded, a new struggle for people's imaginations began: terrorists have been imagined everywhere, thus justifying restrictions of fundamental civic liberties and more freedom for military enterprises. In turn, the exportation of the "war on terror" abroad, with all the casualties it has brought about, has further fomented negative representations of the "West," stirring up hate and fanaticism. All this has not simply increased the power of images, but is substantial to them, as images themselves have become weapons.[2]

Paradoxically, though, in the epoch of the global village, initiated by the diffusion of media on an international scale, we often lack the most relevant information about others and even about ourselves. To paraphrase Susan Buck-Morss (2003:3), we have become a "media-saturated but still information-starved public." Global images are selected by the golden rule of the audience: what "makes news" is only the image that captures the public's imagination. The result is that spectacle prevails over content. We are inundated by images that toy with our emotions and move our imagination, but do not often convey even the most basic and relevant information. Guy Debord's prophecy of a society of the spectacle (Debord 1994) has been fulfilled. The world is no longer just an immense collection of commodities. It has become a collection of spectacles.

However, globalization has brought this process to a new level, which questions some of Debord's assumptions. Today's society of the spectacle is *global* not only because it has annihilated geographical distance but also because it is increasingly difficult to counterpoise it to the reality of facts, as Debord could still do (or, at least, thought he could do). Virtual images are no longer simply commoditized objects reproduced on an industrial scale;[3] they have become processes in need of a perpetual maintenance. More than their authenticity has been lost: the very possibility of locating reality has vanished. Indeed, in the contemporary society of the spectacle, the virtual risks becoming most real.

We are now so accustomed to this condition that it does not come as a surprise to hear that soon after 9/11 videotapes went on sale in China showing the horrific highlights spliced together with scenes from Hollywood disaster movies (Buruma and Margalit 2004:13). The real thing—two flaming skyscrapers collapsing on thousands of people—was not enough: only the veneer of Hollywood imagination could capture the flavor of such catastrophes. The status of reality of the images thus assembled did not matter. We needed a global spectacle and only Hollywood could offer it.

How do we account for the paradox of a world full of images, but deprived of imagination? Have images themselves saturated our political imagination? What has politics become after such a revolution? The aim of this book is to tackle these questions by rethinking the connection between politics and our capacity to imagine. Its fundamental hypothesis is that there is a link between the indiscriminate proliferation of images and the crisis of political imagination understood as the radical capacity to start something new.

To begin, it is important to point out that defining the imagination as simply the faculty to represent what does not exist—the unreal—is inadequate. Such a definition implies that the imagination is relevant only to aesthetic or utopian domains. This view acquired momentum around the eighteenth century, when, as a consequence of the triumph of modern science, imagination was seen as a potential threat to the methodical work of reason and thus was more comfortably placed within the newly constituted field of aesthetics (Friese 2001:7197; Vattimo 1999b:529). This remains a very influential view, not least because it is conveyed by common usage, for example, in expressions describing something as "the fruit of your imagination." However, that is a fundamentally misleading view, because the notion of reality is not an a priori of human understanding that can be defined once and for all and thus used to determine what is purely imaginary and what is not.[1]

Too often, we forget that the definition of reality changes considerably from one context to another. As we will see in more detail in the course of this book, it is significant that the Greeks and the Romans did not even have a word to designate what we today call reality. The term *realitas* was coined relatively recently in history, in late Scholasticism (Abbagnano 1961:733). According to a certain tradition dating back to Duns Scotus, the term denoted every individuality or *haecceitas*. By contrast, for a long time, the prevailing meaning in Scholastic philosophy has been that of *formalitas* or *essentia*, which makes each thing out to be what it is and thus was used to denote the opposite of what we usually understand by reality in common language. Precisely because medieval Scholastic philosophy conceived of *realitas* primarily in reference to the essence (*essentia*) of each *res*, the term *realitas* was used as a synonym for perfection (Courtine 1992a, 1992b; Hoffmann et al. 1992). This explains why God could be called the most real being (*ens realissimus*) and why the real was not opposed to what is purely fictitious (*fictum*) or a mental being (*ens rationis*)—a view that is still echoed in some early modern usages. While a philosopher such as Spinoza, in line with medieval philosophy, could still define *realitas* as perfection,[5] since at least Kant we have come to conceive of it primarily as what accords with the material conditions of experience and therefore also exists outside of our mind (Bottici 2007:64–65; Courtine 1992b:189). Moreover, as we will see in more detail in chapter 1, it is precisely when this view of reality as opposed to the fictitious (*fictum*) became hegemonic that imagination and fantasy started to be systematically associated with the unreal.

However, within the history of Western philosophy there is also another and much broader view of imagination, going as far back as Aristotle, which has recently been recovered by different authors. In this view, imagination is more than mere fantasy: it is the capacity to produce images in the most general sense of the term, independently of whether or not what they represent actually exists; in this view, imagination includes the capacity to represent what does not exist, but it is also not limited to this. It is a much more radical view, in that it includes the production of images of both existing and nonexisting objects. In terms used by Cornelius Castoriadis (1987:336–337), it is the radical faculty to produce images in the sense of *Bilder*, without which there would not be any thought at all.

No other author has stressed the radical character of imagination more systematically than Castoriadis. In his view, imagination is radical in the double sense that, without it, there could not be any reality as such and that it can always potentially question its objects by disclosing possible alternatives (Castoriadis 1987, 1991). Otherwise said, it is radical both politically and ontologically or, even better, it is politically radical because it is ontologically so. His view combines Aristotle with the Kantian insight that imagination is the transcendental faculty of synthesis par excellence in that it is able to unify the manifold into a single image. However, his view also goes well beyond Kant, not only because, as we will see, Kant retreats from this discovery and subsequently relegates imagination to a more intermediary role between intuition and intellect (Arnason 1994; Heidegger 1997; Rundell 1994a, 1994b) but also because Castoriadis does not conceive of imagination as a merely individual faculty.[6] Recovering the insights of psychoanalysis, which has shown that the individual is created through a process of socialization by the imaginary significations of society, Castoriadis argues that we are immersed in the social imaginary in which we have grown up. By emphasizing the importance of social context in shaping the free imagination of individuals, he overcomes the limits of the Kantian approach and the philosophy of the subject that it presupposes.

However, by overly emphasizing the role of social contexts, one risks exchanging a problematic philosophy of the subject for an equally problematic metaphysics of the context. Although Castoriadis is ambivalent on this point, he speaks at times of an "absolute scission" between the two poles of the instituted and instituting social imaginary: the social-historical, on the one hand, and what he calls the "psyche" or "psychical monad," on the other (see, for instance, Castoriadis 1987:204ff). The psyche is said to be monadic because it is "pure representational/affective/intentional flux," indeterminate, and, in principle, unmasterable. Drawing inspiration from his own experience as a psychoanalyst, Castoriadis argues that the process of socialization is always violent and incomplete precisely because of the original unmasterable nature of the psyche. Through socialization, the psyche is forced to give up its initial objects and to invest in socially instituted objects, rules, and the world. As a consequence, it is only through such an internalization of the world, and of the social imaginary significations, that an "individual," properly speaking, is created out of a "screaming monster" (Castoriadis 1991:148).

As some have noted, Castoriadis's thesis about the monadic isolation and fundamental "hetereogeneity" between the psyche and society leads to a highly problematic, and thus untenable, metaphysical opposition (Habermas 1987:327). Once we find ourselves within the monadic isolation of the unconscious, it becomes difficult even to explain how communication is possible in the first place (Whitebook 1989).[7] Castoriadis's problematic metaphysical opposition is the sign of a deeper philosophical problem: if one starts with "imagination," conceived as an individual faculty, then the problem is how to account for the at times overwhelming influence of the social context. If we begin with the concept of the "social imaginary," then the problem is how to reconcile it with the free imagination of individuals. The problem seems unsolvable, and Castoriadis's impasse is the sign that there is no easy way out.

Following the insights of the recent French debate, I propose a theory of the imaginal as the conceptual tool best adapted to overcome such an impasse. *Imaginal* means simply that which is made of images and can therefore be the product both of an individual faculty and of the social context as well as of a complex interaction between the two. The imaginal is a concept that has recently been recovered from a Muslim Sufi philosophical tradition (Corbin 1979) and proposed as a third possibility between theories of imagination and theories of the imaginary (Fleury 2006). In contrast to imagination and imaginary, the concept of the imaginal emphasizes the centrality of images, rather than the faculty or the context that produces them; therefore, it does not make any assumptions about the individual or social character of such a faculty.

Although the term has been attributed to Arabic philosophy, it was originally a Latin term. Imaginal, from the Latin *imaginalis*, denotes something that is made of images. In the current context, developing the concept means embarking on a double Copernican revolution: beyond the philosophy of the subject (imagination as an individual faculty), but also beyond the equally problematic metaphysics of the context (the imaginary as a given social context). The starting point is neither a subject separated from the world nor a world independent from the subject, but simply images. The reason why this is a better starting point is easy to understand: without images, there can be neither a world for us nor a subject for the world. In short, human beings are not only rational animals but also, and even prior to that, imaginal animals.

This is because images, understood as pictorial (re)presentations, enjoy a primacy vis-à vis language and argumentative thinking.[8] As we will see, images emerge before language and contain a surplus of meaning that cannot often be rendered through linguistic descriptions. Thus not only do images appear before language, but they are also at times impossible to translate into words. Indeed, it is a common experience that there are images that cannot be fully put into linguistic descriptions, either because descriptions risk being incomplete or because they may turn into a betrayal of the images. This holds particularly for symbolic images, which exceed our linguistic capacity because the latter is inadequate to render the ambivalent nature of such images: once a symbol is interpreted and thus fixed into a series of linguistic descriptions, it is also somehow interpreted away, as it ceases to display its full multiplicity of meanings.

The emphasis it places on images is precisely what distinguishes the concept of the imaginal from other philosophical traditions that have also tried to find a way to mediate the individual and the social. From the Hegelian notion of the spirit to the phenomenological notion of lifeworld or the Wittgensteinian concept of life-forms, numerous attempts have tried to bridge the gap between the social and the individual, by pointing to a space that lies in between the two. Jürgen Habermas's recovery of George Herbert Mead's intersubjective model, according to which individuation takes place through socialization, can be seen as one of the latest attempts to do so.[9] But none of these philosophical traditions has really focused on the primacy of images as here defined: in all these approaches, images play a crucial role but as part of a linguistically mediated process of socialization. By contrast, the notion of the imaginal focuses on images not only within but also before language.[10]

Thus, the imaginal helps overcome the tension between the social and the individual because it can be the product both of an individual faculty and of a social context as well as the result of an interaction between the two. With regard to the influence of contexts on the free imagination of individuals, the concept of the imaginal is meant to signal the fact that there are different possibilities that go from the freedom of individuals to its erosion in oppressive social imaginaries. Of course, the spectrum has its extremes, but in the middle of it there are many intermediate variants. The imaginal can be understood as a field of possibilities. Yet it is far from being an empty concept: it tells us two important things. First, the human capacity to form images is crucial, and its role must be accounted for. Second, even within a particularly oppressive social imaginary, there is always the possibility for the free imagination of individuals to emerge.

Furthermore, in contrast to the imaginary, which is often associated with the unreal and fictitious in common language, the concept of the imaginal does not make any assumptions as to the reality of the images that compose it. This is particularly clear in the English language, where *imaginal*, according to the *Oxford English Dictionary*, denotes primarily what pertains to imagination or to mental images, whereas *imaginary* primarily means what exists only in fancy and has no real existence and is opposed to *real* or *actual*. The concept of the imaginal, therefore, comes before the distinction between real and fictitious; thus it is particularly adapted to an epoch in which we may be witnessing a change in the hegemonic understanding of reality itself. The imaginal also differs from "imaginative," which, as its etymology points out (*imaginatus*, "imagined"), denotes either the quality of a person endowed with the individual faculty of imagination or an act of imagining that has already taken place.[11] Put in a nutshell, whereas the imaginative is the result of the work of imagination, the imaginal is the medium where such work takes place.

In sum, the aim of this book is to analyze the relationship between politics and our capacity to image, and to do so through a theory of the imaginal. The reason why such an enterprise is important today for critical theory is twofold. On the one hand, as I have already suggested, our capacity to form images is playing an increasing (though ambivalent) role in contemporary politics. As a consequence of the key position that this capacity has acquired in the new economy and media industries—its incorporation in both the processes of production and consumption of commodities (Marazzi 1994)—the imaginal has an unprecedented chance to influence social life and, hence, also politics. On the other hand, we remain ill equipped to face this new challenge. On a philosophical level, the amount of work done on the concept of imagination/imaginary/imaginal is still minimal when compared with the work focusing on reason/rationality/reasonable. Thus there are reasons to suspect that, particularly today, in the conditions of a global society of the spectacle, a more vigorous engagement with the problem of the conditions for a "public imaginal" would be particularly welcome.

Furthermore, not enough work has been done to explore systematically the nexus of politics and our capacity to produce images.[12] Among the philosophers who recovered the Kantian view of imagination and explored its political implications, Hannah Arendt should be remembered. In her *Lectures on Kant's Political Philosophy* she tried to show the crucial role that imagination plays in politics, particularly by virtue of its capacity to strip us of our particularities and thus put ourselves in the shoes of others (Arendt 1982). Nevertheless, her project remained unfinished at the time of her death, so we are left with only a few suggestions in this direction rather than a fully fledged theory.[13] Furthermore, her reliance on Kant makes us suspect that she would not have focused on the ambivalence of imagination—the fact that, as Slavoj Žižek has recently argued, imagination is not only the faculty of synthesis, of putting things together, but also that of madness, of tearing apart pieces of the whole (Žižek 1999b:28–38).

Together with the ambivalence of imagination, Arendt tends also to overlook the social dimension of our capacity to form images. As mentioned earlier, theories inspired by psychoanalysis have pointed out that there is not an autonomous, pregiven subject, since this is the result of a long process of socialization that begins very early, with the first encounters with language. In their conjunction of psychoanalysis and Marxism toward a critique of ideology, different authors of the Frankfurt School have pointed to the political nature of imagination by emphasizing the role that society as a whole exercises in the creation of compliant subjects. However, most of them remained linked to the Freudian view of imagination as fantasy. As Castoriadis notes, although fundamental insights can be derived from Freud as to the nature of imagination, it is a fact that he almost never uses the term (*Einbildungskraft*), preferring instead the misleading term *fantasy* (Castoriadis 1997a:292). As a consequence, in Freud's system, imagination as the capacity to produce images in the most general sense of the term is occulted by fantasy, understood as the representation of what is not immediately present.

This is also largely the case with Herbert Marcuse: he emphasized how, in late capitalistic societies, which create compliant one-dimensional human beings through the manipulation of their needs, the aesthetic imagination unfolds the possibility of freedom (Marcuse 1991:chapter 10). Imagination is here mainly the faculty to represent what does not exist; therefore it is also systematically associated with utopia (Marcuse 1974:141–158). Not by chance, Marcuse, who remains very much linked to Freudian vocabulary on this point, uses imagination and fantasy interchangeably, as if they were one and the same thing (Marcuse 1974:141). This, as we will see, is a misleading or at least an incomplete view.

To help us deal most productively with the problem under discussion here, one can turn to Jacques Lacan and his development of the insights of Freud and psychoanalysis. With his emphasis on language in the socialization of individuals, Lacan went far beyond the idea of imagination as an individual faculty—a break signaled by the new role the concept of the imaginary plays in his theory. In Lacan's view, the Imaginary, together with the Real and the Symbolic, constitutes one of the three fundamental registers. The domain of the Imaginary has its roots in the mirror phase, when the infant not only recognizes himself in the specular image in front of him but also perceives the discrepancy between his fragmented body (over which he has no command) and the unitary image with which he identifies himself. However, such an identification with the specular image is not only a child's experience: the ego itself is formed through the identification with the specular image so that the Imaginary, together with the Real and the Symbolic, comes to be constitutive of the human psyche as such. While in the Imaginary the subject is permanently caught by his own image, the Symbolic order presents itself to the subject as the big Other, the Law, which is counterpoised to the Real (the latter is a sort of limit-concept for what cannot be symbolized and is therefore outside of language).[14]

According to Žižek—the author who has perhaps most vigorously recovered and developed Lacan's insights in terms of contemporary debates—the Imaginary is by definition the place of alienation.[15] Although this does not mean that the Imaginary is simply illusory (Lacan 1999:1:348), as the locus of alienation it is contrasted with the Real. In this perspective therefore, the imaginary is once again primarily associated with the unreal, although in a much more refined understanding of the real and the imaginary, respectively. But if the imaginary is the place of alienation and distinguished from the real, by definition, it becomes difficult to account for the possibility that the imaginary is itself constitutive of the real, which is the hypothesis that we want to test in this work.

Instead of using the notion of the imaginary, which in both common language and philosophical debates is often associated with alienation and unreality, I will explore the potential of the notion of the imaginal. In the contemporary world of virtual reality, it can be problematic to juxtapose the real and the imaginary simply because the latter may well turn out to have become what is most real. Hence the usefulness of a third perspective, that of the imaginal, which looks at the role of images rather than the faculty or the context that constitutes them. In Cynthia Fleury's usage the concept points only to the fact that between the world of sensibility and that of the intellect there is a third possibility, that of the imaginal (Fleury 2006). Although her perspective is helpful to point out that there is a *tertium* between imagination and the imaginary, she does not fully explore the consequences of such a view, in particular, its political implications, which are, by contrast, at the very center of this book.

All the aforementioned perspectives contain important insights regarding the nexus between politics and our capacity to produce images. Yet, for the reasons elucidated, they all present some limits that make them not particularly suited to the current context. A new direction is needed in critical theory, one that focuses more systematically on the relationship between politics and our capacity to imagine as well as on the contemporary transformations of such a nexus. To contribute to this enterprise, I will proceed here in three fundamental steps. Part 1 explores the philosophical dilemmas characterizing theories of imagination as an individual faculty and the theory of the imaginary as a social context (chapter 1, 2) and proposes a theory of the imaginal as the conceptual tool best suited to overcoming them (chapter 3). In this way, the foundations are laid for a theory of the imaginal that will constitute the guiding thread of subsequent arguments. For those who do not particularly like philology and the history of philosophy, I suggest skipping the first two chapters and beginning with chapter 3.

Part 2 investigates the role that the imaginal plays in politics, both when we understand politics in the most general sense of what pertains to the public and when we look at it as a particular part of public life, one that is characterized by the potential recourse to legitimate physical coercion. Chapter 4 traces a genealogy of politics, identifying two big ruptures within it and thus enabling us to identify a very broad and a very restricted meaning as well as the implication of its biopolitical turn. Of course, there are many different understandings of politics, so many so that one can legitimately claim that all political thinkers have given their own definition. Yet all of them move within a spectrum, at the extremes of which there is a very broad definition (politics as whatever pertains to the public) and a very limited one (politics as that part of public life characterized by the threat of recourse to legitimate physical coercion). Using these two extremes, chapter 5 argues that politics in the first sense depends on the imaginal, because it is only through the help of unifying images that a public can exist, while it also shows that politics in the second sense also depends on the imaginal because all the sources of legitimacy (legal-rational, traditional, and charismatic, according to Max Weber's classical typology) tend to rely on our capacity to form images in one way or another.

The subsequent step consists in exploring the contemporary transformations of the nexus of the imaginal and the political by arguing that there has been both a quantitative and a qualitative change in the nature of the imaginal, one profoundly affecting the nature of politics itself. Chapter 6 shows that the quantitative increase causes a tendency toward the spectacularization of politics, whereas the qualitative change implies an increasing virtualization.

Finally, part 3 shows how the theory developed in this book can cast light on peculiar features of contemporary politics and its search for legitimacy within a global spectacle. By recovering Max Weber's typology of the sources of legitimacy, but also adding the conservative reproduction of life as a fourth one (brought onto the scene by the biopolitical turn), it shows why all of them are greatly affected by the transformations of the nexus between the political and the imaginal described in this book. Chapter 7 dwells on the way in which the spectacularization and virtualization of politics affects the search for legitimacy in a more or less invented tradition (what I call the "politics of the past"), whereas chapter 8 explores the imaginal consequences of the repositioning of religion in the public sphere. Finally, chapter 9 analyzes the transformation of the legal-rational grounds of legitimacy by disentangling the paradoxes of the contemporary triumph of human rights discourses.

In sum, this book shows that politics has always been imaginal because we cannot think of politics without imagining a public and a claim to legitimacy. To a great extent, political philosophy has overlooked the importance of this entanglement. We can no longer keep neglecting it because globalization has taken it to a point of no return: the role of images in contemporary politics is such that they no longer simply mediate our doing politics, but now they risk doing politics in our stead.

PART 1

IMAGINING

For philology is that venerable art which demands of its votaries one thing above all: to go aside, to take time, to become still, to become slow—it is a goldsmith's art and connoisseurship of the word which has nothing but delicate, cautious work to do and achieves nothing if it does not achieve it *lento*.

FRIEDRICH NIETZSCHE, *Daybreak*

In common language, the terms *imagination* and *imaginary* are usually associated with the unreal. This can be clearly seen in common expressions, such as: "this is the product of your imagination" or "this is purely imaginary." Faced with such usages, philosophy can reply with a shrug and look for more complex meanings elsewhere by searching for illustrious antecedents in the history of ideas or by attempting to construct a different transcendental perspective. However, whether one tries to bring back the wheel of history through old authorities or attempts the transcendental leap, the result is the same: in either case, we appear abstruse because we go against common sense. One can avoid both roads and instead embrace common usage, adopting a purely analytical approach. Nevertheless, this approach also has its flaws: one is very likely to be understood by one's own epoch, but is also likely to remain imprisoned within it.

The road that I would like to take here is a third one. I will avoid the presumptuous shrug and accept the common usage of these terms, but only as a starting point from which to embark on a genealogical critique aimed at disentangling them.[1] Following Nietzsche, I do not understand the genealogical method as reconstruction of a more or less linear historical path.[2] I am not interested here in historical continuities, nor in faithfully reconstructing the thought of some illustrious theorists of imagination. By contrast, I want to identify conceptual breaks and major ruptures and then look for the underlying interests that have sustained them. In this way it should be possible, if not to transcend our epoch, at least to clarify the forces that may lead to its possible overcoming. To this end, as we will see, a few fragmentary texts will at times be more revealing than lengthy discussions of imagination.

In this enterprise I will largely rely on philology and philologists. A philologist, like an archaeologist, goes in search of more or less fragmentary relicts of the past, and apparently insignificant details can at times be more enlightening than grandiose edifices. As Nietzsche observes in the passage quoted in the epigraph to part I, philology is a "goldsmith's art and connoisseurship of the words," an art that requires great caution (Nietzsche 1982:5). This is the reason why it cannot reach anything if it does not reach it *lento*, through delicate, slow work. By focusing on the unhurried and at times almost imperceptible conceptual moves that crystallize in the usage of words, I will try to emphasize the major conceptual breaks within the genealogy of "imagination." The underlying assumption of this method is that behind the birth of a new word (or of a new usage of old words) there is a deeper philosophical rupture. Creating new words or using old ones in a different way is the result of these breaks. We coin new words or start using them in a different way when the vocabulary that is available to us no longer suffices. It is such an insufficiency that lies at the heart of major conceptual breaks, and the task of philology, as genealogy, is precisely to reconstruct them in order to destabilize our confidence.[3] Following the traces left within the language of "imagination," I will thus first reconstruct the philosophical ruptures that lie behind the concept of imagination (chapter 1) that have led to the coining of an alternative word, the *imaginary* (chapter 2). By assessing the problems left over by those conceptual moves, I will argue that the concept of the imaginal is a promising tool to overcome them (chapter 3).

From *Phantasia* to Imagination

There's nothing more deprived of fantasy than Kant's transcendental imagination.

CORNELIUS CASTORIADIS, *The Discovery of the Imagination*

Imagination derives from *imaginatio,* the Latin term used to translate the Greek *phantasia.* Let us start by considering the latter. If we analyze the list of occurrences of the term *phantasia,*[1] we can immediately see that, besides a few disparate fragments and testimonies,[2] the first authors for whom we can speak of a fully fledged theory of *phantasia* are Plato and Aristotle. This may be the result of the fact that these are the only works that were transmitted to us, and a series of different contingencies could have given us different authors, perhaps even different theories.[3] But for the purposes of a genealogy of imagination, as it has been recorded in relics of our past, it is sufficient to underscore that the view of *phantasia* that emerges from certain passages of both Plato and Aristotle contrasts sharply with the view of imagination as unreal that is encapsulated in today's common usage.[4] It is to the reconstruction of such a contrast between the Greek *phantasia* and the modern *imagination* that this chapter is devoted.

In the *Sophist* Plato presents his view of imagination in the course of an attempt to define a sophist, the sort of expert in the art of rhetoric that emerged in Ancient Greece around the fifth century BCE. In this dialogue the sophist is represented as a troublemaking creature, often speaking merely for the sake of forensic victory. When it comes to the sophist, we must therefore be aware of the possibility of deception. Once we grant such a possibility, Plato observes, "everything will of necessity be full of images and likeness and *phantasia*" (260c). Although for a contemporary reader this may seem to allude to our common usage of the term, Plato is here far from systematically associating *phantasia* with falsity, as we tend to do.[5] *Phantasia* is not necessarily false, but shares the possibility of falsity with both discourse (*logos*) and opinion (*doxa*). As he puts it, "thinking (*dianoia*) and opinion (*doxa*) and *phantasia* all these occur in our soul as true and false" (263d). *Phantasia* can therefore be both true and false, like thinking and opinion. How, then, are we to distinguish between them? Thinking (*dianoia*) here is actually the same as discourse (*logos*), but one can distinguish between them because thinking is the inward dialogue carried on by the soul with itself without spoken sounds, whereas discourse is the current that comes from the soul through the mouth in vocal form (263e). In all of them, assertion and denial can take place—hence the possibility of falsity. When assertion and denial take place in the soul in the course of silent thinking, it is called opinion (*doxa*). When judgment occurs by means of sensation (*diaistheseos*) it is called *phantasia* (264a). For Plato, then, *phantasia* is a mixture of sensation (*aisthesis*) and opinion or judgment (*doxa*), and as such it can be both true and false.[6]

It is well known that Plato's attitude toward forms of judgment or opinion based on sensation is usually negative. In the *Timaeus*, for instance, he distinguishes between the unchanging world, which is eternal, and the changing world, which is subject to becoming (27d–29b). We can have access to the first only by intellection and through reasoning, since such an unchanging world of ideas is translucent to the intellect. The second world is only "like" the first insofar as it is modeled on it. This is the sensible world of becoming which is the object of judgment or opinion (*doxa*) accompanied by sensation (*aisthesis*), which is *alogos*, unreasoning. Since the sensible world is only "like" the first, an image of it, the accounts that we can give of it are equally only "like" the unchanging world. It is therefore clear that, according to this view, the highest form of knowledge is that which can be obtained through the contemplation of the eternal and unchanging world of ideas (*eidos*),[7] but it is equally clear that the opinion based on sensation (*doxa* with *aisthesis*) is also a form of knowledge. Although Plato does not explicitly use the term *phantasia* in this passage, he is clearly referring to it, according to the definition he gave in the *Sophist*. Plato's *phantasia* is therefore associated with *aisthesis* and thus fixed in the world of appearances. Yet we should emphasize that it is a genuine form of knowledge, as he also explicitly says in the *Theaetetus* where, after associating *phantasia* and *aisthesis* with the verb *phainesthai*, "to appear," he observes that "there is *aisthesis* only of what really is" and that this (*aesthesis* of what really *is*) is *episteme*, the word that Plato uses for knowledge (*Theaetetus* 152c).[8] To conclude on this point, the general metaphysics

I have described, which many associate with Plato's theory of ideas, cannot but lead to a skeptical attitude toward any form of appearances rooted in sensation. Nevertheless, the passage from the *Sophist* just quoted shows that Plato does not systematically associate *phantasia* with falsity and unreality, since the latter shares the possibility of falsity with the *logos* itself.

Aristotle, too, roots *phantasia* in sensation. Though the influence of his master is clear,[9] Aristotle goes much further in describing the role that *phantasia* plays in the different spheres of human life by devoting a more systematic attention to it. As has been observed, this is probably due to the fact that Aristotle too believes that true reasoning is the manipulation of pure ideas, but the latter are not for him derived from a supersensible realm, either by direct intuition or through the soul's reminiscence of the ideas it knew before its incarnation (Cocking 1991:18). Aristotle's ideas are derived from the sensible world. Images, therefore, become an essential intermediary between perception and conception (18). Certainly for Aristotle, as for Plato, the best thinking rises *above* images, as it were, but, in contrast to him, can only do so by rising *through* them (18). As he puts it in a famous passage from *De Anima*: "Since it seems that there is nothing outside and separate in existence from sensible spatial magnitudes, the objects of thought are in the sensible forms, viz. both the abstract objects and all the states and affections of sensible things. Hence no one can learn or understand anything in the absence of sense, and when the mind is actively aware of anything it is necessarily aware of it along with an image (*phantasma*); for images (*phantasmata*) are like sensuous contents except in that they contain no matter" (*De Anima* 432a).

The passage deserves a close, attentive reading. Here Aristotle puts forward his (much debated) claim that the mind cannot think without an image or a phantasm (*phantasma*).[10] And, unsurprisingly, it is in this work that Aristotle provides the fullest account of *phantasia*.[11] But what does it mean to say that the soul cannot think without a phantasm? What is *phantasia* and what are the *phantasmata* that it produces? In another passage from the same work, Aristotle defines *phantasia* as "a movement (*kinesis*) produced by a sensation actively operating" and associates it with the root word *light* (*phaos*) by arguing that without light it is impossible to see (*De Anima* 429a). *Phantasia* enables us to produce images that transform all the various bits of our perception (what he calls special sensibles) into a total sensation, a fully fledged appearance.[12] In this sense, *phantasia* appears to be endowed with a peculiar power of unification that explains the very possibility of sense perception. As Aristotle puts it in another work, this is so because "it can make one image (*phantasma*) from many" (*De Memoria* 434a 9–10). We see here an elaborated theory of *phantasia* that goes beyond Plato's scattered references to it: for Aristotle, whenever we think we do so along with an image, since without the unifying power of *phantasia* we could not have perception in the first place, but rather unrelated sensory inputs—a shape, a color, but not yet a brown table.

But images (*phantasmata*) do not only operate during sensation. Precisely because of their constitutive role, they continue to operate even when the perception no longer takes place, so much so that, as we have seen, Aristotle can say that, whenever the mind is actively aware of something, this awareness is always accompanied by an image (*phantasma*). To put it bluntly, *phantasmata* are not phantoms or specters. They are simple images without which even our most elementary mental operations would be impossible. Here the distance between our *fantasy* and the Greek *phantasia* begins to emerge.

This also explains why *phantasia* could be accorded by Aristotle such a crucial role both for cognition and for action. As an ability to produce images (*phantasmata*; De Anima 428a 1-2), *phantasia* transforms isolated and disconnected perceptive inputs into more or less coherent sensations (*De Anima* 428b 18-30). Furthermore, since those images continue to reverberate in us afterward, *phantasia* is also the basis of appetite, which is a form of movement for Aristotle (*De Anima* 433b 29).[13] As he succinctly says, "There is no desiring without *phantasia*" (*De Anima* 433b 29). As a consequence, *phantasia* has both a crucial cognitive and practical role, because without it no account of desiring and thus of action would be possible.

Aristotle returns to this aspect of *phantasia* in places other than the *De Anima*. In particular, a crucial passage from *De Motu Animalium* develops a theory of action as based on *phantasia* by observing that animals who can move become aware of the object of their appetite both when this object is (re)presented through the senses alone and when it is (re)presented in thought (*De Motu Animalium* 701b 34–702a).[14] *Phantasia* thus becomes a necessary ingredient of action on account of its capacity to produce emotionally laden images—a point that also emerges in the *Rhetoric*'s treatment of passions, where Aristotle points out that *phantasia* (again defined as a kind of weak perception) generates emotions (*Rhetorica* 1370a, 1378b).

According to Aristotle, there is a strict connection between *phantasia*, desire (*orexis*), and action.[15] This explains how action is possible, since no purposive motion toward an intentional object could take place without such a combination: if *phantasia* is that interpretative element in perception by virtue of which things in the world "appear" (*phainetai*) to us as certain sorts of things rather than others, then its operation is necessary in order to arouse a specific desire for the thing that generates action itself. Summing up the discussion until now, we find that far from systematically associating *phantasia* with unreality or even falsity, Aristotle sees in it a crucial ingredient of our normal and ordinary mental life.

Aristotle is certainly aware of the potentially negative force of *phantasia*, as is clear in his analysis of melancholia. In his view, the melancholic is somebody who acts without deliberation under the pressure of very intense desires generated by his excessive *phantasia* (*Ethica Nicomachea* VII 8, 1150b 19–28; 15, 1154b 11–12). In this case, the excess of "dark humor" in the body produces movements of imagination that, especially in dreams, can generate monstrous and disordered visions (*De Insomniis* 3, 461a 22; *De Divinatione per Somnum* 2, 463b 17). In its extreme manifestations, this physiological excess can lead to severe depression and even folly.

This excess prevents the melancholic from exercising that temperate and deliberating power of *phantasia* that Aristotle calls *phantasia bouleutike* (*De Anima* III, 434a 6–7). The concept of a *phantasia bouleutike*, literally "deliberative imagination," deserves further attention. The expression designates the capacity to produce and compare the various images (*phantasmata*) with one another.[16] The general idea is that, in order to deliberate upon our actions, we need to calculate future things and compare them with present ones and that we do this precisely through images and thoughts of them (*De Anima* III, 7, 431b 7–10). Aristotle seems to be thinking of operations of breaking down and combining images (*phantasmata*), not dissimilar to those mental acts involved in imagining and constructing geometrical figures (Cattanei 2008:50–51). Calculating our future in relation to our present is a common operation that is absent in the extreme cases of melancholy and folly, when we are completely overwhelmed by the excesses of dark humor. In contrast to other forms of *phantasia*, such as the *phantasia aisthetike*, the sensuous *phantasia* that unites all sorts of animals, the deliberative *phantasia* is a prerogative of the beings endowed with reason (*logos*) because deciding what to do is the task of reasoning (*De Anima* III, 434a 5–8). Therefore, not only is *phantasia* a crucial ingredient of our mental life, but it is also something that, insofar as it enables us to deliberate, is a specifically human faculty associated with reason.[17] The human being is thus for Aristotle not only a *zoon logon echon* (*Nicomachean Ethics* I, 13), that is, an animal who possesses the *logos*, but also, and perhaps even prior to that, an imagining animal who produces *phantasmata*.

Going back to our starting point, we can conclude that Aristotle maintained a very broad view of *phantasia*, which, far from relegating it to the realm of aesthetics, applies it to various spheres of our life: from cognition to deliberation and action. However, for the purposes of this genealogical reconstruction, it is perhaps even more helpful to look at passages where Aristotle uses the term *phantasia* to speak about topics that are not related to his own accounts of this faculty. At times, fragments of ordinary buildings reveal more about daily life than the rest of grandiose palaces. Sure, the latter are those who often set the standard for the generations to come, and the influence of Aristotle's theory of *phantasia* can hardly be overestimated. According to some interpreters, it is indeed the understanding that will dominate at least until the modern epoch, with very little variations by subsequent authors (Abbagnano 1961:453–454). But it is in passages where Aristotle is not concerned with his own theory that we are more likely to grasp what he took to be the common understanding of the term, as distinguished from his own, which may not have been representative of the general usage.

Let us therefore continue our philological investigation by going back to the list of entries for *phantasia* within the body of Aristotle's writings. In two passages of *De Caelo*, for instance, when discussing issues such as the nature of stars and Earth (297b 31, 294a 7), he uses the term *phantasia* to mean the actual vision that we have of the stars (297b 31) or even the true appearance that can be pointed to in order to dissipate the doubts of his adversaries about the circular shape of Earth (294a 7). Here, Aristotle makes recourse to *phantasia*, understood as what literally appears to our senses, as an instance of "actual vision" that can be the basis for demonstrating the truth against his opponents.

This usage of the term, which sounds so strange to modern ears, was common at that time. Moreover, this reading of the passages of *De Caelo* conforms to most philologists' observations that the prevalent meaning of *phantasia* in Greek sources is that of simple "appearance" or "presentation."[18] It is difficult to know whether the awareness of the link between *phantasia* and the verb *phainesthai* (to appear) ever vanished within the linguistic consciousness of ancient Greeks.[19] However, on the basis of the previous analysis of the uses of such words, it is evident that this link was clearly present in the minds of both Plato and Aristotle, who thought their readers would understand such terms if used in this way.

The contrast with the modern view of imagination as purely imaginary could not be greater. The proportions of this rupture are evident in the embarrassment of modern translators who cannot render the Greek term *phantasia* with the literal translation "fantasy" because this would mean the opposite of what Aristotle had in mind when writing those passages. Alternative modern terms are needed to capture the meaning of Aristotle's *phantasia*: "actual vision" or "true appearance," that is, expressions that mean exactly the opposite of what literal translations such as "imagination" and "fantasy" would convey to modern readers. We need completely different words to fill in the gap between a *phantasia* that designates nothing but what really appears to our senses and a fantasy that has lost its contact with reality and has therefore become purely imaginary.[20]

What has happened in between? Why are we unable to render Aristotle's *phantasia* with our "imagination" and, even less so, with our "fantasy"? One may be tempted here to reconstruct the whole history of the term; and indeed, many interpreters have tried to do that.[21] One would then discover that Latin sources use three different terms to render the Greek *phantasia*: *visio, imaginatio,* and *phantasia* (Ferraris 1996:9). The most ancient translation was *visio*—an unsurprising choice, but also one that underscores how distant we are not only from the Greek but also from the Roman understanding of the term. It is only at a much later stage that the term *imaginatio* emerges, and, even then, the latter continues to be used in a sense substantially close to *visio* for quite some time (9). The third term—the postclassical transliteration from Greek *phantasia*—appears even later, not before Quintilian (9). From Quintilian's usage of the term, it is clear that the idea of an association between *phantasia* and unreality was starting to emerge, since he can say, for instance, that the works of Theon of Samos are *phantasiae*, i.e., extravagancies, unreal fictions (*Institutio Oratoria,* book 12, chapter 10, 453).

But, for our philology as genealogy, we do not need to reconstruct the whole history of "imagination." For our purposes, it is enough to underline the great rupture, the gap separating the Greek *phantasia* from our modern "imagination," and all the more from its companion fantasy. In the Latin and in the early European sources both *imaginatio* and *phantasia* (imagination and fantasy) appear. Although in the European Middle Ages there is a tendency to separate the two by underlining the chimerical connotation of *phantasia* in contrast to the realist *imaginatio,* the rule presents so many exceptions that one may wonder whether it actually ever held (Ferraris 1996:10).[22] The relationship between the two terms remained relatively fluid for a long time, so much so that *imaginatio* and *phantasia* were used interchangeably at least until the eighteenth century. By that time, something new had happened.

Whereas in ancient sources *phantasia* is, to a great extent, a synonym of vision and presentation, in the modern epoch it starts to be systematically associated with unreality. In particular, for those philosophers engaged in defining the new scientific method, imagination, far from being a source of light, as in Aristotle, becomes a source of darkness and of potential perturbation of the methodical work of reason (Friese 2001; Guenancia 2006; Vattimo 1999b). A split is then often established between knowledge, on the one hand, which is guaranteed by the enlightenment of pure reason, and imagination, on the other.

Francis Bacon's usage of the term is paradigmatic of this process.[23] He defines imagination as the faculty that "commonly exceeds the measure of nature, joining at pleasure things that in nature would never have come together and introducing things that in nature would never have come to pass" (Bacon 1986:II, 1, 292; 1963:II, 1, 494). As the faculty to arrange all sorts of illegal marriages, imagination has no decisive role to play in cognition, and it can serve human beings only in their poetic creations. In Bacon's view, imagination, together with memory and reason, is one of the three faculties of the mind to which the main divisions of human learning corresponds: poesy, history, and philosophy (Bacon 1986:II, 1, 292). It is therefore given a central role, but one that sets it apart from both cognition and memory of real events. By the time of Bacon's writing, the typically modern split is therefore established: reason and cognition, on the one hand, and imagination and creativity, on the other.

Although Bacon lacked a clear grasp of the importance of mathematics for the new scientific method, his understanding of science was paradigmatic of modernity in many respects, including the new role it attributed to imagination. In the course of the seventeenth century, the great century of rationalism, the critique of imagination became a sort of commonplace for philosophers engaged in the definition of the new scientific method (Guenancia 2006:43ff.; Vattimo 1999b). Let me illustrate this through a few examples taken from different contexts. Like Bacon, the Italian philosopher Galileo Galilei, another founding father of modern science, defines the new scientific method by juxtaposing it to what he calls "mere fantasies" (*mere fantasie*). In *Il Saggiatore* he argues that the "new philosophy" he is proposing is not a mere "fruit of imagination" such as *The Iliad*, precisely because it is written in the vast book of the universe that "stands in front of our eyes" and "whose characters are triangles, circles, and other geometrical figures without which it is impossible to understand a word," without which science would be "wandering in a dark labyrinth in vain" (Galilei 1996:§6, 631; translation mine). A gap is established between the "new philosophy" with its mathematical language, on the one hand (what we would call science), and poetry, the products of human fantasy such as *The Iliad* and *The Odyssey* (*le fantasie d'uomo come L'Iliade e l'Odissea*), on the other.

A similar attitude can be found in Blaise Pascal. Perhaps in no other source is the critique of imagination as clear as in Pascal's famous fragment on imagination. Here the French philosopher and scientist of Port-Royal describes this faculty as "a mistress of errors and falsity" (*maîtresse d'erreur et fausseté*), as a powerful enemy of reason that can control and, at times, even entirely dominate it (see fragment 44/82, Pascal 1963:504). If reason can never completely surmount imagination, the contrary is quite the rule: we are often prey to the wild fruits of our imagination, and reason is powerless in the face of them. This is ultimately due to the corrupted nature of human beings, who, as a consequence of original sin, are "full of natural mistakes, which cannot be eliminated without divine grace" (Pascal 1963:505; translation mine). In this fragment the critique of imagination goes as far as to say that imagination, more than any other human faculty, is the sign of the irremediably flawed nature of human beings, of the original sin that prevents us from simply following the sources of truth: reason and the senses.[24]

This passage from a generally neutral view of *phantasia* (as it emerged in Greek sources) to a negative one, which sees in it a sign of the dark side of human nature (as exemplified in Bacon, Galilei, and Pascal), resulted in a striking semantic break.[25] The outcome of the seventeenth century's great critiques of imagination is the eighteenth century's relegation of *phantasia* to the sphere of the unreal—where, as we have seen at the beginning of this genealogy, it remains to this day. *Fancy*—the contraction of *fantasy*—suffered the same fate. Since then, *fantasy* came to be associated with the ambit of the unreal and the newly constituted sphere of aesthetics (Friese 2001:7197; Vattimo 1999b:529).

What happened in between? How did a word (*phantasia*) that Aristotle could use to mean "true vision" and "presentation" come to mean its exact opposite? What are the values at stake in such a process? It is not hard to recognize in this process the emergence of the autonomy of the individual, which is, according to many interepreters, the very cornerstone of the project of modernity.[26] At struggle in the pages of the supporters of the new scientific method is the individual's need to legitimize himself vis-à-vis theological absolutism (Blumenberg 1983).[27] The struggle is not only metaphorical if we consider that people such as Galilei were imprisoned for questioning the authority of theologians and the church through a new conception of the universe. Circles and numbers were his allies against the fantasies of the theologians. Within a hierarchically ordered world such as the medieval one—in which Earth is not only at the center of the universe, but also ruled by an ordered chain of being culminating in God—there is not much space for the autonomy of the individual. By contrast, within the homogeneous universe of matter and movement of modern science, where Earth is just one among many planets moving in an infinite universe, the human being is assigned no definitive nor special place and is therefore given the chance to assert his autonomy. As a result, the birth of modernity had to take place, to a large extent, through a discussion of a new astronomy. The battle for the birth of a new scientific view of the world is the battle for a different place for the human being within it.

Within this project of modernity, guaranteeing the reliability of the new scientific method becomes the priority. At stake is not just the new image of the universe but also the authority of those who support it. And imagination, with its capricious nature, cannot but raise suspicions. The fight against superstition and the authority of theologians found its best ally in the new scientific method, which opposed numbers, circles, and inviolable mathematical rules to the volatile nature of imagination. Even modern philosophers such as Thomas Hobbes and Baruch Spinoza, who had a broad understanding of imagination that was, in many respects, closer to Aristotle than they would have openly admitted, still saw in imagination, and imagination alone, the sole possible source of errors and superstitious belief.[28]

Yet, as we have seen, if imagination is a source of errors from the point of view of the methodical work of reason, it still has something to offer human beings. This is the capacity to make all sorts of marriages and divorces that, illegal from the point of view of pure reason, find their proper function in the sphere of aesthetics. Indeed, the concept of art as an autonomous domain grounded on the notion of taste is a creature of modernity (Vattimo 1999a:340).[29] The exclusion of imagination from the domain of knowledge goes hand in hand with a process of subjectification of aesthetics that culminates in the modern concept of art (Gadamer 1988: I, II). If science is the domain of reason and understanding—where an *objective* knowledge of the world can be attained—imagination has a function in the sphere of aesthetics precisely because of its capricious, unpredictable, and above all *subjective* character.[30]

Kant's philosophy is a crucial turning point in this respect, not only because he decisively contributed to defining "Enlightenment" as a philosophical category, but also because his attitude toward imagination illustrates the ambivalence of the Enlightenment project on its own terms. Kant notoriously defined the Enlightenment (*Aufklärung*) as the exit from a condition of "self-imposed immaturity" (Kant 1991:54–60). "Immaturity" is the inability to use one's understanding without the guidance of another, and it is "self-imposed" because it derives not from a lack of understanding, but from a lack of courage to use it. The motto of Kant's Enlightenment is therefore *sapere aude*, to have the courage to use one's own reason—otherwise said, be autonomous (54–60). To explore the conditions for the autonomy of reason is indeed the aim of Kant's entire philosophical enterprise. In his view, the main task of philosophy is precisely the investigation of the possibility of an a priori determination of reason in both its cognitive and ethical aspects.

Kant's treatment of imagination shows the Enlightenment's ambivalence with respect to imagination and its products, such as myths and fables. In the first edition of the *Critique of Pure Reason*, Kant emphasizes the central role played by imagination for the possibility of knowledge (Kant 1998 [1781]:A101). He observes that imagination, as the active capacity for the synthesis of the manifold, is the faculty that brings the plurality of intuitions into single images. As such, imagination becomes something like the transcendental condition of knowledge itself (A101). In other words, Kant admits here a sort of primacy of the imagination (Arnason 1994:160). Without such a transcendental faculty of synthesis, knowledge would be merely a chaotic assemblage of intuitions, of disjointed sense data: a form, a color, etc., but not yet a table.[31] Paradoxically, then, the autonomy of reason seems to depend on imagination. Could the herald of the pureness of reason accept this?[32]

In the second edition of the *Critique*, published only six years later, Kant retreats from this perspective and relegates imagination to a more subordinate and intermediary role between intellect and intuition (Heidegger 1997:§31; Arnason 1994; Rundell 1994a, 1994b).[33] The section in which he argued for the transcendental role of imagination as the a priori condition of knowledge (A95–A130) has been replaced by a new one (B129–B169). Here no longer imagination, but so-called transcendental schematism is what plays the crucial role of the synthesis of knowledge. Kant now distinguishes what he calls the figurative synthesis of imagination from its intellectual counterpart, transcendental schematism, and claims that the latter guarantees pure synthesis (Kant 1998 [1787]:B152, B181). Kant says this schematism "is a hidden art" that "we can lay unveiled before our eyes only with difficulty" (B181). However, it is now this obscure "hidden art" that guarantees the purity of reason. The division is neat: images, produced by imagination, on the one hand, and intellectual schemes, produced by the intellect alone, that guarantee the a priori possibility of knowledge, on the other (B181). Purity of reason is guaranteed, no matter what.

Like many other theorists of the Enlightenment, Kant seems to perceive in imagination a potential source of disturbance of the methodical work of reason and thus locates the imagination's proper place in the newly constituted field of aesthetics. Indeed, as mentioned earlier, only in modern times has an autonomous field of aesthetics been established; before the category of beauty was dealt with under the heading of metaphysics (Vattimo 1999a). Kant contributed to this development of aesthetics with the publication of his *Critique of the Power of Judgment*. There he still recognizes an important role for the imagination, but for aesthetic judgments, that is, for judgments about beauty that, as he repeats in many places, do not contribute to the advancement of knowledge (see, for instance, Kant 2000:57, §8, §36).[34] In sum, Kant now mitigates his previous claim concerning the crucial cognitive role of imagination and consequently rehearses a neater division between reason and imagination, science and art, and thus critique and creativity. In this way, critique collapses into cognitivism and the imagination is treated either mediately or aesthetically (Rundell 1994a, 1994b).

Ironically, the imagination that so worried Kant and other theorists of the Enlightenment was already, so to speak, weakened. By the eighteenth century the term *fantasy* had already been associated with unreality (Cocking 1991:vii; Friese 2001; Vattimo 1999b); thus the modern concept of imagination that drove Kant to his recoil was a mutilated one—an imagination, to paraphrase Castoriadis, that was already deprived of fantasy.[35] This is not only because such an imagination is deprived of its capricious nature, but more so because such an imagination never meets the possibility of folly and madness, that potentially destructive side of imagination that had been emphasized by philosophers at least since Aristotle. Kant's transcendental imagination can bring things together, synthesize them, but not tear them apart or dismember them.[36]

This mutilation of imagination that goes hand in hand with the relegation of fantasy to the unreal is far from being the prerogative of Kantian philosophy.[37] This is an approach that I have associated more broadly with the philosophical category of Enlightenment, thus denoting an always possible attitude toward imagination and fantasy. It should now be clear that I am here using the notion of Enlightenment as a category to illustrate a philosophical attitude more than a historical period whose variety is far too complex to be rendered in a few pages. Rather than faithfully reconstruct the past, the genealogy I am pursuing here must be understood as a critique of always possible philosophical attitudes.

As mentioned previously, the Enlightenment's attitude is still reflected in the common usage of these words. As contemporary linguists have argued, imagination and fantasy are, in this respect, former synonyms, since in most contemporary European languages *fantasy* still means "imagination" plus something else, that is, "imagination plus caprice" (Muller 1986:547). In contrast to imagination, to which some modern philosophers still tried to attribute an important cognitive value, its illegitimate sister fantasy is deemed to be unreal (Abbagnano 1961:369).

What are the gains and losses in such a passage? Who are the winners and the losers? To isolate the victor is not difficult: it is reason, whose purity Kant has secured vis-à-vis both experience and the capricious character of fantasy. That triumph realized the promise of liberation from superstition and legitimized a whole epoch that called itself the "new one" for precisely this reason. It may be worth remembering here that *Neuzeit*, the German term for modernity, literally means the "new epoch"—a fact that tends to get lost in the corresponding English term *modernity*. Enlightenment means liberation from illegitimate authorities, exit from a condition of immaturity to an exclusive reliance on pure reason. This is the promise, but perhaps also the "dialectic of the Enlightenment," as Theodor Adorno and Max Horkheimer (1997) would have it.

As they observed, by rejecting myth and imagination as pure subjectivity and superstition, the Enlightenment constitutes itself by reinforcing the subject versus object dichotomy upon which it rests. In this way the Enlightenment hides the fact that myth is already Enlightenment, *Aufklärung*, because it is already a form of explanation or *Erklärung* (Adorno and Horkheimer 1997). Myths tell the origins of things, where they come from, and are therefore already an attempt to "illuminate" or *erklären*. Thus the Enlightenment generates a negative dialectic at the end of which its celebration of the pureness of reason also becomes a mythology of its own. Once pure reason has unified the whole world within its pure relationships and thus completely dominated it, what it finds is no longer the world but rather its own totalitarian abstract categories. The Enlightenment that has rejected myth as subjective has itself turned into pure subjectivity and thus into a myth (Adorno and Horkheimer 1997).

As I have argued elsewhere, by developing the diagnosis of modernity put forth by Adorno and Horkheimer, the Enlightenment can reject myth and imagination because it has also legitimized another view of reality (Bottici 2007:20–70).[38] Within this new conception of reality, imagination becomes "unreal." Imagination and fantasy could be dismissed or relegated to aesthetics as purely "imaginary" because a new conception of reality had, in the meantime, become hegemonic. This is a fact that we tend to forget: the definition of what is "real" is not an a priori of human understanding (*pace* Kant), but rather something that has proved to be particularly variable in different contexts and epochs.

Specifically, as I have already mentioned, whereas the Greeks did not have a word to designate what we would now call reality, we children of the modern revolution tend to conceive of what is "real" as opposed to what is "ideal." In contrast to this understanding, for a Greek, there were only *ta onta*, the things that are, or *to on*, the being as expressed by the nominalized participle of the verb "to be" (*einai*). Whereas all these words come from the verb *einai*, the word *reality* comes from a completely different root: *res*, the thing itself. This different root is the sign of a different approach to the definition of reality. The Greek *ta onta* are only things insofar as they are already conceptually clear, whereas individual things that are given in experience are *ta pragmata*. The things that fall under the umbrella of *ta onta* include the things that reveal themselves for what they are: in this sense, *to be* (*einai*) does not simply mean to exist, but designates a certain mode of existence. This does not mean that *ta pragmata* are not "real." It simply means that they are less "real" or, even better, that they are less *alethes*, or true.

Ancient Greeks conceived of what we would call the real as constituted by different degrees of being (Vlastos 1965). Not by chance, ideas (*eidos*), far from being purely mental contents (as they have been understood from Descartes on), were conceived as thought and reality at the same time—an easily misleading point that has led many interpreters in the English-speaking world to translate Plato's *eidos* with the term *form* rather than *idea*, its closest term.[39] This is because the Greeks, in contrast to us, did not oppose the "real" to the "ideal." Similarly, as we have already seen, medieval Scholastic philosophy conceived of *realitas* primarily in reference to the *essentia* of each *res*, so that *realitas* was used as a synonym of perfection (Courtine 1992a, 1992b; Hoffmann et al. 1992). This explains why God could be said to be the most real being or *ens realissimus*: it is a view very remote from us, but one that explains why God and angels were conceived as being as real as the table in front of me, if not as even more real.

For a palpable example of this shift in the concept of reality, one has only to look at a medieval painting (Bottici 2007:50–60). Medieval figurative art is quite often characterized as "nonrealist," meaning that medieval painters did not paint bodies and objects as they were "in reality," that is, as we perceive them through our senses. However, the point is not that these paintings are not "realistic," but rather that reality itself—*realitas*—was conceived of differently. It is not that medieval painters could not see that their paintings did not reflect the way in which things appear through the senses. Certainly they could. Nonetheless, the way in which things appear to our senses was not as important for them, because it was not the defining feature of reality. There was therefore no interest in depicting bodies and objects from the point of view of how they appear to our senses. Only together with a new *Weltanschauung* where the human being, not God, is the measure of everything, did the way in which things appear to our senses receive a new, crucial importance. But in the medieval great chain of being, God, the most perfect being, sets the standard of what is perfect, and thus real, and what is not.

The fact that one could conceive of *reality* as a synonym of *perfection* is hard to digest for a contemporary mind. Things are perhaps easier to grasp if we consider that the premodern world was conceived to be a qualitative, hierarchically ordered world, which stands in sharp contrast with the mechanically uniform world made of matter and movement depicted by modern science. In contrast to this view, we inheritors of the modern revolution tend to conceive of the real as something that can be experienced, exists outside of our minds, and is thus opposed to the fictitious (Courtine 1992a, 1992b). Kant is again paradigmatic from this point of view, because he defines the "real" as "that which is connected [*zusammenhängt*] with the material conditions of our experience" (Kant 1998 [1781]:321).[40] Precisely because the real came to be defined in this way could fantasy and imagination have been rejected as imaginary and unreal.

The Enlightenment's specific attitude toward imagination proved to be particularly resilient, not the least because this attitude was rooted in a view of reality that was rapidly becoming dominant. But can we define imagination as unreal if the definition of reality is not an a priori of human understanding? Is it legitimate to condemn imagination to the sphere of unreality by changing the terms of the confrontation? More important, are we not implicitly assuming the Enlightenment's definition of the real if we stick to the common understanding of imagination as unreal? If we accept the latter, we are surreptitiously assuming a certain definition of reality, one that equates it with the material conditions of our experience. Moreover, this view emerged relatively late in history (during European modernity) and may well disappear in a not too distant future (particularly as we are increasingly confronted with cultures coming from different trajectories). Alternative definitions of reality that are already available may indeed supplant its hegemonic role.

Thus there is a strict link between the Enlightenment's understanding of imagination and the notion of reality that supports it. Therefore, not by chance, attempts to reevaluate the cognitive function of imagination, such as German Idealism and Romanticism, went hand in hand with an alternative understanding of reality. Johann Gottlieb Fichte, for instance, inverts the relationship between imagination and reality by saying that imagination defines reality and not vice versa. As he openly put it, "Imagination produces reality; but there *is* no reality therein; only through apprehension and conception in the understanding does its product become something real" (Fichte 1982:207). But, together with this inversion of the relationship between imagination and reality, Fichte also puts forward a different understanding of reality, wherein the latter finds all its sources in the ego and has no autonomy of its own: "The source of all reality is the self, for this is what is immediately and absolutely posited. The concept of reality is first given with and by way of the self" (129).[41]

This creative function of imagination became a commonplace in Romantic aesthetics. Novalis sees in such creativity the highest possible good, because it is a power that can liberate us from the strictures of the senses and understanding: whereas the latter are mechanical, imagination is a source of freedom. For Novalis, "imagination [*Einbildungskraft*] is this wonderful sense that can replace all senses for us," precisely because the latter are entirely governed by mechanical laws, while the former is not even tied to the presence and touch of external stimuli (Novalis 1965:II, 650; translation mine). Therefore art, as the domain created by the freedom of imagination, can bring together what the Enlightenment has separated: the subject and the object of knowledge. In this way the capricious nature of imagination, which often caused it to appear to be an inferior form of knowledge during the eighteenth century, becomes the cornerstone for its positive revaluation in the Romantic philosophy of the nineteenth century (Abbagnano 1961:369).

This revaluation will often be accompanied by the distinction between imagination and fantasy that had already emerged in the eighteenth century and that is still reflected in common language where, as we have seen, fantasy tends to be conceived as imagination plus some caprice or extravagance. It is in the latter that the source of artistic genius is to be found. This is the opinion of Hegel, who notoriously grounded his notion of genius in the creative power of fantasy. As he put it in his *Aesthetics*, "First, when we come to the general capacity for artistic production, then, as soon as there is talk of 'capacity,' 'fancy' (*Phantasie*) is said to be the most prominent artistic ability. Yet in that case we must immediately take care not to confuse fancy with the purely passive imagination (*Einbildungskraft*). Fancy is creative" (Hegel 1875:281).

It is significant that in the same passage in which Hegel connects artistic genius with fantasy (*Phantasie*) he also insists on the difference between the latter and imagination (*Einbildungskraft*), understood as passive and mechanical. We find here the same Enlightenment distinction between fantasy and imagination, understood as, respectively, more and less capricious. Fantasy (*Fantasie*) becomes the symbolizing, allegorizing, and poetizing imagination and, therefore, the specifically creative side of it (Hegel 1975:210, 456–457; translation modified).

In sum, despite its critique by Romanticism, the Enlightenment's specific attitude toward imagination proved to be particularly resilient within Western philosophy, in large part because this attitude was rooted in the new view of reality rapidly becoming dominant. Even authors who tried to subvert the Enlightenment often remained trapped within the opposition between imagination and fantasy that it had initiated. As Benedetto Croce (1913:35–36) put it, the aesthetic of the nineteenth century still harbored a distinction between fantasy, as the typically artistic faculty, and imagination, as the extra-artistic faculty: while fantasy is creative and productive of new combinations, imagination is somehow more sterile and mechanical. Otherwise said, imagination is deprived of fantasy.

To conclude, the first great rupture in the genealogy of imagination can be summarized as the passage from Greek *phantasia* to a modern imagination without fantasy. This leaves us with a first philosophical problem: is imagination to be associated with the real or with the unreal? This is a dilemma in the ancient sense of the term, since both alternatives are equally problematic. I will suggest a possible way out of such a tension in chapter 3. However, to do so, we will first need to explore a second rupture in the genealogy of imagination that has been equally crucial for the emergence of the common understanding of the term. One of the first pieces of data that strikes any goldsmith of words attempting to develop a genealogy of imagination is that, in the twentieth century, besides its stepsister *fantasy*, a new term gained prominence next to *imagination*: *imaginary*. It is to this term that we must now turn our attention.

2

From Imagination to the Imaginary and Beyond?

A full recognition of the radical imagination is possible only if it goes hand in hand with the discovery of the other dimension of the radical imaginary, the so-cial-historical imaginary.

CORNELIUS CASTORIADIS, *The Discovery of the Imagination*

We have seen that the first big rupture in the genealogy of imagination is signaled by the passage from *phantasia* to an imagination without fantasy. The second break, one that cannot but strike the craftsman of words, is the appearance and increasing prominence of another term: the *imaginary*. The passage from imagination to the imaginary signals more than just the fact that imagination itself became imaginary, that is, associated with unreality. As I will try to show in this chapter, the problem is not only that of the reality or unreality of the imaginary. The passage from imagination to "*the* imaginary" also points to a passage from a philosophical tradition centered on a philosophy of the subject to a more context-oriented approach—as indicated by the use of the substantivized adjective *imaginary*. As it has been observed, the passage from the word *imagination* to *the imaginary* parallels that from *reason* to the more context-oriented category of *rationality* (Arnason 1994:163).

As before, the terminological shift reflects a deeper conceptual break: a new word was needed because the vocabulary available no longer sufficed. This does not mean that certain problems could not have been thought of before. It means that at some point their significance reached a threshold beyond which the need for a different vocabulary was felt. Indeed, both terms, *imagination* and *fantasy*, encapsulated as they are in the early modern philosophy of the subject, had proven incapable of rendering the novelty brought about by the philosophical developments of the past century. The twentieth century had too thoroughly proven how the individual power of imagination can be annihilated by totalitarian social contexts to still retain a naive belief in its autonomy.

Psychoanalysis and structuralism both contributed to this development—the former with its emphasis on the complexity of psychic life and the latter with a new attention to the products of imagination. Myths, fables, fairy tales, rituals, and totemic practices all have been analyzed as part of the imaginary—one just has to think of psychoanalysis's contribution in this direction or of the structuralist analyses inspired by Claude Lévi-Strauss.[1] All this research focused on the products of imagination, rather than on the faculty that produces them, helping to reconfigure the question of imagination as a new *problematique*: that of the imaginary in which we all are immersed, as opposed to that of the faculty that we possess as individuals.

Although the discoveries of psychoanalysis, with their emphasis on the importance of psychological context in the socialization of individuals, is a crucial development in this direction, it is worth remembering that the terminology of imagination is almost absent from Sigmund Freud's vocabulary. Freud uses *Einbildungskraft*, the German term for imagination, very rarely (see Castoriadis 1997a:247-249), and it is a remarkable paradox for the careful philologist that the father of psychoanalysis—a movement centered on the importance of imagination in our psychic life—does not use the word *imagination*.

Indeed, the concordance for Freud's *Gesammelte Werke* gives only two entries for *Einbildungskraft* (Guttman et al. 1995.1316). Both times the term is used in a rather conventional way, referring to the imaginings of the neurotic. There, the imagination is relegated to the sphere of the pathological. By contrast, Freud makes extensive use of the stepsister of imagination, i.e., *Fantasie*, along with the relative verb *phantasieren*, by giving a very traditional account of it as an activity combining bits of our psychic life. As Castoriadis (1997a:248) observes, commenting on this significant Freudian aporia, "everything happens as if these 'phantasies' were only the product of a recombinative activity, and therefore in no way originary or creative. And when Freud is confronted with the problem of 'originary phantasies' which have no 'actual' real source in life, he will seek a mythical 'real' source for them in phylogenesis." In other words, there seems to be no space in Freud's work for thinking about what Castoriadis called the radical character of imagination—that is, for thinking about an imagination that brings about the new rather than simply recombining pieces of past experience.

There is no easy explanation for this paradox: "The patriarch of the movement, one of whose mouthpieces is the review entitled 'Imago' (founded in 1912 by Hanns Sachs and Otto Rank), the man whose work would be incomprehensible if in the imagination one did not see a central, constitutive power of the psyche, does not want to know anything about it" (Castoriadis 1997a:248). Thus, even Freud, like Kant, seems somehow to recoil before the power of imagination and relegate it to the sphere of fantasy. There are, after all, two basic strategies used to tame the imagination. The first consists in curtailing it by assigning it an *auxiliary* role between intellect and sensation, as in Kant's second edition of the *Critique of Pure Reason*. The second is by seeing in it a mere combinatory activity, as in certain Aristotelian accounts.[2] Freud seems to curtail the radical character of imagination on at least this second front.

The absence of imagination within Freud's vocabulary is even more striking if one considers the centrality that this term assumes in the work of his controversial disciple, Carl Gustav Jung. As early as 1936, Jung was insisting on the differences between imagination (*Einbildungskraft*) and fantasy (*Fantasie*), a differentiation he would make explicit: "I prefer the expression 'imagination' to 'fantasy' because between the two there is that difference that the old doctors had in their mind when they used to say that the *opus nostrum*, our work, must be realized *per veram imaginationem et non phantasticam*—that is through an imagination which is authentic and not illusory. In other words, according to this definition, fantasy is pure unreality, a phantom, a fleeting impression. On the contrary, imagination is an active creation finalized to a certain end" (Jung 1936:62; translation mine).

As we have seen in the previous chapter, by the nineteenth century the term *fantasy*, as well as the corresponding German term *Fantasie*, was more systematically associated with the idea of the unreality of its content than its more illustrious sister *imagination* (or *Einbildungskraft*). It is symptomatic of this split that, for example, when Kant speaks about a transcendental imagination, i.e., of a form of imagination without which no knowledge of the world would be possible at all, he uses the term *Einbildungskraft*—a term that literally translates to the "power to construct" something. He would never have used the term *Fantasie* since, by that time, the term had already moved to the ambit of the unreal and would have immediately suggested the idea of the unreality of its contents—and thus the unreality of sensible experience.

Going back to Freud, there may be several factors influencing this conspicuous absence in his writings. The most plausible seems to me that his general ontology remains linked to a form of realism, according to which reality is, to put it again in Kant's terms, what is in accord with the material conditions of our experience. It is only if the real is understood in this way that dreams as well as the daily imagining of the neurotic can be said to be fantasies.

Although Freud's usage thus remains rather conventional, it is by developing insights from psychoanalysis that the concept of the imaginary—understood as a sociopsychological context—has gained prominence in the last fifty years. This is particularly due to Jacques Lacan's much celebrated "return to Freud," which, as we will now see, is in fact a return that goes a long way beyond Freud in terms of the question of imagination. With his emphasis on language and the importance of society in the socialization of individuals, Lacan went beyond the idea of imagination as an individual faculty; as a result, the term *imaginary* became central to his theory. As we will now see in more detail, in Lacan's view, the Imaginary domain, together with the Real and the Symbolic, becomes one of the three fundamental orders that are constitutive of the psyche (Lacan 1999).

In a seminal text from 1936, the same year that Jung was distinguishing between imagination and fantasy, Lacan put forward his original thesis about the so-called mirror phase, to which the fortune of the concept of the imaginary is largely due. This notion is intrinsically linked to what, according to many, represents Lacan's major contribution to psychoanalysis (Tarizzo 2009:13). The mirror phase consists in that specific moment of infant development (between six and eighteen months), when the infant starts to recognize the image in a mirror as that of his own body. This experience, Lacan (1999:88) observes, is accompanied by an especially jubilant attitude on the side of the infant. Why is this so?

According to Lacan (1999:91, 180), at this stage of development the infant is not yet able to exercise a command over her own body because of the biologically constitutive premature birth of human beings (*prématuration biologique*), that is, the fact that we are born not yet fit for the world we live in. If we compare human infants with other animals, we cannot but perceive a typically human slowness in acquiring a command over the body. At the age of one year and a half, infants still perceive their body as fragmented (*corp morcelé*), that is, as a body in pieces over which they have no control. Therefore, the specific joy derived from recognizing oneself in the mirror at this stage would be due to the fact that the infant perceives herself as a reflected unitary image. Thus a discrepancy arises between the subject on this side of the mirror, which is an I (*je*) without any unity, and the unitary and idealized image (*moi*) that is reflected in the mirror. While the lack of coordination and fragmentation of the former generates a sense of frustration, the image in the mirror gives a reassuring sense of unity and control over one's own body.

As the theorists of *Gestaltpsychologie*—to which Lacan in this phase of his work still makes reference—have shown (Lacan 1999:64, 86), the form of the image possesses a surplus: it adds something that is not in reality itself. This surplus of the form as such gives the infant the peculiar pleasure of unity and also explains the captivating power of the imaginary domain more generally. The latter always provides endless images with which to indentify ourselves as well as a powerful tool to overcome that original specter of the total lack of unity of the fragmented body over which we have no command. Here ultimately lies the seductive power of the Imaginary in Lacan's sense of the term.

Moreover, such identification with the mirror image is not only a child's phase but also an experience that is constitutive of our psyche in general. The ego is formed through identification with such an image, so that the Imaginary, together with the Real and the Symbolic, comes to be one of the constitutive orders of the psyche, as Lacan will put it after the encounter with structuralism in the 1950s. The Imaginary intrinsically captures us with an endless series of imaginary identifications, to which only symbolic interpretation can put an end. Only when the subject comes to identify herself with the father and the whole culture he embodies is a stable identification possible. While in the Imaginary the subject is permanently caught by his own image, the symbolic order presents itself to the subject as the big Other, as the law, which is counterpoised to the Real (that is, what is outside of language and, therefore, cannot be symbolized).[3] In sum, although imaginary identifications are endless, within the process of symbolic interpretation—leading to the recognition of the impossibility of a definitive identification—lies the possibility of liberation. As has been emphasized, despite the difficulties of providing a univocal interpretation of this theory, "Lacan always understood symbolisation as a kind of emancipatory process, releasing the subject from tutelage and stasis, from dependency on an alienating image" (Dews 2002:520).

In sum, we can say that, whereas the Symbolic discloses the possibility of emancipation, the Imaginary is by definition the place of alienation.[4] From the very beginning, Lacan (1999:181) openly states, "the first effect of the *imago* which appears in the human being is an effect of subjective *alienation*." It is the site of alienation in the technical sense of the term, which is so clearly captured by the German word for it: *Entfremdung. Ent-fremden* means that a distance is created whereby a subject projects herself into an other: the latter is by definition an alien; thus the subject becomes split, distant from herself. In Lacanian terms, the gap lies between the fragmented subject (*je*) and unitary image that the mirror gives back as an idealized me (*moi*). Although this does not mean that the Imaginary is always illusory,[5] it remains constitutively the locus of alienation.

For this reason, some have seen in Lacan's notion of the Imaginary "a deeply reductionist approach" that relegates the imaginary to the specular and thus to a merely reproductive activity (Urribarri 2002:48). In this usage of the term, the concept of imaginary is once again limited to the ambit of the unreal—although in a much more refined understanding of the real and the imaginary, respectively. As a consequence, despite the peculiar use that Lacan makes of the concept, with his original reading of the mirror phase, his usage remains paradoxically close to common usage, as when we say something "is purely imaginary." This is because the Imaginary is "essentially meant to be deceiving" (*essentiellment vouée au leurre*) both in the Lacanian and in the most common usage of the term (Laplanche and Pontalis 1992:196).

But what is most relevant for us here is that the imaginary thus conceived is not only associated with what is not real but also transformed into a domain (as opposed to a faculty) wherein the images with which we identify are deposited. This becomes particularly clear after Lacan's structural turn of the 1950s, when the genetic perspective about the origins of the Imaginary of his early writings is abandoned and he begins to investigate the imaginary only to describe it— precisely in the same way in which Lévi-Strauss was describing the structure of mythical thinking by analyzing its products rather than formulating a hypothesis about its origins. Thus the Imaginary becomes a structure constitutive of our being, the context we are immersed in: far from being the autonomous subjects that are presupposed by modern theories of imagination posited as an individual faculty, the underlying idea is that we are captivated and thus constituted by the imaginary in which we live. Simply put, if imagination is an individual faculty that we possess, the imaginary is the context that possesses us.

Together with the influence of psychoanalysis, one should also mention the increasing amounts of historical, sociological, and political works that have focused on specific features of the imaginary understood as a context. In both research inspired by psychoanalysis and empirically driven works there is an implicit shift away from the idea that imagination is an individual faculty that we freely exercise. These strands of research reflect the passage from a subject-oriented research paradigm to a context-oriented one. Novels, melodrama, dress codes, eating habits, as well as social and political symbols all have been studied as means for community building and vehicles of socialization to the social imaginary.[6] For example, when Jonathan Zwicker (2006) speaks of the "social imaginary of nineteenth century Japan," he is using the notion of the imaginary as a specific context, which is both spatially and temporally delimited and within which the role of certain cultural products (in this case, novels and melodrama) can be explored. However, we might also wonder about the boundaries that enable us to speak of nineteenth-century Japan's social imaginary in the singular: is there a discrete, self-enclosed entity that can fruitfully be identified with this name? If the problem with modern theories of imagination as an individual faculty was that they presupposed a problematic metaphysics of the subject, are we not risking here exchanging it for an equally problematic metaphysics of the context?

Recently, the philosopher who has most profitably used the notion of the social imaginary in the English-speaking world is Charles Taylor. By "social imaginary" he means "the ways people imagine their social existence, how they fit together with others, how things go on between them and their fellows, the expectations that are normally met, and the deeper normative notions and images that underlie these expectations" (Taylor 2004:23). In his usage of the term, *the imaginary* is meant to signal the fact that it is not only intellectual schemes that are at stake, but rather the way in which ordinary people imagine their social surroundings as they are conveyed by images, stories, and legends (23). This is because, according to Taylor, while theory is just the possession of a minority, the social imaginary is shared by a large group of people. This leads to a further difference between theory and the social imaginary: the latter is the "common understanding that makes possible common practices and a widely shared sense of legitimacy" (23).

This does not mean that there is no relationship between the two. In the course of his treatment of the specifically modern social imaginary, Taylor explores precisely the relationship between theory and practice. Through the writings of philosophers and intellectuals a certain theory can gradually infiltrate and transform the social imaginary itself (Taylor 2004:28). What is originally an abstract idealization can grow into a complex imaginary by being taken up and associated with social practices. According to Taylor, it is in this way that a theory, the product of the single mind of an intellectual, can come to inform a whole social imaginary, that is, the shared background of our social practices.

In Taylor's usage of the term, the social imaginary includes therefore an understanding that is both factual and normative. It incorporates some sense of how we all fit together in carrying out common practices. In other words, it includes our sense of the way in which things usually go, but also a certain normative stance on how they *should* go (Taylor 2004:24). Although his account probably reflects the influence of the phenomenological notion of lifeworld, Taylor's direct point of reference is what contemporary philosophers such as Hubert Dreyfus and John Searle have called background. The latter is defined as that "largely unstructured and inarticulate understanding of our whole situation, within which particular features of our world show up for us in the sense they have" (Taylor 2004:25). From this and similar passages it is very clear that the reason Taylor used the concept of imaginary rather than the old concept of imagination is because he intends to distance himself from a problematic philosophy of the "disengaged subject" in favor of a new emphasis on the context or what he, elsewhere, calls the "inescapable framework" (Taylor 1989:3).

Notwithstanding the huge differences between authors as diverse as Lacan, Zwicker, and Taylor, their usage of the concept of the imaginary reflects the aforementioned passage from an emphasis on imagination as an individual faculty to the imaginary as a social and psychological context.. The substantivized adjective *imaginary* denotes what we are *immersed* in rather than a faculty that we *possess*. If imagination is a faculty that we have as single individuals, the imaginary is what produces us as social beings. The underlying idea is that we are never pure disaggregated atoms, as in a mythical state of nature, but always already social beings who cannot but exist within a certain background or social context within which we are born.

Who are the winners and losers? What are the interests at stake in such a passage? It is not difficult to see that the context itself is the winner, since it has thickened up to a point where it risks becoming a prison. Some authors have indeed brought this shift of perspective up to a point where social contexts became discrete entities, such as cultures or civilizations, which interact or even clash with each other as if they were individuals.[7] The loser is, potentially, our free capacity to imagine. If we are born within social imaginaries that cultivate us as social beings, how can we escape from them? How do we account for the fact that even within the most totalitarian and oppressive social imaginary, it is always possible to find a moment of friction where the free individual imagination breaks in?

The specter haunting theories of the social imaginary is the same that has been haunting multiculturalism for quite some time now.[8] When we speak of social imaginaries in the plural, as much as when we speak of cultures or even civilizations in the plural, we are often tempted to think of them as more or less coherent wholes, with clear-cut boundaries and a distinctiveness that sets each of them apart from one another. But, as I have argued elsewhere, this is a very misleading view that is often generated from a reductive reading of the notion of background or the Wittgensteinian concept of forms of life (Wittgenstein 1975:19, 23, 241). Unfortunately, Wittgenstein did not fully elaborate this notion, and this left a lot of space for speculation that has led many authors to interpret this concept in overly culturalist terms.

Although this often implies a misleading reading of Wittgenstein,[9] his emphasis on context has often been interpreted as an argument for the distinction and even incommensurability between different cultural contexts.[10] The notion of forms of life and background has often been used to justify a sort of ethnomethodological approach (Coulter 1999), where cultures become self-enclosed entities that interact, dialogue, or even clash with one another as if they were individuals. Indeed, the step from this understanding of contexts in terms of discrete entities to the thesis of incommensurability is much shorter than is usually thought: the specter haunting multiculturalism is one that we can hardly get rid of if we stick to the idea that there are different cultures and social imaginaries juxtaposed to one another as though they were discrete entities.[11]

Lacan, who sees the imaginary as just one element of the structure together with the Symbolic and the Real, can still explain how an exit from the Imaginary is possible.[12] But in Lacan the Imaginary remains a fluid and dynamic domain where we are immersed and does not crystallize into the idea of separated, self-enclosed imaginaries. Therefore, he avoids the specter of incommensurability between different social imaginaries. But when the notion of imaginary is declined in the plural, it comes to suggest by itself the idea that there are different "imaginaries" that can be juxtaposed one next to the other. A craftsman of words cannot but notice that this usage of the term *imaginary* signals a significant shift in the genealogy with which we are concerned.

By speaking about imaginaries in the plural, we risk a reification of contexts.[13] Taylor (1995:146–164) ultimately avoids this risk by recalling the hermeneutic tradition of a fusion of horizons and comparisons between cultures. Other authors, on the contrary, have fully succumbed to this trap by embracing the idea of the incommensurability of cultures or civilizations that, at best, interact and, at worst, clash with one another.

This view appears even more contestable in a globalizing world, where boundaries are increasingly questioned and fluid. As I have tried to argue elsewhere, speaking about multiple imaginaries (or multiple modernities for that matter) can ultimately be just a way of exchanging a problematic *ego*centrism for an equally problematic form of *ethno*centrism (Bottici and Challand 2010:111–122).[14] Otherwise said, we exchange the subject of modern metaphysics for equally self-enclosed social imaginaries or modernities, that is, for a form of solipsism on a larger scale.

As in the case of the tension generated by the first rupture in our genealogy, there seems to be no easy way out. Both alternatives are reductive and uncomfortable, precisely as the two horns of a dilemma in the ancient sense of the term. If the first could be rendered with the alternatives "imagination or fantasy," then is the tension generated by this second break summarized by the alternative "imagination or imaginary?" If we begin with the imagination as an individual faculty, the problem is how to explain the influence, at times overwhelming (because it is constitutive), of social contexts. If we begin with the imaginary understood as a social context, the problem is how to account for the emergence of the free imagination of individuals. The task of the next chapter will be to argue that a helpful way to overcome these tensions is a theory of the imaginal. First, however, let me reconstruct some attempts to go beyond the two dilemmas generated by the genealogy of imagination.

Let us begin with the first: is imagination real or unreal? If we argue along with Aristotle that imagination-*phantasia* is true vision, we risk losing contact with the world we live in—which is certainly very different from Aristotle's. But if we adopt the modern interpretation of imagination-*fantasy* as unreal, we implicitly assume the specifically modern concept of reality that the Enlightenment endorsed. How can we escape it? The problem is not only the fact that this view is deeply rooted in a certain context (the European one) but also that, as we have seen, this view appeared relatively late in history and may well be eclipsed by alternative views in a not too distant future. In a globalizing world, where different views of reality confront each other, would it not be better to begin with an understanding that engages as little of our historically situated heritage as possible?

Among all the attempts to overcome this dilemma, the most interesting one is perhaps that inspired by phenomenology. The aim of the phenomenological method, as elaborated by the early Edmund Husserl, was precisely to put the question of realism in parentheses. The underlying idea is that, since we do not have the means to determine whether our representations of the world correspond to the world as it is "in itself" (if this expression has any meaning at all), phenomenology chooses to leave this question aside and to examine instead the way in which our consciousness relates to the phenomenological world—independently of whether the latter corresponds to a supposed world in itself or not. Consequently, phenomenology is a return to the things themselves, by which Husserl meant that these are phenomena, that is, the original disclosing of reality in consciousness (Husserl 1984 [1901]). As a consequence, phenomenology seems to be much better equipped than other philosophical movements to go beyond the first dilemma of imagination.

Indeed, the aim of the phenomenological method is to describe phenomena as they are given in consciousness in order to grasp their pure form or idea (*eidos*). Therefore, it requires a preliminary reduction through which all common judgments are suspended, which is what Husserl called the *phenomeno-logical epoché*. This means that all theories—ranging from scientific theories to judgments of common sense—are placed in parentheses. Among these theories, Husserl includes naive realism, the belief in the existence of an external world that should be faithfully reproduced by our consciousness (Husserl 1976). We may therefore suppose that we have left behind Enlightenment's view of reality itself.

Yet, when dealing with the issue of imagination, to which Husserl assigns a crucial cognitive and epistemological role,[15] the question of reality, although apparently suspended, keeps returning. Once again, the oscillation between different words is a signal of a certain embarrassment. Terminologically speaking, it is indeed significant that Husserl uses the German terms *Einbildung/Einbil-dungskraft*, and even the transliteration from Latin *Imagination*, as synonyms of *Phantasie*. At times they seem to be almost interchangeable in his writings (Baptist 2008:145). Although in his later works Husserl introduces an important distinction between what he calls pure fantasy (*reine Phantasie*) and consciousness of images (*Bildbewusstsein*),[16] the problem of the reality of imagination seems never to be fully settled.

Already in the *Logical Investigations*, Husserl (1984 [1901]:§10, §23) states that imagination plays an important role in cognition, because every act of perception entails imaginative, perceptive, and symbolic elements. In this way he sets up an analogy between imagination and perception. He does not seem, at this point of his work, to distinguish between the two different forms of imagination mentioned earlier: "pure fantasy" (*reine Phantasie*) and "consciousness of images" (*Bildbewusstsein*). Although this distinction may not be sufficient to fully settle the problem, it is important to emphasize that Husserl clearly opposes the former, which corresponds to an act that poses the object as absent, to the latter, understood as simple posing of the object as an image (Ghiron 2002). Despite the general ontological differences between the two—not least due to the fact that the translation of *phantasma* with "image" is only partially correct for reasons discussed in chapter 1—one cannot but be tempted to see in Husserl's consciousness of images something close to Aristotle's understanding of *phantasia*.

In his later writing, Husserl (1980:4) emphasizes the nature of different forms of presentification, such as remembrance (*Erinnerung*) and expectation (*Erwartung*). In all these cases we have the presentification of something that is not immediately there, but such not-being-there can take very different forms. In some cases it is presentified as not there because it has already been (*Erinnerung*) or because it is not yet there (*Erwartung*), whereas in others it is posed as not there because it is merely possible and thus not real (*Phantasie*). The difference between them is precisely that, in the case of *Phantasie*, what is missing is the consciousness of reality as opposed to what is imagined (4). In the latter case the imagined object is intended to as unreal.

The category through which Husserl explicitly defines imagination/fantasy is possibility. As he puts it, "what I can fantasize about is possible: in itself and for itself" (461). Imagination opens the door to what is possible. As such, it brings to perception the consciousness of doubt and to judgment the negation of what is given. This is also underlined by the terms that Husserl associates with imagination/fantasy: *Freiheit*, *Beliebigkeit*, and *Willkürlichkeit*, which point to the arbitrariness, creativity, and freedom of imagination (see, for instance, Husserl 1980:535). This is in itself a sign that the problem of reality is not yet completely settled, since, by defining imagination/fantasy in terms of what is only possible or not yet there or already past, imagination is once again attached to a lack, to something that is absent. Thus, the question of the reality of imagination/fantasy is not yet completely solved, and Husserl does not fail to confess openly his puzzlement on this point (54-55).[17]

Husserl's phenomenological approach to imagination had a strong influence both within and beyond phenomenology, and it certainly represents the first attempt to go beyond the problems inherited by the genealogy of imagination reconstructed in these two chapters. Yet Husserl's attempts to overcome the dilemma from which we started as well as those inspired by his phenomenological approach do not provide a definitive answer. Despite the important intuitions that can be found in his writings on this point, the constant shift in terminology is a signal that the problem had yet been solved.[18]

But the genealogy of imagination reconstructed in chapter 1 left us with another, and possibly even trickier, tension, that is between the individual and social character of our capacity to imagine. To account for the latter, should we begin with imagination, as one of the faculties with which individuals are endowed, or, rather, with the imaginary as a social and psychological context? Once again, attempts to solve the tension are numerous. Among them, we can distinguish between those authors who tried to solve it by making imagination public and those who moved the other way by trying to render the social imaginary individual. An interesting example of the former is the notion of "public imagination," which has been recently developed by Martha Nussbaum (1995) and Meili Steele (2005). Both speak of "public imagination" in order to underline the social character of our acts of imagining (Nussbaum 1995:3; Steele 2005:6–10), but the way they understand it is diametrically opposed.

Nussbaum uses the concept in her attempt to argue that literature is not a private but a public matter. In her view, by reading literary texts we develop a capacity to imagine what it is like to live the life of another person, an ability "that will steer judges in their judging, legislators in their legislating, policy makers in measuring the quality of life of people near and far" (Nussbaum 1995:3). This is what she meant when she stated that she wanted to consider "the literary as a public imagination" (3). The underlining idea is that literature plays a crucial public role in that it focuses on the possible, thus inviting readers to wonder about themselves and the world they live in (5).

But Nussbaum's *public* imagination is, in the end, only the place where the act of imagining produced by certain individuals meets those of other individuals—and not, much more radically, the place where individuals themselves are made. It is "public" because, as an act of imagining, it has social *consequences*, but not because it is social by its very *nature*—this is why she speaks of imagination rather than of the imaginary. Her ontology is and remains individualistic and is even compatible with a purely Kantian approach.[19] Otherwise stated, her approach remains fully within a philosophy of the subject and thus the dialectic of Enlightenment that it generates. In sum, we remain fully within the second tension generated by the genealogy of imagination, precisely because we are also still fully within the first.

In contrast to Nussbaum, Steele uses the notion of public imagination in order to show how the imaginative social space that citizens inhabit can be the site for political discourse and debate. By public imagination, Steele (2005:6) means "not only the explicit concepts of a culture, but also the images, plots, symbols, and background practices through which citizens imagine their lives." With an explicit reference to Taylor's notion of social imaginary (151), he emphasizes that this notion includes normative languages and assumptions about personhood, history, language, rights, and the like (6). The concept of public imagination is here explicitly invoked to signal that meaning and imagination are not confined to the mental functioning of individuals, but effective and consequential in the world of historical forces, thus moving "beyond the division of subjective and objective approaches" (Steele 2005:7). However, Steele moves via an approach that, like Taylor's, takes the social context as the starting point; as such, he explicitly uses "public imagination" as a synonym of "social imaginary" (Steele 2005:6). In sum, both Nussbaum and Steele try to make imagination "public," but Nussbaum does so by anchoring it in Kantian subjects, whereas Steele ultimately dissolves these subjects in the social context. In both cases the second problem generated by the genealogy of imagination is not overcome, but instead is fully endorsed.

Taking the opposite road, some authors have tried to render the social imaginary individual. Such is the case for Cornelius Castoriadis, who, starting with the premises of psychoanalysis, investigates the space of radical imagination in a way that perhaps no other recent philosopher has done. Castoriadis's (1987) *Imaginary Institution of Society* decisively contributed to the passage from the paradigm of imagination as an individual faculty to that of the imaginary as a social context. Despite the inspiration that he draws from both Aristotle and Kant, his shift toward the notion of the social imaginary stems precisely from the perception of an insufficiency in the vocabulary available. In his view, both the Aristotle of *De Anima* and the Kant of the first edition of the *Critique of Pure Reason* had rightly emphasized the constitutive role of imagination—so much so that he attributes to them nothing less than the "discovery of imagination" (Castoriadis 1997c). However, they both remain entrapped in an ego-logical philosophy of the subject that prevents them from perceiving the intrinsically social nature of imagination. Such a conception is precisely what Castoriadis tries to convey with his notion of social imaginary. As he writes in an emblematic passage,

> There is nothing more deprived of imagination than the transcendental imagination of Kant. And, of course this position is inevitable so long as the problem of imagination and of the imaginary is thought solely in relation to the subject, within a psycho-logical or ego-logical horizon. Indeed in so far as one remains confined within this horizon, recognition of the radical imagination as creation could only lead to universal dislocation. If the transcendental imagination set itself the task of imagining anything whatsoever, the world would collapse immediately. This is why, later on, the "creative imagination" will remain, philosophically, a mere word and the role that will be recognized for it will be limited to domains that seem ontologically gratuitous (art). A full recognition of the radical imagination is possible only if it goes hand in hand with the discovery of the other dimension of the radical imaginary, the social-historical imaginary, instituting a society as source of ontological creation deploying itself as history.
>
> (Castoriadis 1997c:245)

This passage is of crucial importance and deserves a detailed analysis. To begin, let us note that Castoriadis's notion of the imaginary has nothing in common with Lacan's. Castoriadis distances himself very early from Lacan by observing that the latter reduces the imaginary to the specular, to the "image *of* something"

(Castoriadis 1987:3) rooted in the mirror phase and thus also as constitutively alienating. On the contrary, Castoriadis's notion of the imaginary is not the "image *of* something." As he puts it at the beginning of *The Imaginary Institution of Society*, the imaginary "is the unceasing and essentially *undetermined* (social-historical and psychical) creation of figures/forms/images, on the basis of which alone there can ever be a question of 'something'" (3).

We will further discuss Castoriadis's understanding of "figures/forms/images" in the next chapter. Let us here concentrate on his notion of the imaginary. The imaginary is by definition social-historical, since for Castoriadis society is nothing else than alteration, time, and thus history itself (Castoriadis 1987:167–215). Inherited ontology and logic have always tried to cover over this fundamental identity between society and history for one fundamental reason: every society needs to present itself as a given, as always already *instituted,* and cannot recognize its own being always *instituting* because this means accepting the possibility of pure chaos, of social order perpetually standing on the fringes of the abyss (167). The inherited modes of thinking have displayed only forms of logic incapable of thinking the undetermined. "Society is not a thing, not a subject, and not an idea—nor is it a collection or system of subjects, things and ideas" (167). This may be a banality, but one that is worth remembering as it shows how our inherited language is incapable of thinking the undetermined and thus the social-historical itself—here expressed by the fact that we always speak of "a" society or of "this" society (167).

Accordingly, Castoriadis prefers to speak of the "social-historical" (in particular, see 1987:167–215). Society is nothing but history itself, which in turn is temporal alteration produced in and through society. The question of history, for Castoriadis, "is the question of the emergence of radical otherness or of the absolutely new" (172). As a result, Castoriadis, who had been a leading figure of libertarian Marxism in the 1960s, distances himself from Marxism. He goes so far as to say that, by starting from revolutionary Marxism, he finally faced a situation where he had to "choose between remaining Marxist and remaining revolutionary"—between faithfulness to a doctrine and faithfulness to a project of radical change of the society (14).

How crucial experience and militancy within Marxism were for Castoriadis is clearly seen in the structure of his major work, *The Imaginary Institution of Society,* in which the concept of the social imaginary is developed through a critique internal to Marxism. Castoriadis perceived in Karl Marx—and in Marxism more generally—a fundamental tension between two perspectives and modes of explanation that are irreducible to each other. On the one hand, the emphasis on the class struggle points to the possibility of *making* history, in the deep sense of creating something new. To a degree, through this emphasis on the need for struggle, Marx pointed out that human beings literally make their own history. On the other hand, his economic determinism, which reduced history to the conflict between the material-productive forces of society and the existing relations of production, destroys the possibility of thinking history as the radical creation of something new (Castoriadis 1987:30–31).

What Castoriadis ultimately perceives in the historical evolution of Marxism is not a synthesis between these two tendencies, but rather a "triumph of determinism over class struggle" (Castoriadis 1987:30). Castoriadis asks,

> Is the essential factor in the evolution of capitalism the technological revolution and the effects of the economic laws that govern the system? Or is it the struggle of classes and social groups? In reading *Capital* we see that the first response is correct. Once its sociological conditions are established, once what can be called the "axioms of the system" are posited in historical reality (that is the degree and specific type of technical development, the existence of accumulated capital, and of a sufficient number of proletarians, etc.) and under the continuous impetus of an autonomous technical progress, capitalism evolves solely in terms of the effects of the economic laws it contains, and which Marx had formulated. Class struggle nowhere comes in.
>
> (Castoriadis 1987:30)

In this respect, Marx's economic determinism does not differ from all other philosophies of history that, by reducing history to a pregiven logic—dialectical, divine, or natural—destroy the possibility of thinking history as alteration and emergence of the new. "The Marxist knows where history must go" (31), observes Castoriadis, and in this regard, he does not differ much from any other philosophical attempts at covering over the instituting dimension of society—the fact that society itself is history, i.e., alteration. However, I believe that this emphasis on alteration is, paradoxically, the greatest Marxist heritage in Castoriadis's own thinking. The idea of a "revolutionary praxis," of "a conscious transformation of society by the autonomous activity of men" is indeed, by Castoriadis's own admittance, the "most profound and durable contribution made by Marxism" (62), although one that was potentially curtailed by Marx and his economic determinism.

Thus whereas, within a Marxist framework, the problem of imagination and of the social imaginary is treated in terms of the function that it performs within a society,[20] Castoriadis turns this perspective upside down: to speak about a function presupposes the work of imagination/imaginary and not the other way around. Along with Marxism, Castoriadis distances himself from all forms of reductionism that tend to veil the instituting dimension of society—functionalism is the first of these (115). In Castoriadis's view, every act, both individual and collective, without which no society could survive—labor, consumption, love, war, etc.—is impossible outside of the social imaginary (117). All functions performed within any society are, in fact, "functions of something," i.e., they are functions only insofar as their ends can be defined. But these ends, which vary from society to society as well as from one epoch to the other, can be defined only at the level of those social significations without which no social function or need could ever be defined: this is the level at which the "social imaginary" operates. Every society continually defines and redefines its needs, and no society can ever survive outside of the imaginary significations that constitute it and are constituted by it. The institution of a society presupposes the institution of imaginary significations that must, in principle, be able to provide meaning to whatever presents itself.

There are, Castoriadis observes, limits to the social imaginary. First, it must always start from the material that it finds already there. Therefore, the limits posed by nature are primary. For example, societies define the meaning of nourishment, but they must start from the need for it. Second, some limits are posed by rationality, by the coherence of the symbolic edifice. Finally, other limits are imposed by history, by the fact that every symbolism is built on the ruins of the preceding symbolic constructions, so that, to break radically with such constructions, one must begin with these as premises (125).

The way in which Castoriadis addresses the question of the limits to the social imaginary clearly shows that his view does not imply an "all-embracing" or even "all engulfing" conception of imagination, as some have argued (Dews 2002:518, 520). The idea that there are limits intrinsic to the social imaginary derives from Castoriadis's creative reappropriation of Freud's notion of "leaning on" or *Anlehnung* (or *anaclisis* in Greek). He does so because, as Whitebook observes, he remains too much of a Marxist and a Freudian to dissociate the radical imagination from any external anchorage (Whitebook 1989:230). In sum, Castoriadis's imaginary is not everything, despite the fact that it is what provides a meaning to whatever may present itself.

An important difference from Freud emerges, however, precisely on this point: whereas Freud devoted a large part of his work trying to mitigate the radicalness of imagination by constantly trying to root it in real factors such as the biological, the infantile seduction, the primal scene, phylogenesis, and so on (Castoriadis 1987:281; Whitebook 1989:230), Castoriadis does not aim at taming the imagination. His reappropriation of Freud's notion of "leaning on" does not go in the direction of curtailing imagination, but rather points to the fact that imagination operates *ex nihilo*, which does not mean *in nihilo* or *cum nihilo* (Castoriadis 1987:221). Imagination has to start from what it finds already there and the Freudian notion of "leaning on" is meant to explain how this happens, but it does so by fully displaying its radical character.

To put it bluntly, the notion of leaning on implies that "there can be no oral instinct without mouth and the breast and no anal instincts without an anus" (Castoriadis 1987:290). As Castoriadis makes clear, this does not simply mean that the existence of the mouth and breast are mere "external conditions" without which there would be no oral or anal instinct, in the same way in which without oxygen in the circulatory system there would be no psyche and thus no fantasies or sublimation. Oxygen does not directly contribute to fantasies, whereas the mouth-breast and the anus have to be taken into account by the psyche because they support and induce (290). Otherwise stated, the privileged somatic data will always have to be taken up again by the psyche, and, as a consequence, they will always leave their mark on the psychic working (290).

By elaborating the Freudian notion of leaning on in this direction, and transforming it into a quasi-ontological category (Whitebook 1989:233), Castoriadis is able to avoid the danger of an all-encompassing idealistic subjectivism while at the same time rejecting any naive form of realism. Leaning on what is given does not mean being determined by it, as naive realist ontology would have it. As a consequence, Castoriadis can say, for instance, that notwithstanding all the aforementioned limits, the social imaginary has a capacity for virtual universal covering so that any irruption of the raw world can immediately be treated as a sign of something, that is, it can be interpreted away and thus exorcised (Castoriadis 1991:153).

The fact that the social imaginary has to take into account the need for food does not yet tell us why certain animals that are eaten in one corner of the globe are taboo in another (Castoriadis 1987:150). But the power of the imaginary is particularly evident in the fact that even that which collides with its order can be subject to a symbolic processing: transgression of social rule can become an "illness," and completely alien societies that are fundamentally at odds with a given social imaginary can become "strangers," "savages," or even "impious" (150).

At the same time, though, Castoriadis tries to make space for the individual within this theory. He explicitly observes that the major threat to the instituted society is its own creativity: the society that created individuals is at the same time created by them. As we have seen in the passage quoted, the radical imaginary has two dimensions: the social-historical imaginary and the radical imagination. Indeed, the merit of Castoriadis's approach is to point out that the *instituting* social imaginary is always at the same time *instituted*, which means that no society could ever exist if the individuals created by the society had themselves not created it.

Society can exist concretely only through the fragmentary and complementary incarnation and incorporation of its institution and its imaginary significations in the living, talking, and acting individuals of that society. Athenian society is nothing but the Athenians, Castoriadis observes; without them, it is only the remnants of a transformed landscape, the debris of marble and vases, indecipherable inscriptions, and worn statues fished out of the Mediterranean (Castoriadis 1991:145). But the Athenians are Athenians only by means of the *nomos* of the *polis*. In this relationship between an instituted society, on the one hand—which infinitely transcends the totality of the individuals that "compose" it, but can exist only by being "realized" in the individuals that it produces—and these individuals, on the other, we experience an unprecedented type of relationship that cannot be thought of under the categories of the whole and its parts, the set and its elements, and, even less, the universal and the particular (Castoriadis 1991:145).

By speaking of a "radical imagination" together with a social imaginary, Castoriadis (1987, 1997d) suggests that these categories reciprocally imply each other. Even more so: as he puts it in the passage quoted before, the full recognition of the radical imagination implies the recognition of the other dimension of imagination, that is, of the social imaginary. The concept of *radical* imagination has the function of stressing that, as Aristotle maintained, together with an imitative and reproductive or combinatory *phantasia*, there is also what can be called a primary imagination. This consists in the faculty of producing "images in the largest possible sense of the term (that of "forms," *Bilder*), that is images without which there would not be any thought at all, and which, therefore, precede any thought" (Castoriadis 1987:336, 1997d:320–321). Let me dwell on this view more at length because it contains important suggestions as to a possible way out of our two dilemmas.

With regard to the first tension, Castoriadis's notion of a radical imagination helpfully emphasizes that imagination does not imply the nonexistence of the objects of imagination, even though we can also have images that do not correspond to anything in the external world. Images are our way of being in the world, so that one could even say that no world is given for us that is not imagined. According to Castoriadis, the reason why imagination came to be associated with the idea of fictitiousness is that it can create *ex nihilo*—not *in nihilo* or *cum nihilo* (Castoriadis 1987:221).

The traditional Western ensemble logic, which is based on the identity assumption *ex nihilo nihil*, could not, as a consequence, but conceive of imagination as essentially nonexistence. To this identity and set logic, which could never account for the fact that when "x = x" it is always "x = non x," Castoriadis counterpoises the logic of magmas. The concept of magma points to the fact that significations are not "determinate beings," but webs of references or bundles of referrals (*faisceaux de renvois*; Castoriadis 1987:347). These are certainly always determinable, but they are never completely determinate (221). Hence to investigate the nature of the radical imaginary in its two constitutive dimensions we need an alternative logic that is able to think the undetermined.

In sum, the expression *radical imagination* has the function of conveying two ideas. In the first place, *radical* points to the link with the modern project of autonomy (Castoriadis 1987, 1991). Castoriadis recovers such a project, but tries to address it within a theory of imagination informed by psychoanalysis and thus by the observation that individuals are the imaginary products of socialization. *Imagination* is said to be radical in the sense that it can always potentially question its own products, since it can never be completely mastered. Far from being a source of errors and falsity, imagination is seen as a means for critique, and critique is identified as the condition of autonomy, of the possibility to give oneself one's law (Castoriadis 1987:101–107). In the second place, *radical* invokes the concept of creation or the fact that imagination is prior to the distinction between *real* and *fictitious*. In other words, it is because radical imagination exists that *reality* exists for us and that it exists as it exists—and, therefore, one can add, it exists *tout court* (Castoriadis 1997b:321).

The associated concept of the social *imaginary* always reminds us that there is not a subject separated from the society she lives in—there is no punctual ego separated from a reality that she is facing. As we have noted before, the passage from the concept of *imagination* to that of the *imaginary* reflects a change from a *subject*-oriented approach to a *context*-oriented one (Arnason 1994). Thus, Castoriadis's concept of the social imaginary underscores the fact that the definition of "reality" itself depends on the instituting and instituted social imaginary and not vice versa (Castoriadis 1991:147). The fact that the word *reality* has been conceived in so many different ways shows that the social-historical constitutes reality and not vice versa.

This approach to the imagination/imaginary radically subverts the presuppositions of the genealogy of imagination reconstructed in chapter 1. Namely, because imagination exists, reality itself exists, and not the other way around. Once this relation between imagination and reality has been inverted and a new logic for thinking the radical nature of imagination is developed, the tension we have identified vanishes, deprived of its grounding presupposition. Has Castoriadis taken us beyond the dilemmas of the genealogy of imagination? His inversion of the relationship between imagination and reality with the relative emphasis on the radical character of the imaginary has certainly laid the path to go beyond the first tension. The second is much more complicated.

We have seen that, according to Castoriadis, the definition of the real is the result of the dialectics between the instituted and the instituting side of the social imaginary. Behind this idea there is a complex view of the relationship between individuals, who cannot but exist within imaginary significations, and a social imaginary, which cannot but exist in and through individuals themselves. Yet this complexity, which, as Castoriadis points out, cannot be reduced to simple relationships such as that between whole and part, the general and the particular, stands at odds with Castoriadis's own idea of a complete heterogeneity between the monadic psyche and society.

Castoriadis goes so far as to speak of an "absolute scission" between the two poles of the instituted/instituting social imaginary: the social-historical, on the one hand, and what he calls the "psychical monad," on the other (see, for instance, Castoriadis 1987:204ff.). The psyche is said to be monadic because it is "pure representational/affective/intentional flux," indeterminate and, in principle, unmasterable. Drawing inspiration from the theory, but also his own experience as a psychoanalyst, Castoriadis argues that it is only through an always incomplete, violent, and forceful process of socialization that a social individual can be produced. This happens through a process of schooling that starts with the very first encounter with language (in the first place, the language of the mother). Through socialization, the psyche is forced to give up its initial objects and to invest in (*cathecting*) socially instituted objects, rules, and the world. Through the internalization of the world and the imaginary significations created by society, an "individual," properly speaking, is created out of a "screaming monster" (Castoriadis 1991:148).

Castoriadis's thesis about the monadic isolation and the fundamental "hetereogeneity" between the psyche and society seems, therefore, to lead to a highly problematic and thus untenable metaphysical opposition (Habermas 1987:327).[21] Once we find ourselves within the monadic isolation of the unconscious, it becomes difficult even to explain how communication is possible in the first place (Whitebook 1989). Behind this absolute scission there is again the tension between an "individual imagination" and the "social imaginary" from which we started. Although Castoriadis's view has the merit of signaling the problem, his dichotomy between the social-historical and the monadic core is the sign that he has not yet fully overcome it.

There seems to be no easy answer to this tension. If one starts with "imagination," understood as an individual faculty, then the problem is how to conceive of the relationship between individual imagination and social context. If we begin with the concept of the social imaginary, then the problem is how to reconcile it with the free imagination of individuals. The problem seems unsolvable, and Castoriadis's metaphysical opposition between society and the monadic core of the psyche is the sign that he was not fully able to go beyond it. The task of the next chapter is to explore another possible way of framing the issue.

3

Toward a Theory of the Imaginal

> The image is spontaneous, primordial, given with the psyche itself, an essential
> poem at the heart of things.
>
> JAMES HILLMAN, *Healing Fiction*

The genealogy of imagination has left us with a double tension: is imagination
mere fantasy? Is it social or individual? After passing from the imagination to the
more context-oriented category of the imaginary, we need to explore the possibilities of a theory of the imaginal.[1] The imaginal is a category that can lead
us beyond the impasse of a choice between theories of the imagination as an
individual faculty and theories of the imaginary as a social context. The English
language clearly indicates what this is primarily about: *imaginal*, from Latin *imaginalis*, denotes what is made of images (*imagines*). As such, the imaginal can be
both the product of an individual faculty and of a social context as well as the
result of a complex, yet-to-be-determined interaction between the two. As a consequence, the imaginal points beyond the second of the aforementioned tensions.
Moreover, the concept also enables us to solve the first one because, in contrast to
both mere fantasy and the merely imaginary, it does not make any assumption as
to the ontological status of images themselves. This particularly holds, as we will
see, if one understands images as pictorial (re)presentations or appearances that
operate both at the conscious and the unconscious level.

In the first place, we should point out that the concept of the imaginal differs
from that of *imaginative*, which, as its etymology (*imaginatus*) makes clear, refers
to something that has already happened. *Imaginative* denotes either the quality
of a person endowed with the individual faculty of imagination or the quality
of an action of imagining that has already taken place (Simpson and Weiner

1989:7:669–709). The term is used always as an adjective, for instance, when we say that it was a very "imaginative story" or, again, as when we say that "she is a very imaginative woman." We can summarize the difference by saying that while what is *imaginative* is the result of the work of imagination, *imaginal*, as the conceptual ground encompassing the totality of what pertains to images, is what makes the *imaginative* possible in the first place.

The term *imaginal* was introduced into the current philosophical debate by Henry Corbin, who derived it from Islamic philosophy. In his translation of the works of the Persian Platonists, he used the Latin expression *mundus imaginalis* to render the Arab '*alam al-mithal* (Corbin 1979:preface to the second edition). In the authors translated by Corbin the expression denotes a world between pure intellectual intuitions and sense perceptions (ibid.). Despite the label of Platonism, here the influence of the Aristotelian notion of *phantasia*—the faculty of producing *phantasmata*, which makes sensation possible and thus both precedes and enables the work of intellect—is also evident. However, the notion of *mundus imaginalis* does not denote a faculty, as is the case with Aristotle. *Imaginalis* is the adjective used to characterize a *mundus*, a world in itself. It is within this intermediate world—neither material, like the world of pure sensibility, nor immaterial, like that of the intellect—that the so-called acting imagination operates. The latter is the correlate of what medieval thinkers called the acting intellect, namely, the intellect that creates the world rather than simply mirroring it.[2] Similarly, the acting imagination does not simply mirror the empirical world, but is instead endowed with the capacity to create one.

In Corbin, as well as in the works of the Iranian metaphysicians that he translates, the concept of the imaginal has both a strong ontological connotation and a decisively religious flavor. In particular, the acting imagination, whose activity takes place within this realm of the imaginal, presupposes an immortal soul and is the specific site of prophecy (Corbin 1979:preface to the second edition). This idea of an imaginal link between the creative capacity of the soul and the visions of the prophets, established in Islamic philosophy, is transmitted through the Latin Middle Ages all the way into European modernity (Piro 2008:256–258). Although the story is fascinating, the imaginal, as used currently, does not need to make any such ontological—let alone religious—assumptions.

Indeed, whereas Corbin limits the imaginal to this very specific context, the term has subsequently been used in a much wider sense. In the preface to the second edition of his translations, Corbin (1979:23) had already lamented the term's use outside that specific context. For Corbin, the concept has nothing to do with the so-called "civilization of the image"—although, as we will see, it is perhaps not by chance that the need for such a word (and concept) was felt precisely within this context. As I have suggested, the emergence of a new word is often the sign of the emergence of a new problem or at least of a new way of look-ing at a preexisting problem. The fact that we retrieved this third term, *imaginal*, after *imagination* and the *imaginary*, is the sign that something new emerged for which current vocabulary did not suffice. Another word was needed to render the novelty of a culture that has made of the image itself its constitutive moment. And this novel aspect, which our modern vocabulary was inadequate to describe, points precisely to the exponentially increased role of images in contemporary societies. This, as we have mentioned, is very likely to bring about a change in our conception of reality, since in a world dominated by images such as ours, it is the virtual—the unreal by definition—that risks becoming the most real.[3]

Indeed, the reason why Corbin made recourse to a new word is precisely that the available term (*imaginary*) was perceived to be too strictly associated with the idea of unreality to adequately translate the Arabic *'alam al-mithal*. In order to render the idea of a world made of images, but at the same time real, he used the term *imaginal*, importing it from the Latin *imaginalis*. Corbin, and the philosophi-cal tradition associated with his name, used the concept for specific purposes (to recover the intuition of Islamic philosophy), but for our aim it is sufficient to note that, from the very beginning, the concept of imaginal points to the fact that between pure intellect and the forms of sensibility—to use a Kantian expres-sion—there is something else. This intermediate level can also have its appropri-ate cognitive function precisely because it is not relegated to the spheres of the unreal and the fictitious.[4]

Arguably, one of the main contributions of Corbin has been pointing to the distinction between the *imaginal* (*imaginal*), as that which is simply made of im-ages, and the term *imaginary* (*imaginaire*), a term which, particularly in Corbin's native French, is strictly associated with unreality and fictitiousness. It is in this sense that the term has proved to be particularly helpful.[5] As we have seen, even Lacan's peculiar use of the term *imaginary* does not differ much from common sense: it is by definition the domain of alienation. Conversely, the term *imaginal* does away with all the ontological assumptions of unreality or alienation im-plied by the term *imaginary*. Despite the fact that the term is not so common, the *Oxford English Dictionary* already included this peculiar aspect of *imaginal* in its definition more than twenty years ago, by stating that *imaginal* primarily means what pertains to imagination or to images (Simpson and Wiener 1989:2:668). There is no mention here of how real or unreal such images or imaginations are. In contrast, the same dictionary definition of *imaginary* clearly points to the ontological bias of this term insofar as the *imaginary* is said to denote what exists only in fancy, that which has no real existence and is therefore opposed to what is "real" and "actual" (2:668).

Thus, in contrast to the unreal and fictitious, which is associated with the imaginary, the imaginal has no embedded ontological status; it makes no assumption as to the reality of the images that fall within its conceptual domain.[6] The imaginal comes *before* the distinction between "real" and "fictitious" because, to paraphrase Castoriadis, the latter only makes sense within a specific form of the imaginal. As we have seen, the definition of what is real is not an a priori of human understanding, but is something that has evolved continuously over the centuries. This is particularly important for an investigation into the nature of images in the present cultural context, where so many different conceptions of reality compete with one another.

As a consequence, the concept of the imaginal also differs from that of imagery, which is at the center of contemporary philosophical debates about the status of mental images (Block 1981; Kosslyn, Thompson, and Ganis 2006; Tye 2000). As we have seen in chapter 1, according to a philosophical tradition that goes back at least as far as Aristotle, there cannot be thinking without images (or *phantasmata*, as Aristotle would put it). This idea, profoundly influential in Western philosophy, fell out of vogue in the second half of the twentieth century, partly due to the influence of behaviorism in the middle of the century and partly due to the more general difficulty of conceptualizing mental images within a strictly scientific view of the mind (Kind 2001:86).

How can we have scientific evidence of *phantasmata* that have become phantoms? How do we see and register them if they are only mental? How do we account for them, let alone experiment with them, in a universally accessible way? Mental images seem to possess an intrinsically subjective and undetermined status that makes them difficult to assess through universally accessible and verifiable scientific procedures. Even today, long after behaviorism's fall from grace, there remains some skepticism toward the very concept of mental images, so much so that some philosophers prefer to provide accounts of imagination without even mentioning or offering a conceptual account of mental images.[7]

Yet, very recently, a new series of advances in psychology and in philosophy of mind have tried to bring mental images back to the fore. For instance, some have argued not only that certain types of imagining presuppose the existence of mental images but also that any theory of imagination must somehow take into account their crucial role.[8] Since then the debate has mainly revolved around the crucial issue whether such mental imagery is picturelike or something reducible to linguistic descriptions (Block 1981; Tye 2000). But this is precisely the point where the analytic notion of imagery differs from that of the imaginal: as we have already mentioned, the notion of the imaginal, as it has been elaborated within psychoanalysis, points to the primacy of images, or the fact that not all images can be reduced to linguistic descriptions, and thus also the fact that it bypasses the question of the reality of images.

The very term *imagery* mostly refers to the use of pictures in books, films, paintings, etc., to describe ideas or situations—in sum, figures or material representations *of* things (Simpson and Wiener 1989:2:668). As a consequence, imagery essentially refers to representations and manifestations *of* something else. Like the corresponding adjective *imaginary*, imagery primarily refers to what exists in the mind and has no real existence (2:669). It is not by chance, then, that the debate focuses on "*mental* images" and thus mainly on what occurs in the mind. By contrast, the concept of the imaginal does not make any assumption about the reality of images or whether they are mental or not. Thus, while imagery refers to a series of material representations of something else, the imaginal is not essentially a representation *of* anything. This is what I try to convey by saying that the imaginal is made of images that are "(re-)presentations," that is, representations that are presences in themselves, independently of their being real or unreal, mental or extramental.

This brings us to another crucial difference between analytic debates about imagery and the notion of the imaginal as I am using it in this book. The latter refers to the production of images at both the conscious and the unconscious level. Whereas the production of images at the unconscious level is generally contested or neglected within the imagery debate,[9] the concept of the imaginal has an illustrious history of uses in psychoanalysis. This is mainly due to the work of the Jungian psychoanalyst James Hillman, who explicitly referred to Corbin and the neo-Platonist tradition in his usage of the term *imaginal* (Hillman 1972, 2005). As I will try to illustrate now, Hillman's use of the term *imaginal* is close to my own usage, but with some important differences.

By "imaginal," Hillman (2005:56) means the unconscious production of images that, like the old Greek *daimons*, are both real and unreal at the same time. Hillman reads Jung's concept of psychic reality through Corbin's idea of a middle realm, that is, the idea of a world that is as ontologically real as that of the physical objects and the intellect. This psychic reality, discovered by Jung, consists of fictive figures and images that are at the same time real and unreal. A first difference between my and Hillman's usage of the term *imaginal* thus appears immediately: whereas Hillman remains faithful to Corbin's notion of the *mundus imaginalis* as an ontological reality, I propose to use the notion of imaginal in the thinner sense of what is made of images—again, independently of their ontological status. Otherwise stated, whereas the images to which Hillman refers make up a *mundus* that *is* both real and unreal (and thus presupposes a certain understanding of reality itself), the images that my notion of the imaginal presupposes *can* be both real and unreal (whatever meaning we may attach to those terms).

What Hillman wants to signal with this term, even when he uses the expression *imaginal* as an adjective, is the fact that images are so crucial to the unconscious that one could almost say that the unconscious is nothing but images. It is in this sense that the imaginal is primordial. Drawing inspiration from Jung, who, as we will see later on, was one of the first to introduce the notion of *imago* in psychoanalysis, Hillman elaborates a psychoanalytical method that focuses on the free production of images, utilizing this aspect of the unconscious as one of its therapeutic tools. This method presupposes a refusal to reduce images to simple manifestations *of* something else and promote their free development as radical creativity.

While, according to Hillman, Freudian psychoanalysis follows the motto "Where id was, ego shall be" (Freud 1965:100) and consequently treats images as manifestations of a deeper reality that we must decipher,[10] he sees in images presentations and presences in themselves. "Turn to your images," says Hillman, and, quoting Jung, "every psychic process is an image and an imagining ... and these images are as real as you yourself are real" (Hillman 2005:71). Rather than dissipating images by looking for the deeper reality that they (re-)present, Hillman's analytical psychology invites the patient to live by her own images. In his reading, Freudian psychoanalysis would therefore be monotheistic because it considers images to be symptomatic of a deeper reality, and it is to such a reality that it reduces them.[11] In contrast, Hillman's method invites us to accept as psychologically constitutive the multiplicity of forms through which the human psyche expresses itself, rather than attempting to exorcise them by reducing them to a further, deeper reality, be it the Oedipal complex or any other complex of the psyche. Accepting and encouraging such a multiplicity of images is the task of what Hillman defines as a "polytheistic psychology" (Hillman 1971).

The notion of an imaginal ego is thus meant to signal nothing less than a deep revision of the psychoanalytic discipline (Carotenuto 1991:275–276). While the Freudian ego is driven by a monotheistic drive, Hillman's psychology is deeply polytheistic precisely because it takes the plurality of images as primordial and irreducible. To the Freudian ideal of a hero that brings consciousness where the id was, Hillman opposes an "imaginal ego" that lives off of its intrinsic, irreducible multiplicity. Developing an "imaginal ego" thus entails a subtle balance between an active will, an interpretive understanding and the independent movement of fantasies (Hillman 1972:189). The result of this emphasis on the imaginal is that analytical therapy feeds a radical activation of imagination; it is a constant invitation to allow images to rise up and inhabit them without imposing on the patient the need to penetrate to the supposed deeper reality they represent.

It may be worth remembering here that the paradox of the absence of imagination in the Freudian vocabulary goes hand in hand with Freud's extensive use not just of fantasy and its derivatives but also the term representation. As Castoriadis notes, in an only apparently marginal note to his *The Imaginary Institution of Society*, the term *representation* that Freud used almost as many times as the number of pages in his writings is misleading because it surreptitiously suggests that there is something besides what is re-presented (Castoriadis 1987:400).[12] In contrast to Freud's notion of representation, Hillman's concept of the imaginal has the advantage of stressing that unconscious images are presences in themselves, and not manifestations *of* something else.

Hillman's theory of imaginal has been an important step in the current configuration of the concept. In the first place, he has, so to speak, secularized Corbin's notion of the imaginal by rooting it in the immanence of the unconscious production of images. The unconscious expresses itself through images. In a way, it is nothing but images. Or, to be more precise: it is images well before being language. In my view, this is something Freud himself would have agreed with (despite the fact that he would probably have spoken about fantasies). But Hillman radicalizes this stance. As he puts it, "the image is spontaneous, primordial, given with the psyche itself, an essential poem at the heart of things. The primary datum is the image ... this is the soul presenting itself, straight on" (Hillman 2005:75). Indeed, what is the unconscious besides a stream of images? Language plays a crucial role in the structuring of the unconscious, but, even before that, the unconscious itself speaks in and through images that cannot be reduced to linguistic descriptions.

However inspiring Hillman's notion of the imaginal may be, my understanding of the concept is, at the same time, both broader and stricter than Hillman's. It is a more restricted usage because by imaginal I mean what is made of images in the sense of pictorial (re)presentations. In contrast to this understanding, Hillman includes all sorts of unconscious images in his notion of the imaginal: pictorial, sensorial, and even behavioral (Hillman 1972:189). Indeed, he explicitly says that the "imaginal ego" is not a pictorial ego (189). On the contrary, in this work

I will focus mainly on pictorial appearances that can be both presentations and re-presentations.

The notion of picture or picturing can be understood in a broader or in a more restricted meaning. In the former, it includes whatever appears and is therefore close to Aristotle's notion of *phantasmata*. In this sense one can speak for instance of logical pictures.[13] In the more restricted sense, to which I will primarily be referring in this work, images are pictorial (re)presentations, because they differ from logical, auditory, olfactory, and other mental productions.[14] In other words, the imaginal in this more restricted meaning of the term means something that is visualizable, which does not necessarily mean that it is visual, in the sense of a retinal image actually taking place.[15] By visualizable I mean something that can potentially be visualized, even if it is not actually so.[16]

The reason why I use the notion of the imaginal in this more restricted sense will become clear in the course of the argument. Despite the fact that a full account of the imaginal should also include the nonvisual, in the course of this investigation I want to focus on the pictorial side of images understood as (re)presentations precisely because this is the aspect that is most relevant for the transformation in the nature of politics I am interested in here. Thus, images here should be understood as pictorial (re)presentations, independent of whether or not they are actually visualized. They are (re)presentations because they *can* be representations of something else, signs of things; but they can also be simple presences in themselves, as is often the case with unconscious images and symbols. Again, the *epoché* is radical. If Hillman detranscendentalizes Corbin's imaginal world, I go one step further in that I try to deontologize it.

This means that the imaginal is not for me a third world between the sensible world and the intellectual world. In other words, whereas for Hillman the imaginal is both fictitious and real because it is a world in itself that participates in both ontological properties, I argue that it *can* be both or either—depending on the definition of reality one assumes. The imaginal is not a world, but it is what makes a world possible in the first place. I radically suspend the issue of reality, because, as we have seen, the definition of reality itself varies too much from one context to another for one to naively believe (with Kant) that "reality" is given to us as an a priori category. To put it bluntly, the imaginal is a field of possibilities.

But my use of the concept is also broader than Hillman's because by imaginal I mean what is made of images, be they produced at the conscious or at the unconscious level. This reflects my conviction that the dividing line between what is conscious and what is unconscious can at times be very thin, so that what is conscious can become unconscious minutes later and vice versa.[17] This is something already suggested by Jung in *Psychological Types* (1962:554) when he observes that images can be the expression of both the unconscious and the momentarily conscious situation at the same time.

It may be worth remembering here that Jung, in contrast to Freud, clearly distinguished between imagination and fantasy on the basis of the observation that fantasy is usually associated with the illusory, whereas imagination is an "active creation finalized to a certain end" (Jung 1936:62; translation mine). This is also conveyed by his psychoanalytical usage of the term *imago*. He used the Latin term *imago*, rather than the usual word *image*, precisely to point out that what he has in mind are not images in general, but subjective images, or, even better, the unconscious schemes through which a subject experiences others. It is in this sense that he speaks of the maternal, paternal, and fraternal *imagos*.[18] In my view, it is within this Jungian notion that we should look for the origins of Hillman's imaginal.[19]

But my usage of the term *imaginal* is also broader than Jung's *imagos* in the sense that it includes both images and *imagos*, that is, both conscious and unconscious images. Besides the Jungian use, the term *imago* has been subsequently employed in psychoanalysis to denote more generally any subjective determination of the image (Evans 1996:95–96). In contrast to the term *image*, the Latin word *imago* thus denotes both visual representations and the feelings that are attached to them. As we have seen in chapter 1, the idea that images are vehicles of emotions and desires goes at least as far back as Aristotle; what is new here is the emphasis on their unconscious dimension. This is the reason why some psychoanalysts, such as Lacan, went as far as to say that "it is possible to designate in the *imago* the proper object of psychology, exactly to the same extent that Galileo's notion of the inert material point formed the basis of physics" (Lacan 1999:188).

I take this sentence to mean that there is something in subjective images themselves that can be investigated only by psychoanalysis and that this is the reason why it is its "proper object."[20] Whereas linguistic expressions of the unconscious can be approached through other means (such as linguistics and literary theory, to mention only the most obvious), unconscious images cannot always be translated into linguistic descriptions. Some images, as Hillman suggests in the passage quoted in the epigraph to this chapter, are primordial and therefore cannot be reduced to anything else. The most we can do is visualize or live by them. Translating them into linguistic descriptions means bringing them to an end. By assigning them a meaning, their symbolic value is explained, but thus also explained away. Once a symbol finds its "proper" meaning in a linguistic expression, it dies. The same is true for unconscious images. This also settles, at a different level, the central question of the imagery debate concerning whether or not images are picturelike or mere linguistic descriptions. Even admitting that all conscious images could be reduced to linguistic descriptions, this is hardly the case with unconscious images. Translating unconscious images into linguistic descriptions means curtailing their evocative power. To sum up, extending the notion of the imaginal to both conscious and unconscious images has the effect of emphasizing that there exists a part of our mental life that is consubstantial to images themselves and cannot be reduced to something else.[21] This does not mean that unconscious images are mute: it means that they communicate with means *other* than words and linguistic descriptions. And this is the reason why the imaginal is primordial, spontaneous, given with the psyche itself. To put it bluntly, whereas imagination, as the faculty to represent what is not there, can be understood as the sign of a lack, the imaginal is the result of an abundance.

But my usage of the term imaginal also reflects a different definition of the unconscious, one that distances itself from both Jung's and Hillman's. In the first place, by unconscious I mean very generally what we are unaware of.[22] Unconscious in this sense is both what has been repressed and what has simply never come to the level of consciousness. For instance, it is well documented that we are able to process only a minimal part of information we receive (Fromm 2001:98; Hopper 2003:127). The rest gets stored somewhere in the psyche, in a place that some have called the preconscious in order to distinguish it from the unconscious that results from repression.[23] As a consequence, the unconscious I am concerned with in this work encompasses all that we are unaware of, including, therefore, both the subconscious and the preconscious.

My usage of the term *unconscious* does not necessarily refer to the mainstream definition of the unconscious as result of the repression of a part of individual experience; even less so does it presuppose the Jungian concept of collective unconscious. Hillman's imaginal directly refers to Jung's collective unconscious since, in his view, it is Jung's notion of archetypes and the collective unconscious that opens the path to the imaginal world. For Hillman, images are always archetypes, that is, universals of the unconscious psyche that recur in different cultures and historical contexts (Hillman 1972:190, 2005:63).[24] Archetype refers to the unconscious patterns that go beyond individual identity and link us to the entirety of humanity insofar as they are deposited in our biological constitution (Jung 1990).

On the contrary, the concept of imaginal as I have defined it leaves the issue of the individual or archetypical character of the unconscious production of images open. Imaginal is what is made of images, that is, of pictorial (re)presentations, be they produced at the individual or social level. I use here the alternative "individual" or "social" because, together with the concept of individual unconscious, I want to refer to the concept of "*social* unconscious" as an alternative to Jung's collective unconscious. Let me explain what I mean by this term.

The concept of social unconscious has been used by Erich Fromm (2001:128) to point out that "what is unconscious and what is conscious depends on the structure of society and on the patterns of feeling and thought it produces."[25] By emphasizing the constraints that society itself unconsciously exercises on its members, Fromm combined Freud's insights on the unconscious life of the psyche with Marx's observation that it is society that determines the life of its members.[26] Given its emphasis on the social and thus historically and geographically variable character of such unconscious constraints, the notion of the social unconscious distances itself from Jung's and Hillman's collective unconscious. Furthermore, like Fromm, I also understand the term in the strictly operational sense. As he puts it, properly speaking the "unconscious is a mystification" because there is not such a thing as "the" unconscious (Fromm 2001:98). Like the society of which Castoriadis speaks, the unconscious is not a thing—a banality that is always worth remembering. There is not one thing called the unconscious: there are only some experiences of which we are aware and others of which we are unaware, that is, of which we are unconscious (98).

More recently, in his work on the notion of a social unconscious, psychoanalyst Earl Hopper defines this concept in the following way: "The concept of the social unconscious refers to the existence and constraints of social, cultural and communicational arrangements of which people are unaware: unaware, in so far as these arrangements are not perceived (not 'known'), and if perceived not acknowledged ('denied'), and if acknowledged, not taken as problematic ('given'), and if taken as problematic, not considered with an optimal degree of detachment and objectivity." And he later specifies that "constraint" is not meant to imply only "restraint," "inhibition," or "limitation" but also "facilitation," "development," and "even transformation of sensation into feelings" (Hopper 2003:127).

There immediately emerges here an important difference from Fromm's own definition. Whereas Fromm (2001:88) defines the social unconscious "as areas of repression which are common to most members of society," Hopper speaks about the "arrangement of which people are unaware."[27] This notion of social unconscious is thus closer to my understanding because "unconscious" here is not only the result of mechanisms of removal and repression of parts our experience. In this view, the social unconscious can also be formed through the simple exposure to contents of which we are not aware.

I call it social to point out the fact that it is the result of specifically *social* experiences. It can also be the result of forms of repressions, but it is not necessarily so. In this respect, we can distinguish between a weak and a strong version of the social unconscious: while the strong corresponds to the notion of unconscious as synonymous with the repressed, the weak version is represented by Hopper's broader approach that takes "unconscious" to simply mean "what we are unaware of" (Bottici and Kuehner 2011). This is a notion of unconscious that is much more flexible than both Freud's and Jung's usage. It is more flexible than Freud's because it also includes what he would have called the preconscious,[28] thereby pointing to the fact that there are certain images that express both the conscious and the unconscious situation of the psyche at the same time and that what is unconscious in a certain moment can become conscious the minute after and vice versa.

But it is also much more flexible than Jung's collective unconscious because it does not presuppose the existence of universal archetypes. Although the idea of a collective unconscious is less contestable than it may prima facie appear in its many vulgarizations (first and foremost because it is a hypothesis and not a metaphysical entity),[29] the social unconscious differs from it because it is not the same for all human beings.[30] The notion of social unconscious seems to be a better tool, then, to investigate unconscious dynamics in postmodern societies where the nuclear bourgeois family, with its three crucial figures (mother, father, siblings), is being challenged. This is not only due to the fact that in other parts of the globe the mononuclear family has never been the rule but also because even in Western societies the typical family structure changes considerably as a consequence of the growing importance of same-sex parents and single-parent children. It is tempting to argue that, in a certain sense, the family is back. But it is undeniable that what has come back is not the same thing that had gone away. To investigate the consequences of such an epochal change is beyond the scope of this book, but this transformation of the family is one that we should keep in mind if we wish to equip ourselves with more flexible tools for taking these consequences into account.

To employ the social unconscious as a more flexible tool is also a great advantage in empirical research. If one uses the notion of a collective unconscious in the study of dynamics of exchange in the context of globalization, the results will be oriented toward universality and sameness from the very beginning. On the contrary, the employment of the notion of social unconscious seems more apt to render ongoing processes of questioning old boundaries and the concomitant creation of new ones—what some people have tried to render with the neologism "glocalisation" (Robertson 1992).[31]

Precisely for its capacity to register contextual differences in unconscious patterns, the notion of a social unconscious is not primarily rooted in biology. While the collective unconscious has its roots in the biological constitution of the human being and is therefore transmitted through heredity,[32] the social unconscious is always the mediated result of our social experience and cannot be taken to be the same for every human being. As a consequence, it does not derive from our biological constitution but rather from social experiences such as language, shared images, and other social practices. The social unconscious thus understood changes not only in space but also, and most significantly, in time.

Bringing together the different threads of the discussion, we can say that the imaginal can be both conscious and unconscious, social and individual. It is a field of possibilities in the production of images understood as (re)presentations. The latter can indeed take place at all these different levels, and it would be problematic to leave one of them out. Keeping all these different dimensions potentially open is thus a helpful strategy in the current context where, as a consequence of the exponential increase in the imaginal produced by contemporary capitalism, the proliferation of images has become more constitutive of subjectivity than it has ever been in the past. Otherwise said: Hillman's imperative—"turn to your images"—may no longer be the remedy, since images themselves, both at the conscious and the unconscious level, may turn out to be no longer "ours" in any significant meaning of the term. As Mitchell has pointed out, there are things that pictures, in our late capitalist societies, simply "want from us" (Mitchell 2005), and this may be different from what we do.

This brings us to a crucial point: are the images that compose the imaginal a source of alienation, as Lacan would have it, or a source of liberation, as Hillman seems to suggest? I would argue that it can be either, depending on the context. When Lacan writes that "the first effect of the *imago* which appears in the human beings is an effect of subjective *alienation*" (Lacan 1999:181), he is referring to a particular kind of images—as signaled by the word *imago*, which has the function of emphasizing the subjective determination of the image. In the case of the specular image, with which the infant identifies herself, we can hardly deny that the image is alienating in the technical sense of the term—and that it is constitutively so for both infants as well as socialized adults. Without a doubt, images *can* be alienating.

But this is only one part of the story. Images are neither good nor bad as such.[33] And not all images have the deceptive effects of the *imagos* composing Lacan's Imaginary. This does not only hold for conscious images, such as that of this computer in front of me. It is equally valid for unconscious images. As we have seen, the unconscious is a ceaseless production of images, and it is through such a production that it expresses its creativity. The unconscious is imaginal, because, to paraphrase Castoriadis, it is the essentially undetermined and ceaseless creation of images (Castoriadis 1987:3). As we have seen in the previous chapter, Castoriadis uses the notion of images in a much broader sense than I do. This is clear from the very beginning of *The Imaginary Institution of Society* when he speaks of the imaginary as the creation of figures/forms/images as if all of these are one and the same thing (3). He can do so because he understands them in the broadest sense of the term *images*, that is, he takes images to mean forms—whereas, for the purposes of this book, I refer primarily to the notion of pictorial (re)presentations. Notwithstanding this important difference, Castoriadis's emphasis on the radicalness of imagination/imaginary contains a central contribution for any psychoanalytical account of our capacity to imagine.[34]

Nevertheless, as was mentioned in the previous chapter, Castoriadis remains entrapped in the second tension of the genealogy of imagination. In particular, he is led to postulate a monadic core of the psyche precisely to be able to explain how creativity is possible, even if individuals themselves are formed by the process of socialization to the imaginary significations of society through what he calls the "triadic phase" (300). As he says, it is through a violent process of socialization that the society imposes on the psyche "an organization which is essentially heterogeneous with it" (298–301). In some of the strongest formulations, Castoriadis pushes this heterogeneity so far as to say that the psyche is "in no way 'predestined' by nature" to socialization, so much so that this imposition "amounts to a violent break, forced [on it] by its relation to others" (300–301).

Despite the fact that, as Whitebook (1989:236) observes, there are passages in Castoriadis that seem to contradict this idea of an inherent asocial and monadic core of the psyche,[35] the more general question arises of whether it is necessary to postulate such a heterogeneity between the psyche and society in order to be able to explain the autonomy and radical creativity of the imaginal. This is a crucial question. In the first place, even within a view of the self inspired by psychoanalysis, there is no need to conceive of the psyche in terms of monadic isolation. Rather, it could be argued that our basic instinct even before we enter the world is to *relate* to the other—in particular to the figure of the mother. We are not monadic selves that become dependent on each other through a violent socialization. We are, from the very beginning, *dependent* beings, notwithstanding our monadic drives.

The psyche is better understood as always already open to the discourse of the other rather than as essentially heterogeneous to it. As Gauchet (2002:7–8) observes by commenting on Castoriadis, we are characterized by "constitutive polarities," caught up in a permanent instituting process that is sustained by an original openness to being formed, which goes side by side with our monadic drives. Constituted by such opposite drives, we live strung between two equally impossible and potentially mad poles: that of a total subject and that of a Leibnizian monad without doors or windows. Note that this is a view that is very much compatible with Castoriadis's own magmatic logic, according to which things are determinable but never determinate. In Castoriadis's own magmatic terms, we could say that the psyche *has* to be at the same time social and monadic. One could even argue that this is the necessary consequence of the essentially *undetermined* nature of the psyche and that it is precisely because it is undetermined that it cannot be monadic.

The reason why I think Castoriadis is led to postulate such a heterogeneity is that, like many philosophers who preceded him, he looked at the human being primarily as a being-toward-death. Death is indeed the only event in our life when we are completely monadic. All other acts that accompany our lives—from love and hate to language and thinking—take place with others. Even thinking, apparently one of our ordinarily solitary practices, presupposes the presence of others because it presupposes the existence of language.[36] As Arendt (1982:10) put it, quoting Kant, "company is indispensable for thinking."[37]

Death is the only act in our life that does not presuppose the presence of others. Death can be more or less painful, more or less remembered by those who assist to it, but it is essentially a monadic business. The body dies alone. Despite this peculiarity of death vis-à-vis all other events in human life, surprisingly enough, it is the moment to which most philosophers have concentrated their attention, with the result that the human being that most of them have portrayed is an individual in the strong sense of the term.[38] This is the consequence of the privileged attention that, at least since Plato, philosophers gave to end of life over other experiences of it—and, most notably, over its beginning.[39] Not by chance, Greek philosophers called human beings the "mortals" (*brotoi*; Cavarero 2009:55).[40] They privileged death over life because they conceive of philosophy as an activity that unties the soul from its bodily imprisonment derived from birth itself. That is, they conceived of philosophy as a preparation for death (Cavarero 2009:21–39).

On the contrary, if we take the opposite road and look at human beings as beings-after-birth, a completely different perspective emerges.[41] In the first place, it immediately comes to light that we have arrived on the scene literally to-gether with an-other human being.[42] Even before being born, we were accompanied. Communication begins in the womb and never stops thereafter. Only death will put an end to it. At the very beginning, it is a prelinguistic form of communication, but precisely for this reason it is perhaps an even stronger one based on the sharing of the same body. This bodily unity is broken at the moment of birth, but not the communication going on there—a communication mediated by images and sounds prior to being mediated by words. It is a fact that birth is a traumatic event, and this probably explains why philosophers are so eager to forget about it. But it is equally a fact that we are all born and that we are never born alone.

The body that dies alone is always born in company. Thus, if it is true that we are beings-toward-death, it is truer still that we are beings-after-birth. Philosophers are always eager to remind us of the former, but are surprisingly keen to forget about the latter. Yet birth, and thus company, is our primordial experience since we can be beings-toward-death only because we are beings-after-birth. If it is striking to see how many *dispositifs* human beings have envisaged through the centuries to forget about death, even more striking is to note how many they have devised to make us forget that we have been *given* birth to.[43]

Going back to the point that interests us here, if we look at human beings from this perspective, as beings-after-birth, it is not only the essentially social nature of the psyche that comes to light but also the fact that there is a fundamental openness to the other. The emphasis on the fact that each of us is born also reminds us that each of us has brought to the world something that was not there. Despite the fact that human beings today enjoy a control over the deepest mechanism of life that was unthinkable only fifty years ago, it is still the case that every birth is a miracle: literally a new thing, something whose sex and features we are (still?) unable to decide, is brought to the world.[44] As a consequence, there is no need to postulate a monadic core of the psyche in order to explain how creativity and thus autonomy is possible even within a particularly oppressive social imaginary. To put it in Hannah Arendt's words: "The miracle that saves the world, the realm of human affairs, from its normal, "natural" ruin is ultimately the fact of natality, in which the faculty of action is ontologically rooted. It is, in other words, the birth of new men and the new beginning, the action they are capable of by virtue of being born. Only the full experience of this capacity can bestow upon human affairs faith and hope" (Arendt 1958:247).

Following Arendt, but also taking her remarks much further, we can say that the capacity to produce new images does not derive from a presumed monadic core of the unconscious, but rather from the creativity of the unconscious itself as ontologically rooted in natality. This is the miracle that can potentially save us from the specter of a world of total subjects. If the notion of the imaginary can therefore explain how the social context can shape our being up to the point of possessing us, that of the imaginal, as the production of images rooted in natality, can equally explain how freedom can always unexpectedly break through. And this essentially undecided nature of images, which can be either alienating or liberating according to the different contexts, impels us to leave the question of their status of reality open.

But by leaving the alternative of "social" or "individual" open, the concept of the imaginal takes us also beyond Castoriadis and the alternative between the social imaginary as a context and the imagination as an individual faculty. With regard to the influence of contexts on the free imagination of individuals, the concept of the imaginal is meant to signal the fact that there are different possibilities, which go from the spontaneity of imagination as an individual faculty—ontologically grounded in natality—to its disappearance in oppressive social imaginaries. These are, of course, extreme poles of a spectrum in which there are many degrees of possibility; as I have mentioned, the imaginal must indeed be understood as a field of possibilities. However, it is far from being an empty concept because it tells us two important things: first, that the human capacity to form images is a primordial one and that its role must be accounted for; second, that even within a social imaginary that is particularly oppressive and closed there is always the possibility for the free imagination of individuals to emerge.[45]

Following this line of thought, one could even say that the concept of the imaginal is similar to that of the reasonable. Just as the passage from imagination to the imaginary parallels that from reason to rationality, the further step toward the imaginal is in many ways similar to the move toward a theory of the reasonable. The latter can be seen as a way to go beyond the opposition between the concept of reason understood as an individual faculty and that more context oriented of rationality. At least in its original Rawlsian formulation, it denotes a way to mediate between the universal and the particular, between the absolute claims of an unbounded reason and the particularism of contexts that are characterized by the unelimitable fact of pluralism.[46] Similarly, the concept of imaginal is a minimalist concept, a way to go beyond the opposition between the unrestrained freedom of an individual faculty and its disappearance in historically situated contexts. If the two concepts—imaginal and reasonable—converge in that they are both meant to mediate between the power of an individual faculty and the influence of contexts, the main difference is that the reasonable does so by subtracting a minimal core of agreement from the influence of contexts (the overlapping consensus), whereas the imaginal remains open to a variety of possibilities that go from the absolute freedom of an individual faculty to a potentially overwhelming influence of contexts.

In conclusion, the concept of the imaginal leads us beyond the tensions generated by the genealogy of imagination we have reconstructed in the previous chapters. In the first place, by focusing on images understood as pictorial (re)presentations, no ontological assumption is made about their status of reality—whatever meaning we attach to the word. In the second place, by shifting the focus onto images themselves, independently of the faculty that produces them, the concept of the imaginal also goes beyond the alternative between the notion of imagination as an individual faculty versus the imaginary as the social and psychological context that determines us. In the current context, developing the concept of the imaginal means embarking on a double Copernican revolution: beyond the philosophy of the subject (imagination as an individual faculty), but also beyond the equally problematic metaphysics of the context (the imaginary as a given social context). The starting point is neither a subject separated from the world nor a world independent from the subject, but, simply, images. The reason for this is easy to understand: without images there can be neither a world for us nor a subject for the world. Human beings are not only rational animals but also, and even prior to that, imaginal animals. We now have to see the consequences that this has when it comes to politics.

PART 2

POLITICS

Mephistopheles:
> For just where meaning fails, you see,
> a new word will come in—good at need!
> JOHANN WOLFGANG von GOETHE, *Faust*

We have seen in part I that the genealogy of imagination left us with two tensions and that the concept of the imaginal provides us with the tools for addressing them. First, the imaginal, as that which is made of images, of pictorial (re)presentations that are always also presentations in themselves, can be more or less real, according to the different contexts and definitions of reality one refers to. Second, the category of the imaginal can be the result of both the individual imagination and the social imaginary—as well as of a complex yet to be determined interaction between the two.

Having thus defined the imaginal, we can move to the question of what role, if any, such a category plays in politics. Can there be politics without images thus understood? Or is politics always imaginal? And, if so, why start calling it imaginal only now? Otherwise stated: If Mephistopheles is right in saying that a new word arrives precisely when meaning fails, what is the failure of meaning that makes the notion of an imaginal politics necessary or, perhaps, simply useful?

The purpose of the second part of this book is to address these questions by first proposing a genealogy of politics that identifies a broader and stricter meaning of the term (chapter 4) and then showing why both of them depend on the imaginal as we have defined it (chapter 5). Politics will thus be proven to have always been imaginal, although the biopolitical turn we are experiencing has exacerbated this feature of politics. This latter claim will be demonstrated by examining the transformation of the relationship between politics and the imaginal. By looking at both the quantitative and the qualitative transformation of the imaginal, it will be argued that such transformations have been gradually producing both an increasing virtualization and spectacularization of politics (chapter 6). This will also explain why, to paraphrase Mephistopheles, a new word has come in—"good at need!"

4

A Genealogy of Politics

From Its Invention to the Biopolitical Turn

From these things therefore it is clear that the polis is a natural growth, and that man is by nature a zoon politikon, and a man that is by nature and not merely by fortune without a polis is either low in the scale of humanity or above it.

ARISTOTLE, *Politics*

L'homme, pendant des millénaires, est resté ce qu'il était pour Aristote: un animal vivant et de plus capable d'une existence politique; l'homme moderne est un animal dans la politique duquel sa vie d'être vivant est en question.

MICHEL FOUCAULT, *The History of Sexuality*

It is well known that the meaning of the term *politics* has significantly changed from one epoch to another. While Arendt could write in the 1960s that the experience of the Greek city-state (*polis*), from which the word *politikos* derives, will stay with us as long as we keep using the word *politics* (Arendt 1969:49), other authors have identified major ruptures in our understanding of politics, which have brought the term far afield of the Greek meaning. Following the genealogical method described in part 1, I would like to focus here on two major ruptures in the genealogy of politics. Again, such a genealogy must not be understood as a history of the concept, but rather as the critical attempt to identify major conceptual breaks that have left their traces in the usage of words themselves. Once we have reconstructed such ruptures (chapter 4), it will be possible to show why politics, both in the largest and the strictest understanding of the term, depends on the imaginal (chapter 5).

The first rupture in this genealogy occurs with the invention of the term *politics* itself. Despite its Greek derivation from the adjective *politikos* (generally indicating whatever concerns the *polis*), the use of the substantive *politics* is to a large extent a modern invention. This is an old story for historians and philologists,[1] but it is a story that we tend to forget: *politics* has not always been there.

This rupture most clearly emerges if we consider that the ancient Greeks did not have a single substantive to denote a specific kind of activity within the more general sphere of the public. For them there existed the *polis,* the typically ancient

Greek city-state they lived in, as well as the adjective *politikos*, denoting the things pertaining to the affairs of the city-state. This means that the realm of the *polis* was thus conceived to be coextensive with the entirety of public life in general and *not* as indicating a specific kind of activity within the public sphere. This is further evident if we consider that the *polis* was distinguished from the *oikos*, from the sphere of the household where familial relations and economic activities aimed at the reproduction of life took place.[2]

The more abstract terms used by the Greeks to indicate what we would call politics were expressions such as *politike techne*, which denotes the art of leading political affairs, and *ta politika*, the plural substantivized adjective literally meaning "the things concerning the *polis*." But both expressions refer to the sphere of the *polis*, understood broadly as the site of public life in contrast to private life, and not a specific kind of activity within it. As a consequence, it is not an exaggeration to say that the Greeks, to which so many philosophers attributed the invention of politics itself, did not have a word to designate it.

This of course does not mean that one cannot use their experience as a model for what politics is or should be.[3] You can have the thing and not name it or have it and name it differently. However, we should be aware that when we speak about the ancient Greek understanding of politics, we do so with a word that was invented at a much later stage. Strictly speaking, it is an anachronism. And this invention signals that something new had in the meanwhile happened, which the available vocabulary was insufficient to designate. By contrast, in their own daily usage, ancient Greeks felt that the *polis*, the concrete space where they exercised their public life, was sufficient to indicate the activities we normally term politics. When they wanted to speak about it in the most abstract terms, they did not feel the need for *politics*, but most often used an expression (*ta politika*) that denotes both the "things relative to the *polis*" and "the knowledge about the *polis*."[4]

This is a point worth emphasizing before we move on. The expressions used by the Greeks to indicate politics, *politike techne* and *ta politika*, mean both the thing itself and the knowledge about it. The term *techne* in Ancient Greek not only means a neutral technique but also implies a specific knowledge. Equally, *ta politika* is a term that is used to refer to books written about the *polis*. As well known, *ta politika* was the title given to Aristotle's books on what we would call politics and, as we will see, it is to a great extent thanks to the influence of such a book that the term *politics* has entered our vocabulary.[5] This should not come as a surprise if we consider that Aristotle famously defined there the human being as a *zoon politikon*, as a political living being, thereby grounding the existence of what we would call politics in human nature itself. As we read in the passage quoted in this chapter's epigraph, the *polis* is a natural growth, so much so that whoever lives without it must be either below or above the scale of humanity. We will later discuss the implications of defining the human being as a *zoon politikon*. For the time being, it is sufficient to note that, even here, *ta politika* denotes both the thing and the knowledge about it.

The lack of a word for *politics* in Ancient Greek is something that cannot but strike any careful crafter of words. Even more puzzling is the complete absence of such a word from classical Latin. The Romans, according to some the most "political" of all ancient peoples,[6] did not feel a need for the word *politics*. This may be due to the fact that the Romans were so political that, for their linguistic universe, politics occupied the entirety of public life; thus they did not feel the need to distinguish between politics and other spheres of public life. This seems to indicate that for both the Greeks and the Romans the semantic field corresponding to what we would today call politics was so broad that they could not even name it.

Nevertheless, it remains a striking fact that in classical Latin there is not even the adjective *politicus*, the term that literally corresponds to the Greek *politikos*. Indeed, *politicus* appears only once in classical Latin, as an unusual Grecism, whereas the substantive *politica* enters into common usage only in the Middle Ages, after the translation of Aristotle's book on politics (*ta politika*) (Rubinstein 1987:41; Viroli 1992).[7]

This is perhaps the most puzzling twist in our story thus far: the Romans, this eminently political people, who imported so many things from the Greeks, did not feel the need to import *politikos*. Like the Greeks, they did not have a substantive that corresponds to our *politics*; however, neither did they have an adjective corresponding to our *political*, for which the Greeks used their native *politikos*. The Romans had their own words—and perhaps also their own different things: they had the adjectives *civilis*, *publicus*, and *socialis*—literally "civil," "public," and "social"—and such words were enough for them to accurately designate what they wanted to say about politics.

The substantive *polis* was rendered by the Romans as both *civitas* and *societas*, a usage that is still attested to in early modern sources.[8] And instead of *politics* they notoriously made use of other terms such as *res publica* (the "public thing"), the *publica negotia* ("the public affairs"), and the *res civilis* ("the civil thing").[9] The only attested use of the term *politicus* in classical Latin appears in a passage by Cicero where he speaks about "political philosophers" (*politici philosophi*)—and here political does not denote the thing itself but rather the knowledge about it. Note, furthermore, that (as I mentioned before) this usage of the term was an unusual Grecism, one that remained without a sequel; in general, the Romans did not feel the need for it. For them, the space of what we would today call politics was adequately covered by other terms.

The fact that the space of the political was thought of in terms of *publicus*, *civilis*, and *socialis* is very significant. Together with *civitas*—literally, "city"—the Romans translated the Greek *polis* with the term *societas*, which, like the corresponding adjective *socialis*, comes from *socius*, meaning "ally," "associate," "partner." This is an important innovation, because it is the first step toward the birth of the social and thus of the distinction between society and politics. Yet, as both are still thought of in terms of *publicus*, we can conclude that the Romans did not conceive of "politics" as a separate field within the more general realm of the public and the social—or at least that they did not perceive such a distinction to be so crucial as to feel the need to name it.

I will not enter here into the details of the birth of *politics*.[10] What is important to emphasize is the fact that it is a modern invention. In this respect, the rupture from previous usages could not be greater. For some, this pathbreaking innovation is the result of the curious fact that, when Wilhelm von Moerbeke translated Aristotle's book on politics (*ta politika*) into Latin (around 1260), he did not use the standard words Latin had used for centuries, but directly imported from Greek the terms *politicus, politica*, and *politicum* (Sternberger 1991:153). Among the terms imported by von Moerbeke, there is thus not just the adjective *politicus*, but also the substantive *politica*, a very eccentric translation for that time, yet one that was full of decisive consequences.

Dolf Sternberger attributes this unusual choice to the fact that von Moerbeke was probably not so sure about the precise meaning of those terms and decided to leave them in the original, with a slightly Latinized version (*politicus* instead of *politikos, politica* instead of *ta politika*). Is the birth of *politics* just the result of an inaccuracy? Even if this is the case, and the actual birth of *politics* ultimately derives from a bad translation, this still does not explain why the term *politics* successfully eclipsed the more illustrious Latin words that writers had used for more than a millennium. Furthermore, the very fact that von Moerbeke was uncertain about their usage is already a sign that something had in the meanwhile changed: the political world of thirteenth-century Europe perhaps could not be rendered through words that the Romans and Latin Christianity had used for centuries.

The fact that the word *politica* comes into modern Latin through von Moerbeke's translation of Aristotle's *Politics* will not come as a surprise to those familiar with the Middle Ages. For centuries, at least since the foundation of the Sacred Roman Empire, the crucial political debate was about the relationship between temporal and spiritual power. According to supporters of the former, the temporal power of the emperor derives directly from God and is thus independent of that of the pope. By contrast, for the supporters of the latter, temporal power had to be subordinated to the spiritual power in the same way in which our life on Earth must be subordinated to eternal life. After centuries of debates and political struggles between the two factions, the translation and circulation of Aristotle's *Politics* proved to be a particularly powerful weapon to support the autonomy of temporal power.[11] If the *polis* derives from the fact that, as Aristotle puts it, man is a *zoon politikon*, then it is rooted in human nature and possesses, therefore, its own autonomy. By the fourteenth century this argument had become crucial for the opponents of Augustinism or the idea that, as Augustine put it, without divine justice human political associations (*regna*) can only be *magna latrocinia*, gangs of criminals (*De Civitate Dei*, book 4, chapter 4), thus necessitating that the temporal power be subordinated to the spiritual one.

However, despite the appearance of the term *politica*—and the fact that this brought with it a new series of arguments for thinking of what we would call the autonomy of politics—we should not forget that for centuries the Latin term *politica* kept being used in the ancient meaning of the art or science of government. Like the corresponding terms *physics*, *economics*, and *ethics*, the term *politics* denoted the works devoted to the study of the things related to the *polis* and not the thing itself (Bobbio 1990:800). As late as 1603, the great Johannes Althusius would still call his major work about the foundation of the *consociatio politica* (what we would today call the state) precisely *Politica methodice digesta*, literally meaning "the science of politics methodically digested." This testifies to the great importance that Aristotle's *Politics* had in our tradition, so much so that it does not appear exaggerated to say, with Arendt, that the experience of the Greek city-state (*polis*) will stay with us as long as we keep using the word *politics*. However, it was not until the modern epoch that we began to use the word *politics*, and this is largely because it was only after the exit from the Middle Ages that politics began to be perceived as an autonomous domain.

According to some interpreters, the decisive moment for the birth of *politics* thus understood was the revolution initiated at the dawn of modernity by the theorists of the "reason of state" (Viroli 1992). Among them, the influential Giovanni Botero used this expression to refer to the knowledge of the appropriate means to establish, maintain, and enlarge a state, defined as a "firm empire [*dominio*] over a people" (Viroli 1992:490). For Maurizio Viroli, it is only with this revolution that the term *politics* ceases to have its ancient meaning of civil philosophy—the knowledge about the affairs of the *polis*—and instead assumes the specifically modern meaning of the art of preserving and enlarging the state and thus the activity taking place within it. In other words, behind the fortune of a translator's seemingly chance introduction of the term *politica* into Latin, there is the puzzlement that emerged in response to a political novelty: that of the sovereign state, of a firm domain over a people within a territory defined by clear-cut boundaries. The modern state, which appears in Europe between the sixteenth and seventeenth centuries,[12] was indeed an unprecedented form of political community, whose novelty is manifest if one considers that medieval Europe had been characterized for centuries by a chaotic and overlapping system of authorities where no political power could claim sovereign authority over a defined territory. It is only, then, to designate and to emphasize this novelty that the passage from a knowledge of the thing ("politics" as civil philosophy) to the thing itself ("politics" as the activity concerning the affairs of the state) took place.[13]

Note that, despite what is usually assumed, it took a long time before the term *politics* affirmed itself. In the sixteenth century Niccolò Machiavelli, to whom many attributed the invention of the modern concept of politics (in its autonomy from both ethics and religion), does not use the word *politics* (*politica*) and only makes recourse to the expression *vivere politico,* "political living," a handful of times, by which he means living according to certain laws as opposed to living under a completely arbitrary power.[14]

A century later, Spinoza, following the Ancient Greek usage, called his books in political philosophy *Tractatus Theologico-Politicus* and *Tractatus Politicus,* respectively; yet he uses the adjective *politicus* only a few times in his writings and even less so the substantive *politica.*[15] When he speaks about politics, he uses mainly the classical terms *civitas, societas, publica negotia,* and *res publica.* For instance, it is significant that when dealing with the problem of the foundations of politics as a peculiar kind of activity he uses the expression *fundamenta civitatis,* meaning the principles leading to the foundation of the city (*Ethics,* IV, prop. 37, sch. 1).

However, this should not come as a surprise if we consider that Thomas Hobbes, one of the first great theorists of the sovereign state and, in many respects, a major source of inspiration for Spinoza, did not even feel the need for the adjective *politicus* to name his works in political philosophy. When referring to what we would call politics, he follows the traditional Latin usage and speaks about the commonwealth, a literal translation of *res publica,* opposing it to the natural condition of mankind.[16] If it is true that Hobbes has to a great extent invented English philosophical language (since before him Latin was the official language for philosophy), then we have to conclude that politics was not yet an integral part of it.

Wherever one locates the birth of *politics*, it is clear that the use of the term implied a significant *shrinkage* of the semantic field previously designated by older terms. The passage from the Greek adjective (*politikos*) to the substantive, as it appears in the different European languages (*politics, Politik, politica*, etc.) meant, therefore, also a significant restriction in the semantic field of *politics*: *politics* no longer meant the whole of public, civil, and social life, as it was conveyed by the classical sources, but just one section of it. In sum, precisely because both the Greeks and the Romans were more political people than we are, they did not feel the need to name *politics* that is, to distinguish a peculiar subcategory within the general life of the *polis* or of the *res publica*. The birth of politics is thus the consequence of the serious limitation that has in the meanwhile occurred with respect to the semantic range of this term.

There is neither the space nor the need for discussing the vicissitudes of the modern term *politics*.[17] Here let me simply point out that by the time Max Weber takes up the term at the beginning of the twentieth century, it is reduced to its minimal semantic core: no longer a knowledge about the whole of public life, but rather a small part of the thing itself—that peculiar kind of power characterized by the potential recourse to the use of legitimate physical coercion.[18] Weber was obsessed with definitions, so much so that his mastodontic *Economy and Society* can be described as an attempt to provide definitions for almost any aspect of our social life. This, together with the fact that he is considered one of the founding fathers of sociology, explains why his definitions have been so prominent in the literature. In particular, Weber's characterization of politics still exercises a significant influence in contemporary debates (Bobbio 1990). For our genealogy, it is important to note that the success of a definition of politics that reduces it to the state is inseparable from the fact that it clearly reflected the change occurring in political life itself: it is because of the emergence of the modern state—a form of political community characterized by the sovereign monopoly over legitimate coercion within territorial boundaries—that people felt the need for a new word.[19] People confronted with what politics had become within modern nation-states felt a sense of novelty, and *politics* was the term they chose to convey it.

As I mentioned before, Weber's definition is still widespread, not the least because it is the most frequent in common language. If we read the entry "politics" in *The Oxford English Dictionary* (Simpson and Weiner 1989:33), for instance, we learn that, after the old historical definition of politics as the science or study of politics,[20] the common meaning is strictly associated with state politics: politics means here the "activities or policies associated with government, esp. those concerning the organization and administration of a state, or part of a state, and with the regulation of relationships between states." This centrality of the notion of the state in the common understanding of politics may be due to the fact that the sovereign state appeared for centuries as the culminating point of political life, the privileged object of inquiry for political theorists.

Yet, we should not forget that the modern state is a relatively recent discovery in the history of humanity and, more relevantly, one that has been limited to European modernity until very recently. Exported to the rest of the world through European colonialism, the division of the whole world into sovereign states does not predate the second half of the twentieth century.[21] It is thus a very recent innovation, and one that may turn out to be particularly short-lived if talks about the end of the sovereign state system are to be taken seriously. Maybe the modern state is not dead, but it does not seem to be in a very healthy condition either, as we will see later on.

For the purposes of our genealogy, it is crucial to notice that it is the appearance of the new political form of the state that inaugurates the separation between politics and the *whole* of public and social life, whereas in early modern Latin sources the three semantic areas are still overlapping. This is because, whereas in antiquity and during the Middle Ages politics could hardly be separated from other aspects of common life, with the modern epoch politics starts to be perceived in its autonomy, first from religion and ethics and subsequently from social life as a whole.[22]

Vis-à-vis such a restricted view of "politics," many felt constrained. The resistance to such a constraint heralds the second great break within the genealogy of this concept, to which I will now turn. Different authors, in the belief that something had been lost, looked to classical antiquity to expand the concept again. Among them, perhaps most notable is Hannah Arendt, who saw in the Athenian model of democracy the epitome of what real politics is about.[23] Arendt attributes to the Greeks the invention of politics, whereas she sees in modernity the moment of the rise of the social, illustrated in exemplary fashion by the emergence of the social question during the French Revolution (Arendt 1958). It should be evident by now that, from a philological point of view, this is, properly speaking, an anachronism, because the Greeks did not have the word *politics*. Modernity could give birth to the social only because it had also given birth to politics itself, in its separation from both the public and the social.

We will come back to Arendt later on, but for the moment what is most important to emphasize is that she and other authors perceived the identification of politics with the activity taking place within modern nation-states as too narrow. Their response was to attempt to forcibly expand the language in use by imposing new and alternative meanings on the term *politics*. In most cases, the result has been an enlargement of the semantic core of the term and not an impossible return to the ancients.

For a philologist as genealogist, it is important to note that the attempt to widen the semantic core of this term also signaled another recent linguistic rupture: the emergence of the expression *the political*. The term *the political* gestures at a return to the adjective which, as we have seen, extends back a long way from modernity; however, the emphasis this time is on the substantivized form: "*the political*." What are the consequences of this change of terms? Has politics transformed again to the point that other words are needed to indicate such a novelty? It is perhaps too early to say whether the fortune of the term *the political* will continue and eventually replace that of *politics*, but it is clear that the recourse to *the political* signals an insufficiency of the available vocabulary.

Reflecting on the meaning of this shift from *politics* to *the political*, Pierre Rosanvallon argues that it implies a deep change of perspective: from politics as the Weberian struggle for the monopoly of legitimate coercion within modern states to an examination of the background, of the ontological conditions for the existence of politics as such (Rosanvallon 2003). Some authors, following Carl Schmitt, found such conditions in the couple friend and enemy, whereas others, such as Rosanvallon, prefer to identify it with the *sadro d'ensemble*, all that makes a city (*cité*) above and beyond institutional life and the competition for the exercise of power that takes place within the formal structure of state politics.[24] In both cases the result is an enlargement of the semantic range. Despite the different directions in which the concept of the political has been taken, it is important to stress here that they all indicate such an extension. Like the expression *the imaginary*, the passage to *the political* reflects a shift of emphasis toward a more context-oriented framework. Whereas the term *politics* indicates the thing itself, *the political* is meant to signal a renewed emphasis on the background, on the conditions that have to be met for formal politics to take place.

But, together with *the political*, a new term has recently appeared on the scene: *biopolitics*. In the past few decades, there has been a diffuse perception of a radical novelty that perhaps explains the proliferation of so many new words.[25] Some have proved to be more resilient than others, and biopolitics seems to be one of them. The term, introduced by Michel Foucault in the 1970s,[26] has gained prominence in contemporary debates,[27] along with all the corresponding terms constructed with the prefix *bio*: *bioethics, biolaw, biomedicine, biotechnology, bioterrorism,* etc., are all new words that point to a different or at least a more significant role of the notion of life (*bios*) itself. Note that, despite the huge differences with the ancients, the concept of biopolitics maintains the modern attention to the institutional mechanism of power while at the same time enlarging it to include a kind of knowledge, as was the case for the ancient meaning of the term *politics*.[28] To put it bluntly, politics is, for both Weber and Foucault, something that has to do with power, but with this fundamental difference: for Foucault power is pervasive because it is inseparable from knowledge. As a consequence, like *the political*, the term *biopolitics* also denotes a semantic enlargement.

As is well known, Foucault introduced the term *biopolitics* to denote a change in the nature of modern political power. In his view, while traditional sovereignty has always been a power aimed at controlling life by threatening it with the possibility of death, the new form of power that emerges in the mid-nineteenth century is that of a power aimed at inciting and preserving life.[29] While the sovereign power—not by chance symbolized by the sword—was essentially a power to kill, a power to take life or let it die, the new biopower manifests itself as a power to *make* live and let die (Foucault 1990:136, 1997:241). Hence the increased significance of biological life as the medium where political power displays itself.

In Foucault's analysis, it is indeed in the nineteenth century that "power's hold over life" emerges; this would be the moment when the biological came under state control or at least the moment when the tendency toward state control of the biological emerges (Foucault 1997:239–240). The rise of biopolitics is manifested in the systematic inclusion of disciplines such as demography, public hygiene, birth control, etc., in the practice of government. This change attests to an attempt by political power to directly control life, no longer by simply threatening to inflict death (the power of the sword) but also by inciting, promoting, and, in a word, disciplining life.

While in Foucault's view there is therefore a difference between classical forms of sovereignty and biopolitics, according to other interpreters of the biopolitical turn the latter began with modernity itself: far from being a break in the modern paradigm, biopolitics is inscribed in the bones of modernity from the beginning. According to Giorgio Agamben, the paradox of modern sovereignty is precisely that it has always been simultaneously within and outside the juridical order, because its power derives from its capacity to decide on the state of exception and thus to inflict death (Agamben 1998:chapter 1). While the modern paradigm, at least since Hobbes, has justified its own existence in terms of its capacity to guarantee the security of its citizens, Agamben shows the striking paradox that lies at the very origin of this move: the sovereign is the sovereign because it can guarantee our security by potentially killing us with impunity. In that respect, as the title of his work reminds us, we are all *homines sacri*, "sacred men," sacrificial human beings, which, like the corresponding figure in Roman law, can be killed with impunity (79–83).

Precisely because of its capacity to exercise power over life, Agamben observes that modern sovereignty is from the beginning biopolitical: "Contrary to our modern habit of representing the political realm in terms of citizens' rights, free will, and social contracts, from the point of view of sovereignty *only bare life is authentically political.* This is why in Hobbes the foundation of sovereign power is to be sought not in the subjects' free renunciation of their natural right but in the sovereign's preservation of his natural right to do anything to anyone, which now appears as the right to punish" (Agamben 1998:106). Agamben can thus claim that the authentically political is bare life itself, since the sovereign, who retains the right to kill with impunity, is at the same time inside and outside the juridical order. This is evident in its capacity to decide on the state of exception that makes the Nazi concentration camps not a deviation from modernity but rather the epitome of its very biopolitical paradigm (129–131). Thus, whereas according to Agamben the ancient Greeks could still distinguish between *zoe* (bare life) and *bios* (the qualified life, as in expressions such as *bios politikos* or *bios theoretikos*), and therefore also between the sphere of the household (*oikos*) and that of the *polis*, this possibility would be lost for us, because life itself becomes the political question par excellence (13).

Despite the fact that Agamben locates the birth of biopolitics at the very beginning of modernity, he thus agrees with Foucault's fundamental insight: whereas for millennia man remained what he was for Artistotle, a living animal with the additional capacity for a political existence, the modern man is an animal whose politics places his existence as a living being in question (as the Foucauldean passage quoted in the epigraph to this chapter indicates). Thus racism of the kind inherent in Nazism is for both authors the culminating point of the biopolitical turn: Nazism only took the interplay between the sovereign right to kill and the mechanism of biopower that is inscribed in the working of every state to the paroxysmal point of the extermination camp (Foucault 1997:260; Agamben 1998:129).[30] Otherwise stated, for both authors biopolitics culminates in a form of *thanatopolitics*.

But is this the only way to think about biopolitics? Does biopolitics always negate life while sustaining it? Roberto Esposito has tried to reverse the thanato-political paradigm of Nazism into its opposite and thus elaborate an affirmative model of biopolitics that configures itself not as a politics *over* life (*sulla vita*), but as a politics *of* life (*della vita*; Esposito 2008: 159–215). The three sites where Nazism displayed its biopower—the body, the birth, and the norm—can all be recast in affirmative terms, which potentially divest the biopolitical turn we live of its lethal outcome. At the end of his *Bios*, Esposito tries to do so by drawing inspiration from different strands of vitalistic philosophy. However, in my view, he ultimately does not manage to succeed in this task because he remains captive to the Hobbesian paradigm that links the existence of the political community to the possibility of death.

Since his earlier work on the notion of community, Esposito has thought of the notion of community (*communitas*) as the possibility of living *cum munus*, that is, with *munus*, meaning at the same time a gift and an obligation that we have toward the other when contemplating the possibility of death (Esposito 1998). Despite the fact that Esposito thus reverses the traditional thinking of the community as the fatherland depicted by certain communitarians and points to the fact that community is a debt and a gift (according to the etymological meaning of *munus*), he still remains attached to the idea that this being-in-common of the community is defined by our own fragility with respect to the possibility of death.

A Heideggerian heritage is lurking deep in his thinking, which, however, as we have mentioned in part 1, is an attitude that reaches far back in the past. Most philosophers, at least since Plato, looked at human beings as beings-toward-death. Very rarely did they take the opposite perspective of looking at them as beings-after-birth,[31] a puzzling fact on its own, given the ontological priority of birth over death. For, while it is true that we are beings-toward-death, it is equally true that we are so because we are in the first place beings-after-birth. Philosophers, as we have suggested in the previous chapter, like to remind us of the first truth, that we will die, but tend to forget the second one, that we are born.

If we look at biopolitics from this perspective, then a different strand of considerations comes to the fore. In the first place, we should notice that what is authentically political is life itself, not because it is *killable*, as Agamben argues, but because it is *born(e)*. From Hobbes to Weber, and thus from its very birth, politics has all too often been conceived in relationship to the possibility of death. Obsessed with the latter as the defining feature of our existential horizon, modern philosophers have neither been able to wrest themselves from this heritage nor to find a more powerful justification for the existence of sovereign political power other than attributing to it the guarantee of our security vis-à-vis the possibility of death.

This emphasis on the possibility of death has led us to neglect the crucial political role that life itself has always had. The conservation of life and its needs has always been at the center of our life in common, so much so that we can say that, to a certain degree, politics has always been biopolitics. Even in Aristotle the distinction between the household (*oikos*) and the sphere of the *polis* does not mean that life has no role to play in the *polis*. Life and its needs are central to politics because without them there could not be any life in common in the first place. It is not by chance that both Plato and Aristotle agree that the *polis* derives from the satisfaction of needs, that is, from the fact that we are incapable of providing for our life and our most basic needs in isolation (*Republic* 368b and *Politics* 1252b 30).

Aristotle was well aware of the centrality of life, as seen in the fact that when he defines man as the *zoon politikon*, he uses the expression *zoon*, which literally means "living being." The Latin rendering of *zoon* as "animal" is misleading because the term *animal* has a connotation of inferiority. On the contrary, *zoon* (from *zoe*, "life itself") simply means every "en-souled" or "living" being (Jonas 1973:123). As a consequence, it is no exaggeration to say that even Aristotle was well aware of the fact that we can be political beings only because we are *living* beings or, what is the same, because we are born. By inverting the Foucauldean quotation in the epigraph of this chapter, we can therefore conclude that man has always been a creature in whose politics its existence as a living being was in question or, otherwise stated, in whose politics the very fact that he was born is at stake.

We come here to the second crucial point. Life has always been at the center of politics, not only because life and its needs are crucial political issues, but also because, as Arendt reminds us, birth is the political moment par excellence.[32] If it is true, as we argued in chapter 3, that death is the moment where we are necessarily alone, whereas birth is always in common, then we have to conclude that birth, rather than death, should be at the center of our thinking about politics. We can die more or less surrounded by other people, and we may even commit collective suicide, but it is a fact that our body dies alone, whereas at birth it is always accompanied: there is no birth which is not in common.

If politics then has to do with our social life, with the fact that our passage on this earth is accompanied by the presence of others, we then must conclude that birth comes well before death as the crucial political moment. The fact that this basic truth has so often been neglected does not only have to do with the circumstance that most philosophers, historically speaking, are men. Having gone through the experience of birth only at the beginning, it is all too easy to understand why they tend to forget about it. A vastly different genealogy of politics would probably have been written if women had had a larger role in it.

Another striking paradox in the history of philosophy is that the person who most emphatically stressed the importance of birth as the political moment par excellence is a woman, Hannah Arendt, who nevertheless would have dismissed the word *biopolitics* as a contradiction in terms. In a rightly famous passage, which goes against a few millennia of politico-philosophical speculation, Arendt states, "since action is the political activity par excellence, natality, and not mortality, may be the central category of political, as distinguished from metaphysical thought" (Arendt 1958:9).

This passage not only shows that Arendt was well aware of the fact that politics has to do with the condition of plurality—that is, with men as a plurality of individuals of the same species (Arendt 1958, 1982). For Arendt, politics depends on birth because it depends on the possibility of action understood as the capacity to bring about the new. It is in this sense that she can, for instance, write that natality, in which the capacity for action is ontologically rooted, is "the miracle that saves the world, the realm of human affairs, from its normal, natural ruin" (Arendt 1958:247). The fact that newborns constantly come into the world does not only explain how the new is possible, but why and how plurality comes about. What Arendt does not sufficiently emphasize is that this also explains why we are fit for political life understood as being-in-common.

This is, to a great extent, due to the fact that Arendt, with her interpretation of the Greek model, defined politics as the sphere of speech and action that is opposed to that of the *oikos*, where the basic needs for the subsistence of life are provided. For her, the emergence of political modernity and thus the problem of needs—the social question—marks the end of politics rather than its birth. Modernity is the moment when politics is eclipsed by the social, when the question of the conservation of life comes at the center of politics—hence also her criticism of Marxism and the whole socialist tradition that had put the question of needs at the top of the agenda of political philosophy.

For Arendt, politics begins when the problems of the subsistence of life are resolved, not when they are put at the center of the discussion. Debate, not satisfaction of needs, is the very stuff political life is made of (Arendt 1968b:237). It is not by chance that Arendt interprets Aristotle's definition of man as *zoon politikon* as strictly linked to his other definition of man as *zoon logon echon*, as the living being that possesses the *logos* (Arendt 1958:27). While interpreters since the Middle Ages have translated the latter expression as "rational animal" (*animale rationale*), Arendt more cautiously leaves the term *logos* untranslated. The *zoon logon echon* is indeed not only the rational animal (or, to be more precise, "rational living being") but also, and foremost, the being that has the capacity for speech, that is, for *logos*—the reason, argument, and word. Driven by this definition of politics, Arendt could never accept the expression "*biopolitics*. Hence the paradox noted before: one of the earliest theorists of the biopolitical turn of modernity would never have used that expression, unless to sharply criticize it.

This has in my view also prevented Arendt from realizing that since its very birth politics has always been biopolitical. This is not only because, in contrast to what she seems to assume, the term *politics* is a recent invention, very much linked to the emergence of the modern sovereign state. Politics has always been biopolitical because, in whatever way we want to conceive of it, it is our existence as living beings who have been *born* that is in question there, as suggested by the proposed reversal of Foucault's epigraph. Politics is biopolitical because it is *genopolitics* well before being *thanatopolitics*.[33]

At this point in the argument, one may rightly ask: why, if politics has always been biopolitics, did this term emerge only now? One reason is capitalism's rapidly transforming tendency to intensify the link between politics and life. Through the technological developments of the past half-century and the incorporation of life in the mechanisms of production itself, human beings have become capable of penetrating the inner mechanisms of life in a way that was never the case before. Literally, not only death, but life itself can now be inflicted by political power. Hence the term *biopolitics* emerges to signify the appropriation by the state of the power over biological life. Just as the birth of modern states gave to politics an autonomy that it had never possessed to such an extent before, thus justifying the birth of a new term (*politics*), so, equally, the capitalist transformations we are witnessing have made of life itself such a crucial political problem that a new term, *biopolitics*, was needed. Life has always been crucial to politics, but never to the degree that it is today. It is to signal such a novelty, as well as the failure of the available vocabulary to designate this fact, that a new term has emerged.

That the technological developments of late capitalism have given life such a crucial position also points to the fact that "bare life" never existed for us.[34] Biopolitics does not begin when we can no longer distinguish between *zoe* and *bios*, between bare life and *bios*, because bare life has never been accessible to us. Or better: "life," let alone the place that it occupies in politics, is inseparable from the image that we have of it. Here we can begin to see why biopolitics is also imaginal: our being-in-common is mediated by images well before being mediated by words. We are *zooi politikoi*, political living beings, because we are at the same time, and in that very moment, also imaginal beings. The task of the next chapter is to spell out why this is so.

5
Imaginal Politics

As to the visual elements, the stage designer has a more powerful art at his disposal than the poet.

ARISTOTLE, *Poetics*

The previous genealogy of *politics* showed us that the semantic core of this concept went through a process of shrinkage and that the emergence of the notions of the political and of biopolitics points to an attempt to broaden it. What is then the relationship between this semantic ambit and the notion of imaginal introduced in part I? The task of this chapter is to address such a central question.

Let us begin with the broadest meaning. If we understand politics as whatever pertains to life in common and the decisions concerning its fate, the link is quite clear. Politics coincides with the sphere of public life and therefore includes all that concerns the social and the political. Politics thus understood depends on the imaginal because it is only by imagining it that a public comes into being.

This holds for large communities such as modern states, but also for small ones. The former are patently "imaginal beings" insofar as it is only by imagining them that one can perceive a sense of belonging with strangers inhabiting a territory. The same holds for the latter: even in small communities, based on face-to face relationships, the subject in question needs (re)presentation through an image in order to make it exist out of a simple collection of individuals. Communities cannot exist except as imaginal beings. What a given subject sees gathered together in the public square (the *agora*) is a set of bodies, not (yet) a *polis*. In order to perceive a *polis*, something that unifies all those scattered bodies, you need a pictorial (re)presentation that can include all of them. This can be given by the image of the *agora* itself or by the walls of the city, as was often the case in antiquity, or some other image of the common territory, but, in any case, it must be conveyed through a certain image that defines its boundaries.

There are innumerable ways to imagine a community: through metaphors, such as that of the collective body; metonyms, such as the portraits of the rulers; or synecdoche, using a part to signify the whole of it (e.g., the walls that stand for the whole community). However, a community is not *a* community until it is gathered together and unified in a pictorial (re)presentation. The metaphor of the body politic is a particularly influential form of such community-engendering (re)presentation.[1] The analogy between the human body and the political community goes far back into antiquity, but it found its greatest expression in the time between the Middle Ages and the late Renaissance, when systematic reference was made to the organic image of the body (Cavarero 2002:99).

Despite its ancient origins, we should, however, notice the crucial difference between previous uses of the metaphor of the body politic and modern usage. Although in antiquity the analogy had the function of emphasizing the organic nature of the community—the *polis* appeared as a whole superior to the parts, but also inconceivable without them—the modern idea of the state introduces something new: the state, as a person, becomes an autonomous actor, an abstract legal subject and bearer of rights and duties (Schild 1990). In sum, it becomes a separate juridical person.

This is a crucial novelty, inseparable from the appearance of the modern notion of political representation and its corresponding theory of sovereignty. By contrast, classical jurists had not developed a proper notion of the juridical personality of the state. Roman law, for instance, does conceive of communities as legal subjects independent from their members: the Roman people (*populus romanus*) cannot be conceived as a legal subject independent of the body of the concrete *universitas civium*, the universality of the citizens (Albanese 1983).

Classical law has the concept of *persona*, or "person," understood as a general category indicating every human being independently of the physical differences between them. According to some, this term derives from the Greek *prosopon*, literally meaning what is placed in front of the eyes, i.e., a theatrical mask. As such, the concept of person came to mean by extension the role impersonated and the actor (Cotta 1983:160). According to others, it would instead derive from the Etruscan word *phersu*, whose precise meaning is unknown (Albanese 1983:170). But despite differences of interpretation with respect to the origin of the term, there seems to be agreement about the fact that the modern notion of the personality of the state added something that was not there before.

A decisive contribution to the development of the modern concept of juridical personality comes from canon law. Medieval legal science had to face the challenge of elaborating a concept to represent the fact that institutions such as monasteries, churches, religious confraternities, and charitable institutions could legally possess a distinct patrimony independently of the people that composed them (Campitelli 1983). Although the extent to which the Germanic and the Roman tradition respectively contributed to this development is still a matter of debate, some interpreters have suggested that the concept of person in canon law is derived from the Pauline idea of the mystic body (*corpus mysticum*)—that is, from the idea of an entity of a clearly distinct rank separate from that of the members comprising it (Campitelli 1983:183).

This derivation would seem to support Carl Schmitt's thesis, according to which the central concepts of modern political theory are, originally, theological concepts (Schmitt 2005). This concerns in particular the modern notion of sovereignty, a power that recognizes no superior on Earth, which, according to Schmitt, derives from the theological concept of God as *legibus solutus* (iii). The fortune of the notion of political theology is linked to the fact that it seemed to explain the ambivalent nature of the modern concept of sovereignty, encapsulated somehow between the two extremes of an absolute presence and a total absence. But the modern sovereign's absent presence is not (or no longer) based on a transcendent external theological order that justifies it, but rather on the immanence of human social relationships that generate it. And it is precisely representation that explains how such a sovereign power can be attributed to a single source that at the same time "stands for" but also alienates it from the multitude of the subjects that gave rise to it.

Representation as such is not an invention of modernity, but the idea of a specifically political representation is: whereas in the medieval epoch the representatives were simply delegates—that is, executers of the will of somebody else—in modernity they become autonomous interpreters of such a will and the interests of those represented (Cotta 1983:955).[2] Even more so, without representation there cannot be sovereignty as such because it is only through representation that a multitude of scattered bodies becomes a people and thus, properly speaking, comes into being. What is specific to the modern notion is that representation is absolute. As Carlo Galli observes, absolute representation is indeed the central category of modernity: without the "doubled image" of a people that is at the same time unity and multiplicity there cannot be sovereignty and thus political modernity (Galli 1988:53, 62).[3]

This paradox of a sovereign body that comes into being only when it alienates the sovereignty that constitutes it, as we will see in more detail, is very well illustrated by Hobbes's theory of the sovereign state. Once constituted, the artificial person of the state becomes independent from the subjects that produced it; in so doing, the subjects conceded their authority (*auctoritas*), or the right to be author, to the sovereign. It is because they have done this that the state has the right to "personate" (Leviathan, part 1, chapter 16). Notice here that Hobbes insists on the *artificial* nature of the person of the state, and there is thus for him no reference to the natural character of such an order as in ancient organic usages of the corporeal metaphor.

Whether the derivation of the modern notion of the personality of the state from theology is historically correct or not, the crucial point for us is that the modern notion of sovereignty depends on the imaginal, since the idea of a community that possesses juridical personality independently from its members needs the synthetic power of images to represent it even more than previous forms of politics (admitting for the time being that we can use this anachronism). However, it should be emphasized that this does not always need to be a theological image: as we will see, means other than theological ones were often used to render the paradox of a community that is at the same time dependent and independent from its constitutive members. To put it bluntly, to say that there cannot be politics without the imaginal does not mean that there cannot be politics without the theological. The imaginal is not the transcendent, but rather the *transcendental* of political modernity.

In big political communities, including heterogeneous territories and populations such as empires or modern nation-states, unifying images were (and still are) often provided by maps. The latter are representations, usually on a flat surface, of the features of an area of Earth that portrays them in their respective forms, sizes, and relationships according to some convention. Maps are representations that reproduce a reality "out there" and of necessity express the idea of what people think this reality is, what they have *chosen* as worthy of representation. A map reproducing exactly the reality it is meant to represent would be pointless. Any map is an image, but an image that reflects a choice. And modern maps are representations that reflect the choice of the state. As McKenzie Wark (2004:219) has argued, "the politics of representation is always the politics of the state. The state is nothing but the policing of representation adequacy to the body of what it represents."[4]

While ancient maps were qualitative and made out of the sea-perspective, and thus mainly used as an orientation tool for travelers, modern maps are quantitative and made from the ruler's perspective. With the modern epoch and the rise of sovereign states defined by clear-cut boundaries, political maps—bidimensional representations of political communities whose boundaries separate the inside from the outside—began to proliferate. Properly speaking, a bidimensional and thus a *political* map is only possible in sovereign states insofar as they identify clear-cut boundaries within which a single absolute authority is exercised.

Whereas the Middle Ages were characterized by an overlapping system of authorities in which it was often impossible to determine where the jurisdiction of one power ended and another began, with the emergence of the modern state the political space became homogeneous. This is the revolution entailed by the concept of sovereignty, defined as the *summa potestas superiorem non recognoscens.* This notion refers to the fact that within those specific boundaries there is just one supreme power that does not recognize any superior within that territory. Hence the emergence of *political* maps: whereas physical maps are full of objects represented (mountains, rivers, lakes, etc.), the space of the sovereign state is, tellingly, empty.

It is worth remembering here that the emergence of political maps went together with a more general revolution in the representation of space.[5] Space is not an absolute quantity; it is a human one, a function of the time that man uses to traverse it. Space widens and narrows according to the technical evolution of mankind. It was once the human body that measured space: distances were then fathoms and feet. After the modern revolution, the qualitative space of traditional communities became the objective and quantitatively measurable space of Renaissance perspective and modern science. As a consequence, the way in which space was represented also changed: while medieval charts were used to reproduce all the human and natural elements that a traveler could see, modern maps represented an objective and homogeneous space.[6]

The emergence of the modern organization of power thus implied a process of conquest and definition of space that would not have been possible without this revolution in its perception. For a modern conception of political power to be accepted, it was necessary for space to be perceived as a uniform and objective reality, subject to the exercise of a unique sovereign. This is the reason why control over maps was so important: they were the direct means by which to control the representations of political space and thus politics itself.[7] Political maps of the territory, which, as a homogeneous and univocal division of political space, would have been impossible during the medieval age, became in modern times the most common way of representing and thus rendering political power perceptable and thus effective.

This also explains why modern politics, far from emancipating itself from the imaginal, has to rely on it even more than previous forms of politics. This was clearly illustrated by Hobbes when, in order to explain the puzzle of modern sovereignty in his *Leviathan*, he has to elaborate the typically modern notion of representation. How else would he have been able to explain the fact that the sovereign power is nothing but a merely artificial creature? How could he explain that the greatest power on Earth, which has no superior above himself—as we read in the quotation from Job in the frontispiece of *Leviathan*—is a mere fiction?

We read in the crucial chapter 16 of the *Leviathan* that the commonwealth has authority, that is, the "right to do any actions," because it has the capacity to "represent" somebody else (*Leviathan* part I, chapter 16, section 5). Hobbes further explains that the Leviathan can do this because it is a person, defined as "he whose words or actions are considered, either as his own, or as representing the words and actions of an other man, or of any other thing to whom they are attributed, whether Truly or by Fiction" (*Leviathan* part I, chapter 16, section 1). Thus the sovereign has authority because, as an artificial person, he has the capacity to represent others.

The consequence is that the subjects to the Leviathan can recognize themselves in the actions of the sovereign because he bears their own person. This is the crucial moment in the institution of the sovereign body, because otherwise it would be impossible to understand how it is that individuals cede their right to do whatever they want to the sovereign. Only the latter can exercise that right because a multitude of scattered bodies is replaced by a Leviathan that represents them all. Otherwise stated, it is thanks to such a unitary image of the political body that the latter comes into being. Before the institution of this image, neither the representative nor represented people exists. This is clearly expressed by the frontispiece of *Leviathan*, to which Hobbes devoted particular attention, where the sovereign is literally represented wearing the persons of its citizen as if they were just the innumerable scales of its armor.

Hobbes does not hide that there is thus a fiction at the basis of the modern understanding of sovereignty. He also states that the term *person* derives from theater, where it originally indicates the "disguise or outward appearance of a man, counterfeited on the stage, and sometimes more particularly that part of it which disguiseth the face, as Mask or Visard" (*Leviathan* I, 3). He is well aware then that the sovereign is thus nothing but an "authorized actor" (Galli 1988:6). Yet, as a good nominalist, he knew quite well that this does not mean the drama of the sovereign state does not have extremely real effects.[8]

As Simon Critchley (2012) has also recently observed, fiction is crucial to politics because it is what ultimately explains how it is possible that the majority is unified into a minority.[9] Without such a fiction, or even a supreme fiction—a fiction we know to be a fiction, as Critchley puts it, recovering the term from the poet Wallace Stevens—there can be no politics (90–93). There can thus be a "fructuous collision" between politics and poetry, in that poetry permits us to see fiction as fiction, that is, to see the fictiveness of the world we live in (91). And in this sense it has a crucial critical function, in the Kantian sense, "as demystifying any empiricist myth of the given and showing the radical dependency of that which is upon the creative, ultimately imaginative, activity of the subject" (91).[10]

In sum, the Leviathan, as the modern sovereign state, is nothing but an imaginal being. If it is true that "politics" is a creature of modernity, then we have to add that it is an imaginal one. Both for small and large political communities you need a pictorial representation of the border of the *polis* in order to perceive a single community instead of a heterogeneous territory inhabited by a set of bodies. In this sense, politics has always been imaginal, since it has always been representative in the most general sense of the term. This is what Agamben (2007) tries to convey by saying that power needs its own apparatus of "glory."[11]

But the fact that politics, and in particular modern politics, has always been imaginal does not mean that it is not real, as should be clear at this point of the argument. It is for this reason that we have introduced the notion of the imaginal as an alternative to that of the imaginary: the concept of the imaginal does not make any assumption about the ontological status of images themselves, whereas that of the imaginary, as commonly understood, is mainly associated with the idea of unreality.

Indeed, both small and large political communities are imaginal beings. I say *imaginal* beings, and not imagined beings, to emphasize a fundamental point: in contrast to the imaginary, imaginal beings are not only the product of the actions of individuals but also, in turn, what shapes the imagination of the individuals themselves.[12] This is a further advantage of the notion of the imaginal over alternative concepts such as imagination or the imaginary: the states we live in are not (only) the fruit of the imagination of individuals but (also) what shapes the imagination of individuals and thus, in a way, what constitutes them. At the same time, states would have never come about if, at some point, the free imagination of individuals had not led them to first depict them. Thus the imaginal dimension of sovereign states is a (re)presentation constituted by and constituting the imagination of individuals.

Politics is thus imaginal because it depends on the possibility of depicting commonalities between a set of bodies, but also because, as we will now see in turning to Arendt, it depends on the possibility of freeing oneself from one's own particularities and creating images of what is not immediately in front of us. In her political reading of Kant's notion of taste, Arendt stressed precisely this point.

Her project in the last years of her life was indeed that of a theory of judgment based on the concept of imagination, a project left unfinished by her sudden death. Instead of a fully fledged theory, we are left with a few fragments of a possible theory, collected in her *Lectures on Kant's Political Philosophy* (Arendt 1982).[13] Note that the reason Arendt attributed the invention of politics to the Greeks is that she understood politics in the specific sense of a moment of acting together and perceived in the talkative *polis* of the ancient Greeks a model for such an activity (Arendt 1958). For Arendt, it is debate itself that constitutes the essence of political life (Arendt 1968b:237), and politics thus becomes a space of appearances—not a physical space, but one in which I appear to others and others appear to me (Arendt 1958:198).

If we consider her emphasis on the link between politics and action, understood as the capacity to bring about the new, it is striking to see that imagination plays almost no role in her early writings (McGowan 2011). It is not by chance that imagination appears only a few times in her *Human Condition*. Only later in her life, after the experience of the Eichmann trial, is she led to consider the role of image production in a different light. What strikes Arendt is precisely Eichmann's lack of imagination, his incapacity to look at things from the standpoint of others (Arendt 1964:48–49, 286). His failure is precisely his inability to produce those living images of the mind and experiences of others. And it is after this experience that Kant's *Critique of Judgment*, with its reference to the notion of imagination, becomes appealing for her.

It is within this background that we must locate Arendt's claim that Kant's *Critique of Judgment* contains his genuine political philosophy (Arendt 1982). According to Arendt's reading, our capacity to imagine is what mediates between the particular and the universal in judgment and therefore it is what enables us to take the point of view of others—what Eichmann simply could not do. As she wrote in her commentary on Kant's third critique, "an enlarged mentality is the condition *sine qua non* of right judgment; one's community sense makes it possible to enlarge one's mentality. Negatively speaking, this means that one is able to abstract from private conditions and circumstances, which, as far as judgment is concerned, limit and inhibit its exercise. Private conditions condition us; imagination and reflection enable us to liberate ourselves from them and to attain that relative impartiality that is the specific virtue of judgment" (Arendt 1982:73).

Following Kant, Arendt seems to have a predominantly intellectualist understanding of imagination. In *Lectures on Kant's Political Philosophy*, she goes so far as to say that another name for imagination is what Parmenides called the *nous*. For Arendt, imagination is indeed the faculty to represent what is not in front of us

(Arendt 1982:65). As such, it is the faculty that enables us to abstract from our peculiar situation and represent what is not there. However, as it is often the case with Arendt, the aforementioned passage about a community sense as necessary for enlarging one's own mentality highlights another strand of thought in her writings that emphasizes the importance of images for both our mental and political lives. It is indeed this line of argumentation that can helpfully be recovered in the perspective of a theory of imaginal politics.

By developing some Kantian intuitions, especially as they are elaborated in the first edition of the *Critique of Pure Reason*,[14] Arendt observed that imagination is the faculty that mediates between the universal and the particular by providing both schemata for cognition and exemplars for action (Arendt 1982:72ff, 79–85). As Kant had already argued in order to explain how is it possible that a series of sense data can be recognized as a unitary object—say, a table—we need to possess an image of what a table must be like. "This—Arendt argues—can be conceived of as a Platonic idea or Kantian schema; that is, one has before the eyes of one's mind a schematic or merely *formal table* shape to which every table somehow must conform. Or one proceeds, conversely, from the many tables one has seen in one's life, strips them of all secondary qualities, and the remainder is a table-in-general, containing the minimum properties common to all tables: the *abstract table*. One more possibility is left, and this enters into judgments that are not cognitions: one may encounter or think of some table that one judges to be the best possible table and take this table as the example of how tables actually should be: the *exemplary table* ('example' comes from *eximere*, 'to single out some particular'). This exemplar is and remains a particular that, in its very particularity, reveals the generality that otherwise could not be defined. Courage is like Achilles, etc." (Arendt 1982:76–77).[15]

My contention is that this exemplary table can be fruitfully understood as an imaginal table. It is a pictorial (re)presentation, that is, a representation that is a presence in itself. Equally imaginal are exemplary figures such as Achilles, to whom Arendt herself refers. Achilles is an image of courage and thus a representation of something that is absent but still present precisely for its exemplary validity, namely, for being individual and social at the same time. Examples are fundamental both in cognition as well as for action.[16] This is because, as she puts it, by recovering a Kantian expression, "examples are the go-cart of judgments," that which sustains us when we formulate judgments. "The example is the particular that contains in itself, or is supposed to contain, a concept or a general rule" (Arendt 1982:84). How is one able to judge an act as courageous? If one were an ancient Greek, Arendt argues, he would have in the depths of his mind the example of Achilles. The imaginal is central here because it makes present to our mind what is not in front of us, and it does so through an image that recalls a whole series of more of less conscious feelings.[17] If we say of somebody that he is good, Arendt adds, we probably have in the back of our mind an example such as Saint Francis or Jesus of Nazareth or some other example of goodness (Arendt 1982:84). Otherwise stated, we have some imaginal beings in mind.

If we consider these passages about the role of exemplary images alongside the passage about the need for an enlarged mentality, it becomes clear why politics is imaginal. In order to assume an enlarged mentality, we need to be able to put ourselves in the shoes of others, and imagining things from their point of view is the chief means to do so. "Political thought," Arendt writes, "is representative" (Arendt 1968b:237). Hence the crucial role of literature: it is by representing the conditions of others through the vivid pictorial representation of their situation that, to paraphrase Arendt, we can train the imagination to go visiting.[18] As we will see in chapter 9, Arendt is ambivalent on this point because she combines her emphasis on the importance of storytelling with a sharp critique of empathy.[19] Arendt criticizes sympathy because she sees in this emotion a danger for the impartiality of judgment. Hence the metaphor of "visiting": when you visit somebody you do not completely indentify with them, but do so by retaining your own identity (Dish 1996:141-171).

By contrast, as we will see in the chapter 9, the imaginal is crucial to politics precisely because of its capacity to move our emotions and sympathies. We will come back to this later, but let me here note the significance of the fact that the syllabus for her lectures on Kant's political philosophy included mainly literary texts as required readings.[20] This shows Arendt's awareness that the vivid, pictorial (re)presentations provided by literary texts are a means to train our imagination and thus to create that sense of community that enables us to assume an enlarged mentality.

With her emphasis on the role of examples, Arendt thus brings Kant's treatment of imagination and images further. Whereas, by relegating imagination to the realm of aesthetic judgments that have no cognitive values, Kant restated a conventional division between creativity and critique, Arendt brings the analysis of images much closer to a theory of the imaginal. It comes as no surprise to find that Arendt, in comparison with Kant, is therefore conscious of the potentially disruptive force of imagination. The experience of totalitarianism left her with a burning awareness of the power of imaginary worlds.

This may also explain why, the moment she emphasizes that imagination is crucial for the possibility of action—understood as the capacity to begin something new—she also maintains that this is only one side of the story. Our capacity to represent what is not in front of us is the source of the basic ambivalence of imagination—and of an imaginal politics more generally, we may add. As she points out at the beginning of "Lying in Politics," a characteristic of human action is that it always begins something new in the world and that this does not mean that it starts *ab ovo*, but simply that it adds something (Arendt 1972:5). This capacity to begin something new depends, in its turn, on our capacity to mentally remove ourselves from our physical location and imagine that things might well be different from what they actually are (5). This capacity to change facts, or to act, fundamentally depends on imagination. But, as Arendt observes, from the same faculty also depends the capacity, so often met in politics, to deny factual truth (5). The ambivalence of our capacity to form images of what is not in front of us thus brings us face to face with the equivocal nature of imaginal politics.

We will come back to this later on. For the time being, let me here sum up the different threads of the argument by saying that the imaginal is central to politics understood in the broadest possible sense of the term, with all the ambivalences recognized in imagination at least since Aristotle. Politics, understood as whatever pertains to the *polis*, to the life in common, is imaginal because we need an image of the public to make it exist, but also because politics presupposes the capacity to consider the point of view of others and thus to form images of what it must be like to find oneself in their shoes.

Moreover, the imaginal is also central to politics if we understand it in the more restricted sense of the term. We have seen in the previous chapter that Weber's definition of politics reflects a significant shrinkage in the semantic range of the term: no longer the whole of public life, but only a subsection of it. For Weber, politics is a specific activity within the more general public and social life, one that is characterized by the potential recourse to legitimate coercion.[21] Political power is a specific form of power, where power in general is the chance that one actor has to carry out his own will despite resistance (Weber 1978:53). In this sense, political power differs from other forms of power precisely because it can have a recourse to physical coercion that is held to be legitimate. As Weber put it, quoting Trotsky, every state is based on force, but in order for it to be something more than sheer force it needs to be a legitimate form of power (Weber 2004:33). But to be perceived as *legitimate*, political power needs to make sense within its imaginal constitution. If it fails to do so, it ceases to be political power and becomes mere violence, physical force. This is ultimately the reason why it must rest on the imaginal.

Castoriadis also notes that political power (what he also at times refers to as "explicit power") is essential to every society. This is because the fundamental ground power exercised by the instituting dimension of a society can never completely succeed in its attempt to forge compliant subjects. The instituted dimension of the social-historical will always reemerge because no society can ever completely subsume individuals within itself. For Castoriadis, there has always been a dimension of the social institution in charge of this essential function: to reestablish order, to ensure the life and operation of society against whatever endangers them (Castoriadis 1991:154).[22]

Whether such a power is necessary in principle, as Castoriadis argues, or whether it is not necessary, as far as it exists, it indubitably relies on the imaginal. To quote Castoriadis:

> Beneath the monopoly of legitimate violence lies the monopoly of the valid signification. The throne of the Lord of signification stands above the throne of the Lord of violence. The voice of the arms can only begin to be heard amid the crash of the collapsing edifice of institutions. And for violence to manifest itself effectively, the word—the injunctions of the existing power—has to keep its magic over the "group of armed men" (Engels). The fourth company of the Pavlovsky regiment, guards to His Majesty the Czar, and the Semenovsky regiment, were the strongest pillars of the throne, until those days of February 26 and 27, 1917 when they fraternized with the crowd and turned their guns against their officers. The mightiest army in the world will not protect you if it is not loyal to you—and the ultimate foundation of its loyalty is its imaginary belief in your imaginary legitimacy.
>
> (Castoriadis 1991:155–156)

Here we can easily change the term *imaginary legitimacy* to *imaginal legitimacy* and it will be clear why politics, insofar as it implies the notion of legitimacy, has to be imaginal. Politics has to adorn itself with the dress of legitimacy, it needs its own apparatus of glory; otherwise it amounts to sheer violence. This is pivotal to Weber's notion of political power, but was already present in Augustine when he observed that without justice there would be no difference between states (*regna*) and criminal gangs (*magna latrocinia*) (*De Civitate Dei*, IV, 3, 4, 33).[23]

There can be innumerable sources of legitimacy. But, if it is true that there can be no world for us without images, we have to conclude that for power to be endowed with legitimacy it has to make sense within what Weber called *Weltbilder*, or what I have rendered with the notion of the imaginal.[24] In his monumental *Economy and Society*, Weber groups the possible sources of legitimacy into three ideal types: tradition, faith, and rational enactment (Weber 1978:37).[25] The traditional grounds for legitimacy rest on a belief in "the sanctity of immemorial traditions and the legitimacy of those exercising authority under them (traditional authority)" (215). In the case of charismatic grounds, the belief in legitimacy rests "on devotion to the exceptional sanctity, heroism or exemplary character of an individual person, and of the normative patterns or orders revealed or ordained by him (charismatic authority)," while in the case of rational grounds it depends on "a belief in the legality of enacted rules and the right of those elevated to authority under such rules to issue commands (legal authority)" (215).

It is not difficult to see why all such ideal-typical sources of legitimacy have to rely on the imaginal in one way or another. The latter is crucial to traditional power, because no tradition can be respected without imagining it at the same time. You cannot believe in a tradition without an image, or a series of images, that connects the present to the past. Moreover, the imaginal is essential in the case of charismatic authority too, since people obey commands because of their faith in the sacred or heroic image of the charismatic person; one needs an image or a series of images to perceive the exceptional sanctity or exemplary character of such a person. Finally, the imaginal is crucial for legal authority as well. In order to believe in the legality of institutions, you need to possess a certain image of what law must be like, an exemplary law, to use Arendt's expression. It comes as no surprise then if we discover that even law has always had its politics of images (Douzinas and Nead 1999).

At this point of the argument, it should be emphasized that the three sources of legitimacy we have described are pure ideal types that are almost never given in reality in such pure form. Most of the time, different sources of legitimacy are intermingled with one another, so that we have claims made on the basis of both tradition and charismatic grounds, as is often the case with national leaders. But, as Weber observes, in modern societies the most common form of legitimacy is the belief in legality, the compliance with enactments that are formally correct, so that it is impossible to imagine a political authority advancing a claim to legitimacy today without resting in one form or another on a legal-rational ground of legitimacy.

In part 3 we will analyze the contemporary transformation of these ideal-typical sources of legitimacy in more detail. I would like to mention here, however, that, as a consequence of the biopolitical turn described in the previous chapter, a fourth source of legitimacy seems to have come into prominence: the reproductive conservation of life (Esposito 2008:160). The two parallel processes, the biologization of the political and the politicization of the biological, have made of the conservation of life such a crucial ingredient for the belief in the legitimacy of political power that a revision of Weber's three ideal types is needed.

However, as already mentioned in the previous chapter, biopolitics is inevitably a form of imaginal politics because there cannot be a belief in political power over life without an image, or a series of images, of what life must be like. Particularly in an epoch when technological developments have given us the potential to intervene in the most basic mechanisms of life, from birth to death, we cannot perceive life without an imaginal representation of what it must be like to be alive. Endless political debates about when life begins and when it ends are a stark reminder of the fact that, even admitting that the Greeks could still distinguish between bare life (*zoe*) and qualified life (*bios*), this distinction is lost for us: life, today more than ever, is what we make of it.

We will deal with the consequences that this has for contemporary politics in the following chapters. For now I will sum up the thread of the argument thus far by saying that, if the imaginal is essential to politics, it is so with all the ambivalences that had been noted about imagination already a long time ago. The imaginal is radical because it can make present what is absent in the double sense of creating something new as well as the denying of facts. The creation of images is central to our capacity for action, our capacity to begin something new in the world, but also to our ability to lie. In both cases we deny what is given because we depict something that is not there.

Hence it is necessary to rethink the imaginal in connection with a critical approach that focuses on this crucial question: in what condition is the imaginal a means for critique? And when does it turn into a means for oppression? Drawing inspiration from Castoriadis, we could say that it is in the radical capacity to question one's own images that the possibility of critique lies. On the contrary, a closure of meaning and thus of interrogation is operative when social arrangements are presented as the result of an extrasocial source that is outside the possibility of questioning, e.g., God, traditional ancestors, or even the immutable laws of history.

As we have seen in the previous chapters, the emphasis on the project of autonomy and a revolutionary praxis was indeed the crucial heritage that Castoriadis retains from Marx (we could also add Freud to the list). Further guided by his own reading of the history of the Athenian *polis*, he pushed the argument as far as to postulate a distinction between the concept of the political and that of politics. While *political* denotes politics as commonly understood (what Castoriadis also called "explicit power"), politics, such as that created by the Greeks, amounts in his view to the explicit putting into question of the established institution of society (Castoriadis 1991:159). Castoriadis here goes against the common understanding of terms, but he does so to put forward the idea that true politics was discovered by the Greeks, and thus to point to the fact that there cannot be true politics without autonomy. With this terminological twist he wants to emphasize the importance of the possibility of critique. Not by chance, then, he attributed to the Greeks the discovery of both politics and philosophy: Greek thought amounts to the putting into question of the most important dimension of the institution of society, namely, the representations and norms of the tribe and the very notion of truth.

Whether the Greeks invented both philosophy and politics in Castoriadis's sense is at least disputable. If by philosophy we mean a rational attitude toward the world, it appears at best naive to believe in the idea that nobody philosophized about the world before Thales looked around him and came up with the idea that water is the principle of everything.[26] Equally contestable is the idea that the Greeks invented democracy, if it is true that other people had similar forms of organization of power before.[27] But even if they did so, we should rather call it democratic politics. The fact that Castoriadis talks about "true politics" or "politics properly conceived" (Castoriadis 1991:160), that he needs to add those two little words, *true* and *properly*, is a sign that he is trying to persuade us of something that goes against common understanding. In contrast to Castoriadis, I think one should be allowed to violate the maxim *nomina non sunt multiplicanda praeter necessitatem* if one needs to. There are moments when the creation of a new word is necessary to render a novelty we are witnessing—and, in a way, this book is nothing but a long argument about the need for a new word. However, in this case, there is no real lack of vocabulary to describe what Castoriadis has in mind. We already have a word for it: *democracy*.

The reason why Castoriadis insists on calling democracy "true politics" should not escape us. If politics, since the very birth of the term, has to do with our being-in-common, then we should conclude that democracy is "true politics," because it is the moment when politics becomes reflexive. Democracy, as the form of government where the people (*demos*) exercise power (*kratos*), is the moment when the people are reflexively aware that their destiny depends on their being-in-common and take their political destiny into their own hands.

This brings us to a crucial question: is the imaginal something that favors or, rather, hinders the possibility of democracy? How do the current transformations of the nexus of politics and the imaginal impact the possibility of democracy itself? The task of the next chapter is precisely to focus on this question. The fact that politics has always been imaginal is perhaps a banality that immediately appears if we consider that images are consubstantial with our being in the world, because there could be neither a world for us nor a subject for the world without them. Politics is imaginal because it needs a world in order to be in the first place. Yet, as we will now see, the reason why we need to name it now is that the imaginal itself has undergone such a deep change in contemporary conditions that we have reached a critical threshold. Politics has always been imaginal, but the difference is that today we can no longer ignore this fact. That is why we need a new word here and now—as Mephistopheles says, "good at need!"

6

Contemporary Transformations Between
Spectacle and Virtuality

> People think they come together in the spectacle, and it is here that they are isolated.
>
> JEAN-JACQUES ROUSSEAU, *Letter to d'Alembert on the Theatre*

We have seen why politics is imaginal; there can be no politics, either in its narrowest or broadest senses, without the imaginal. We need now to analyze how the nexus of politics and the imaginal changes within contemporary conditions. If we look at the political role of the imaginal—understood to be what is made of images, of (re)presentations that are always presences in themselves—we cannot but perceive a puzzling tension: the imaginal has been both exponentially inflated as well as paralyzed at present.

On the one hand, contemporary politics is overwhelmed by the imaginal. It depends on images not only because images mediate our being-in-the-world as such but also because they allow us to communicate with one another. But there seems to be more going on here—a sort of hypertrophy of the imaginal. In the first place, this is due to the massive diffusion of the media. If one thinks of what politics used to be before streams of images started to enter our homes through television, it is clear that the quantitative increase in the number of images has also produced a qualitative change in the nature of politics itself. Our political experience has become inconceivable outside the continual flow of images that appear on our screens every day. Images are no longer only the medium by which we communicate our political activities, but have also become an end in themselves: the very stuff that politics is made of.

This emerges most clearly if one considers what politics was a few centuries ago. While it is true that (insofar as there cannot be a political community without images) politics has always been imaginal, it is also equally true that before the media revolution ordinary people had very little visual contact with their rulers: they needed and possessed far fewer images of them. Portraits and maps were from the very beginning political, as I have argued in the previous chapter, but they were not as widely circulated as they began to be in the age of industrial reproducibility.

The increase in the number of images went hand in hand with the progressive extension of the suffrage and rise of representative democracy. When rulers need the consent of their subjects, their relentless search for legitimacy has to even more regularly make recourse to the support of images—the medium that can capture people's imagination in the most immediate way. However, particularly today, the imaginal that enters politics is no longer the wild fruit of individual creativity: it is the result of carefully planned and manufactured images. Given the power of images produced on an industrial scale today—a transformation that some have tried to capture by speaking of a "civilization of the image"—it does not come as a surprise to learn that mass-marketing techniques have entered the workshops of power. As studies on the introduction of such techniques into political campaigns have showed, in an age when images are manufactured on an industrial scale, the careful planning and staging of pictorial (re)presentations has become consubstantial to democracy. There is no political regime that does not rely in some way on the "mass marketing of politics" (Newman 1999).

The term imaginal, which suspends the question of reality, is particularly relevant here. The mass marketing of politics does not only mean that politicians have become obsessed with their image because this corresponds to what they are or to the impact that they expect certain images to have on the audience. As Thomas Meyer has observed, politicians behave *as if* the images transmitted by the media were reality itself, independently of their actual impact on peoples' minds. No policy is undertaken, nor is any decision made by contemporary politicians, without first (and foremost) considering how this will affect their image in the media (Meyer 2002), a phenomenon that Meyer has referred to as the "theatricality of contemporary politics."[1] Politics has become theater because politicians behave according to an expected imaginal appeal on the audience, independently of whether and how this will actually turn out to be.

As we have seen in the previous chapter, sovereignty has always been representational, so much so that, in order to explain the paradox of the fictitious character of the Leviathan, Hobbes had to make recourse to the notion of the *persona* or mask taken from theater. But, whereas in Hobbes there is still the idea that the subjects can recognize themselves in the actions of the sovereign who bears their person,[2] what is new is that politicians behave according to the forecasts of mass-marketing experts, independently of whether this actually has an impact on their audience or not. This obsessive reliance on the image is the result of the exponentially increased role that the imaginal has in contemporary politics.

Nevertheless, this political world that is full of images seems to lack imagination—understood here in the traditional sense of the capacity to question what is given through the production of images of the new. In an epoch in which politics has been reduced to governance—simple administration within a general neoliberal consensus—there seems to be no space to imagine things differently. It may be worth remembering here that the term *governance* was coined in the 1980s to denote the politics of the World Bank. This occurred in a juridical context that denied the World Bank the right to exercise functions of government—that is, to mingle in the political affairs of a sovereign country. Since then, *governance* has become synonymous with a way of doing politics that does not imply government and therefore amounts to mere technique.[3] Once again, the rise and fortune of such a new term is the consequence of a change that available vocabulary was not able to render: the fact that you can have politics without government because the former has been reduced to mere technique.

The term *governance* was indeed originally coined to denote a form of authority not fully political: *governance*, as opposed to *government*, denotes a politics that is not politics, that is, politics without vision. Since then, the term has been extended to denote a particular networklike form of authority that situates itself above that of nation-states.[4] David Held and colleagues have influentially used the term to denote the "multilayered global governance" that has emerged as a consequence of globalization (Held et al. 1999). While the idea of government implies some sort of centralized structure, governance has come to mean a networklike form of global authority that is not, or at least pretends to be, nonpolitical. As such, the concept has been associated with the crisis of nation-states and of the traditional sites of democracy that gradually yield authority to transnational and supranational bodies that escape the traditional mechanisms of representative democracy.[5]

The term *governance* is thus associated with the structural crisis of representative democracy brought about by globalization and the much celebrated (or criticized) "end of politics." (Boggs 2000). Globalization in its numerous aspects—economic, financial, environmental, technological, political, and cultural—has created a situation in which events, decisions, and activities in one part of the world can have significant consequences for individuals and communities in opposite parts of the globe. As such, *globalization* became a catchphrase for a set of processes that shifts the spatial form of human organization and activity to transcontinental and interregional patterns of activity, interactions, and exercises of power.[6] Globalization involves a stretching and deepening of social relations and institutions across space and time such that, on the one hand, day-to-day activities are increasingly influenced by events happening on the other side of the globe and, on the other, the practices and decisions of local groups or communities can have significant global reverberations. This means that our lives increasingly depend on peoples and activities taking place in remote regions of the globe; consequently, we feel increasingly less able to master our destinies. This perception of impotence is the result of a structural crisis undermining the modern model of democratic representation. Whereas the social chains of interdependence have stretched themselves to the extremes of the globe, politics—and particularly democratic politics—remains anchored to its traditional boundaries.

A promoter of globalization, the sovereign state seems also to be its most illustrious victim. The exercise of sovereign power in the modern age has been associated with the capacity for rational control over territory and its resources, a capacity that the current predicament throws into question. But the crisis of modern sovereign states also brought with it a structural crisis of the modern model of representative democracy. The latter, centered as it was on the notion of popular sovereignty, was indeed based on the idea of the congruence between decision makers and their addressees (Held 1995).

What globalization and the emergence of a multilayered system of global governance questions is precisely this solution. Together with sovereignty, democracy itself is in danger. By stretching the social chains of interdependence, the symmetry between decision makers and the addressees of such decisions—a symmetry upon which democracy itself ultimately rests—breaks down at a number of important points. The territorial anchorage of the state, its correspondence to precise territorial and functional boundaries, was at the same time the limit and the force of the modern state: it enabled the modern state to control a territory as well as to define the body of the citizens called on to participate in the democratic process.

As Jürgen Habermas has pointed out in reference to this territorial anchorage, the expression globalization evokes the image of fluxes that undermine the control of frontiers, threatening the whole democratic edifice. In other words, the ruler is no longer he who controls the territory, but is rather she who has at her disposal the maximal speed.[7] The compression of space and time that has been brought about by globalization implies a tendential depletion of the "attrition of distance" that guaranteed the modern state the possibility of controlling the space in which it exercised its sovereignty—as defined by its territorial bound-aries.[8] The globalization of capital and liberalization of the labor market have engendered a condition in which economic activities tend to get rid of spatial constraints. Crucial sectors of production, particularly those in high technology, now have transnational scope. Thanks to a communications revolution, which enabled the costs of transportation to be reduced and complex information to be transmitted, the production process has become fragmented and different seg-ments of production have been displaced to remote regions of the globe. In this way global elites can easily escape territorial constraints and the social burdens and responsibilities that these define.[9]

Even more striking is the erosion of state sovereignty due to financial activi-ties. Contemporary communication technologies and the liberalization of mar-kets have made it impossible for a single state to control financial transactions. The speed by which bytes travel from one computer to another has canceled the distance separating Wall Street from Tokyo and Shanghai. This has not only changed our way of imagining of the world but also contributed to the increased role played by financial transactions: the electronic herd traveling instanta-neously from one side of the globe to another has reached such proportions as to be able to determine the destiny of individuals, groups, and even entire commu-nities. In no other case is the equation *power = speed* as evident as that of financial activities. While the financial transactions of ancient times brought with them the image of the ruler (the exergue of coins), today flux of financial exchanges brings with them the questioning of local power and thus also a different image of the world (from Wall Street to Shanghai we are all on the same boat).

In the security field as well, technological changes have undermined the at-trition of resistance that space once provided. Environmental and security issues are another significant example of the equation *power = speed*. As for the applica-tion of technological innovations to military strategy, we can see present condi-tion as the last stage of a process in which the quantitative growth in our de-structive capacities has ended in a qualitative change marking the passage from one epoch to another. Just as firearms once made the creation of large political spaces possible, enabling the sovereign power to overcome feudal castles, today nuclear and chemical weapons undermine single states' capacity to defend their boundaries; just as the former marked the passage to the political modernity of sovereign states, the latter might accompany a significant paradigm shift toward a postmodernity demanding new political maps.[10]

Another threat to the capacity of single states to defend their citizens is rep-resented by environmental issues. This is perhaps the case in which the stretch-ing of the social chains of interdependence is more significant, not only because issues such as global warming have an irremediably global impact but also because they mark the point where the expansive dynamics of modern capitalism encounter a limit, i.e., the limits of available spatial and natural resources. This is the argument put forward by scholars such as Albrow (1996), who argue that modernity, with its expansive dynamics, has come to an end and we have moved toward "a global age": if the projecting rationality is the characteristic feature of modernity, and if territorial and natural resources are the ground for its realization, then globalization—as the point where the limits of these resources are encountered—cannot help but mark the beginning of a new age characterized by the production of the world as a whole (ibid.).

This process of divesting traditional sites of politics of their authority resulted in the perception that politics itself had come to an end. The paradox of a world full of images but deprived of imagination must be understood within this scenario. The widespread sense that "there is no alternative" is the consequence of the emergence of neoliberal forms of global governance that question traditional ways of conceiving democracy, divest them of the power they have had until recently, and replace them with a multilayered system of governance that escapes democratic accountability. This is a process that, by questioning the modern image of a world of sovereign states, can also potentially point the way to new, more global political maps. But the capacity to envisage new images of the world seems to be threatened by the saturation of our political imagination.

The structural crisis we have described is indeed occulted by the spectacle of politics paraded across our screens every day. This spectacle is indispensable because it has to conceal the death of traditional forms of democracy. The paradox of a world full of images but deprived of imagination thus rests on the growth of the more *passive* side of the imaginal, which happens at the expenses of its more *active* side. Otherwise said, we are so image saturated by the spectacle clamoring for screen time that it becomes increasingly difficult to *create* new ones.

This is the consequence of a change in both the *quantity* and the *quality* of the images produced in the global epoch, which we will now consider. With regard to the quantitative increase, we have already mentioned the exponential growth in the quantity of images that enter our political life. In particular, the quantity of images produced by the media has reached such a level as to also determine a qualitative leap: images have become an end in themselves, weapons in the hands of skilful artisans who have developed novel and powerful mass-marketing techniques.

Take elections as an example. Many authors have noticed that elections have always had the function of a ritual, since, by virtue of mere repetition, they reinforce a certain model of society by providing it with visible continuity.[11] But today the quantity of images that accompanies elections in most Western countries has become such that the spectacle prevails over the content. Images are now overly abundant, and so they need to be selected and filtered by the media in some way. The golden rule of the audience does the job: only those images that can capture people's attention so as to prevent them from turning to something else are selected, hence the prevalence of images in the register of spectacle.

However, the electoral battle dramatized on our screens hides the fact that no real battle is taking place, because the real clash is not among the official candidates (who most often have very similar policies), but offstage, hidden in the wings. The real fight is between the political options that are touted by the candidates, left and right, and those that are not even taken into consideration. The decisive distance is not between candidates, but between those who get a role in the spectacle and those who are left out of it.[12] In sum, the reduction of politics to governance has gone together with the spectacularization of democratic processes, because it is by participating in these empty spectacles that the addressees of democratic institutions are blinded to the fact that they are not the authors of their destinies.

As Castoriadis observed, the real purpose of elections in so-called representative democracies is not to choose, but rather "to educate people in the conviction that they are unable to manage the problems of society, that there exists a particular category of men endowed with the specific ability to govern" (Castoriadis 1976:15). This is the reason why the affirmation of representative democracy went together with professionalized politics and political apathy. The spectacle of elections occults the fact that we are mere consumers of political decisions rather than active producers of them.

This is the reason Castoriadis does not hesitate to say that the typically modern idea that democracy is equivalent to representation is "political mystification" (15). Whereas in premodern times representation always took the form of mandate and was therefore revocable, with modernity representation becomes permanent. As we have seen in chapter 5, Hobbes very clearly pointed to the representative nature of modern sovereignty when he observed that the sovereign is he who can bear the person of its subjects—to represent them—in order to act as if they were present even when they are absent. But the ballot box, whereby the power to decide is delegated to representatives, is not the beginning of democracy: it is the end of it. If democracy means government by the people, the moment when the right to govern is alienated to representatives cannot but be the moment when it ceases. As Castoriadis puts it, "being irrevocable (even if formally limited in time), the permanent delegation of power to representatives is a form of political alienation. Political power is appropriated by the representatives. But to decide is to decide for oneself. It is not a matter of deciding *who* is going to decide" (15). This is the reason why the spectacularization of politics had to go together with its alleged democratization: the spectacle of election has to hide the fact that potentially active citizens have been transformed into purely passive spectators.

In his *Letter on the Spectacle*, published in 1758, Rousseau, a harsh critic of representative democracy, issued a stark warning about the dangers of spectacles for a democratic polity (Rousseau 1960). Of all Rousseau's writings—including the political texts where he directly criticizes Hobbes and puts forward his arguments in favor of direct democracy—this is his most anti-Hobbesian, since it is the one in which the combination between representation and sovereignty is most decisively shown to be detrimental to political life.[13] In the spectacle, as Rousseau argues in the passage quoted in this chapter's epigraph, we come together, but it is also there that we are most isolated (17). This is because the spectacle renders us distant spectators of what is going on. As he puts it, "everything that is played in the theatre is not brought nearer, but made more distant" (25–26).

There is indeed something like a systematic distortion inscribed in the very nature of spectacles. A spectacle has to entertain, and if it fails to do so it ceases to be a spectacle. Rousseau, who regularly attended theater when he was in Paris and was a playwright himself, knew this very well. According to him, the spectacle can never present the true relation between things: "For in general, the poet can only alter these relations in order to accommodate them to the taste of the public. In the comic, he diminishes them and sets them beneath man; in the tragic, he extends them to render them heroic and sets them above humanity. Thus they are never to his measure, and we always see beings other than our own kind in the spectacle" (27; translation modified).[14]

According to Rousseau, this systematic distortion of the spectacle generates in turn a certain taste and habit of counterfeiting. The talent of the actor is indeed "the art of counterfeiting himself," of systematically putting on an aspect other than his own and thus appearing different than he is, "of becoming passionate in cold blood, of saying what he does not think as naturally as if he really did think it, and, finally, of forgetting his own place by dint of taking another's" (79). If we consider that this habit, which constitutes the very essence of the talent of the actor, can be transferred to the whole of society as a consequence of the proliferation of spectacles, it is not difficult to understand why Rousseau deems it highly inappropriate for a true republic.

In his view, these problems are compounded by the fact that, together with the taste for systematic distortion, the spectacle also fosters a spirit of inaction, a passive attitude in which the subject watches and receives instead of acting and producing (65). In conclusion, according to Rousseau we should be aware that the spectacle renders us distant and passive spectators, mere receptacles of a distorted truth that can never be lived but only passively observed.

The problem becomes even more serious if we consider, along with Guy Debord (1994:thesis 4), that the spectacle is not just a collection of images, but "a social relation among people, mediated by images." The reference to Debord is not accidental. Despite the fact that Debord never quotes Rousseau on the spectacle, the similarities between their two diagnoses are striking. Nobody after Rousseau has, in my view, captured the essentially spectacular nature of society as well as the leader of the Situationist International. Like Rousseau, Debord knew from practice what a spectacle was; however, in contrast to Rousseau, he elaborates his diagnosis within the context of late capitalist societies, hence his focus on the language of political economy.

If Marx had already emphasized the spectacular nature of capitalism through his pathbreaking analysis of commodity fetishism, Debord extended this analysis so as to make the spectacle the central category in the analysis of the constitutive dynamics of contemporary capitalism. Thus if Marx began *Capital* by saying that "the wealth of societies in which the capitalist mode of production prevails appears as an immense collection of commodities" (Marx 1976:125), Debord opens his *Society of the Spectacle* by observing that "in societies where modern conditions of production prevail, all of life presents itself as an immense accumulation of spectacles. Everything that was directly lived has moved away into a representation." (Debord 1994:thesis 1). Notice the opposition between "directly lived" versus "moved away into representation." According to Laurent Jenny, it is precisely this opposition between being and appearing, between lived experience and spectacular appearances that is shared by Rousseau's and Debord's approach to the spectacle (Jenny 1990:110; McDonough 2011:44).[15]

However, I would also note the strong emphasis by both authors on the fact that the spectacle produces isolation and alienated separation. As Debord writes in a passage that sounds almost like a reformulation of Rousseau, albeit in the language of political economy:

> The spectacle originates in the loss of the unity of the world, and the gigantic expansion of the modern spectacle expresses the totality of this loss: the abstraction of all specific labor and the general abstraction of the entirety of production are perfectly rendered in the spectacle, whose *mode of being concrete* is precisely abstraction. In the spectacle, one part of the world *represents itself* to the world and

is superior to it. The spectacle is nothing more than the common language of this separation. What binds the spectators together is no more than an irreversible relation at the very center that maintains their isolation. The spectacle reunites the separate, but reunites it *as separate*.

(Debord 1994:thesis 29)

Thus the spectacle becomes not simply a form of entertainment but also the quintessence of contemporary capitalism, which produces separated spectators at the moment that it brings them together. As Debord (1994:thesis 34) put it in his typically laconic style, the spectacle is nothing but "*capital* to such a degree of accumulation that it becomes an image." It is when capitalist exploitation has reached the ultimate threshold of the whole globe that capital has to become spectacle in itself in order to find new imaginary markets. This is the reason why the spectacle can no longer be simply a form of entertainment achieved through a collection of images, but has become "a social relation among people mediated by images," thus marking the moment when the commodity has attained the total occupation of social life (theses 4, 42). As a consequence, the spectacle is no longer merely a crucial ingredient of commodity fetishism and thus of the moment of capitalist consumption. It is, much more radically, a relation that pervades all social relationships in late capitalist societies. Debord with Marx, but also beyond Marx.

Writing in the 1960s, Debord was able to identify a crucial change in the nature of contemporary capitalism that brought about the exponential increase of the imaginal many associate with globalization and the rise of so-called cognitive capitalism. Commenting on the premonitions of Debord, Franco Berardi has recently written,

the situationist movement dissolved when Paris started featuring the graffiti "power to the imagination." 1968 was realising the dream of historical vanguards, Dadaism and Surrealism: the dream of the abolition of art and the routine of daily life and above all of the fusion of the two, the dream of a life where difference prevailed on repetition. But, as we later found out, imagination became crystallised in the Image and the predominance of the Image paralyzed the imagination. Machines of homologated production of the Image have infiltrated the collective mind and wired it up by introducing psychic, linguistic, and relational automatism. We must recognise this: real society is no longer capable of imagining anything that has not been produced in the laboratories of the Global Homologated System. In his most celebrated work, Debord called this homologating effect of imagina(c)tion the "Spectacle." The spectacle is what must be seen but can never be lived.

(Berardi 2011)

With his prophecy that a society of the spectacle would be the last product of capitalism, Debord also predicted early on that contestation of the 1960s was doomed to fail. Giving all the power to the imagination is not enough when the latter has been colonized by machines of the homologated production of images. Whereas Marcuse—who was mainly concerned with the Fordist mode of production, that is, with a mode of production that is alienating because it reduces human work to the mechanical repetition of a single gesture on the assembly line—could still perceive in imagination and art a way out of a "one-dimensional" society (Marcuse 1991), Debord went one step further.

In this respect, Debord has been a visionary of the change in the nature of capitalist production itself, a change that some associate with the post-Fordist transformations of capitalism. There are at least two different versions of such a diagnosis that are particularly crucial for our purposes, because it is such a transformation of capitalism that lies at the basis of the biopolitical turn described in chapter 4 (Bazzicalupo 2006; Lazzarato 2011).

The first variant is the post-Fordist hypothesis strictly understood. According to such a paradigm, there has been a shift in contemporary capitalism aptly summarized by the idea of a "linguistic turn in the economy" (Marazzi 1994). While Fordist production was based on the alienating repetition of a mute laborer, after such a turn language and communication become crucial ingredients of the process of production itself. This has been capitalism's reply to the criticism raised by the social movements of the 1960s. The latter criticized capitalism for alienating the working class through repetitive mute work and invoked the "power of imagination" as a possible weapon against such alienation, but post-Fordist capitalism accepted such a challenge by becoming flexible and systematically incorporating creativity in participative management.[16]

This does not mean that post-Fordist capitalism realized the aspiration for a liberation from alienation invoked in the 1960s. Quite the contrary, if Berardi is right in the passage quoted before, we can say that it has rendered such an emancipation even more difficult. Now that the obsessive proliferation of images has dried up our capacity to create new ones, because it has become consubstantial to the productive process itself, it seems even more difficult to find a way out.

Indeed, participative management, networks, and creativity do not abolish either alienation or social antagonism. On the contrary, the capitalist mode of production becomes even more authoritarian, because "creativity" ends up being an imperative within a context where its possibilities are already predetermined: the product must be sold even before it is produced and the most efficient way to do so is to follow the trends, as mass-marketing techniques have shown us. Hence the tendency toward a multiplication of the number of images in our lives, but also our increasing difficulty to produce radically new ones.

The fact that, with such a post-Fordist turn, "mute labor" is being overcome by the newly central role of "immaterial labor" (Lazzarato 1997) does not mean liberation. Within the factories, this simply takes the form of a decentralization, with the emergence of diffuse factories and production on demand—the so-called just in time. This further challenges the possibility of an organized form of political antagonism because workers are rendered even more isolated than in the past. Outside the factories, the rise of immaterial labor is most evident in the exponential growth of the tertiary, where it is not material commodities that are produced but rather services that require an even more sustained integration of creativity and imagination (Lazzarato 1997; Marazzi 1994).

A more radical version of this diagnosis has been developed by Carlo Vercellone, who criticizes the post-Fordist hypothesis for remaining prey to an industrialist bias, with its emphasis on factories and the industrial mode of production (Vercellone 2007). Capitalism, Vercellone observes (14), began a long time before industrialization and is currently surviving it in advanced modern societies in the form of a "cognitive capitalism," which can be best observed outside of factories. As he points out, the centrality of knowledge to capitalism is not new per se, as the notion of a general intellect developed by Marx in his *Grundrisse* demonstrates. According to Vercellone, the introduction of computer technologies in the production process itself has indeed rendered Marx's thesis of the general intellect particularly timely: computer technologies, telematic and microelectronic innovation, can only work in contexts of diffused intellectuality—that is, in contexts where the relation of capital to labor is marked by the hegemony of knowledge. But the systematic recourse to computer technologies that operate through icons implies a quantitative and thus also qualitative change in the role of the image. And that is the reason why the "linguistic turn" in the economy is also an imaginal one: words became crucial to the production process, but images are even more primordially so.

According to Vercellone (2007:16), this new phase of the division of labor is accompanied, on the one hand, by the crisis of the law of value labor and, on the other, by the strong return to mercantile and financial mechanisms of accumulation that can sustain constant innovation. The crisis of the traditional model of value labor relations is determined by the fact that value becomes difficult to calculate, since we are all constantly producing value insofar as we create new knowledge that can be subsumed by capitalism. And Marx's prediction of the rise of a general intellect, of diffuse intellectuality as the next stage of capitalist production, here shows its striking timeliness.[17] The only difference is that the general intellect is, to a great extent, also an imaginal one.

It is precisely this transformation in contemporary capitalism that has fulfilled Debord's prophecy, but has also brought the whole process to a further stage. Because of the new central role that the production of images plays, not only in the moment of consumption of commodities—as in the classical diagnoses of the phantasmagoria of the commodities—but also in production itself, the society of the spectacle prophesized by Debord has become more prominent than ever before: the spectacle is no longer just a form of entertainment for some, but a social relation that pervades society as a whole.

However, as is often the case, the realization of this prophecy also somehow announces its overcoming, so that the need emerges to further consider some of Debord's assumptions. Significantly, the opening thesis of his *Society of the Spectacle* quoted earlier is followed by another passage where Debord (1994:thesis 1) states, "everything that was directly lived has moved away into a representation." The opposition between representation and reality, or spectacle and reality, pervades his entire work, but the idea that we can still counterpoise the representation to the reality itself is something that the present work is trying to contest. The society of the spectacle has become *global*, not only because it has annihilated geographical distance but also because there is no longer the possibility to contrast it to the reality of facts. To put it bluntly, there is no more "outside" to the spectacle. Rather, the spectacle has become a pervasive social relation from which there is no possibility of escape.

This has to do with a qualitative transformation in the nature of the imaginal itself, to which we will now turn. Together with the quantitative increase of the imaginal, contemporary capitalism has also brought with it a change in the quality of images themselves. Virtual images are not only commodities that can be reproduced on an industrial scale.[18] They have become ongoing processes requiring perpetual maintenance. As a consequence, not only has their authenticity been lost, but the very possibility of determining their status as real or unreal has vanished. In the contemporary society of the spectacle, the virtual risks becoming the paradigm for what is most real.[19]

Let me further illustrate this point by focusing on this intrinsic *qualitative* change in the nature of images—a change that also deeply affects the link between the political and the imaginal. Behind the virtual revolution there is indeed a deep revolution in the nature of images that has been enabled by the introduction of computer technologies. Virtual images are not only commodities subject to the laws and treatment of all other commodities, but they are now also malleable to an extent that has never been the case before. Images are not only *reproducible* in series, but they are also *modifiable* up to a point where they have completely lost their link with the "here" and "now."

A way to illustrate this point is to start from Walter Benjamin's remarks on the work of art in the age of its technological reproducibility (Benjamin 2002). Benjamin begins with the observation that, as a consequence of their industrial reproducibility, works of art have lost their "aura." The aura is defined as "a strange tissue of space and time: the unique apparition of a distance, however near it may be" (104–105). Artistic images, as is clearly evident in photography and cinema, have lost their being *hic et nunc*, here and now. A piece of music can be repeated in different spaces and times in a substantially identical form so that we cannot say that it is precisely that concert, played by X and Y in the moment Z and not another one. Similarly, a photograph can be reproduced ad infinitum without it being possible to distinguish between the original and the copies.

With the advent of virtual images, we have reached a further level of this process. Photography and cinema, it can be argued, still had a connection with the *hic et nunc*. A picture needed to be taken before being reproduced. So too, a film needed to be shot in the first place. Even if they could be both cut and assembled in different ways at different times, they still had their original here and now: the moment when they were taken, turned, created. All this is overcome by virtuality. There is no *hic et nunc* in a virtual image and therefore no authenticity to be preserved and no original to orient us. Virtual images are not objects that can be created at once, but ongoing processes. There is no original creation, but only a process of perpetual maintenance.

This is clearly shown by the practice of contemporary photography and the way in which Photoshop and other computer programs have modified not simply the practice of photography, but the very nature of images. In 2009 a photography exhibition called "Manipulating Reality: How Images Redefine the World" gathered artists from all over the world to show how new techniques had changed the nature of contemporary photography.[20] Their work now consists mainly of a constant process of reworking images, so much so that walking through the exhibition one had the impression of going through works in progress. Some of those images consisted of the obsessive repetition of singular architectural units, so as to produce new objects out of the simple repetition of the same image over and over again. In these cases it is very clear that the process can potentially continue ad infinitum so that it becomes difficult to say when it began and even less so when it will stop.

What are the potentially political uses of such techniques? In 2006 a reporter from Reuters was covering news about the Israeli bombing of Lebanon in July and August. The image he used to illustrate the story depicted a city so covered in smoke that it aroused suspicion about the veracity of the picture. The reporter claimed he had just been trying to remove dust marks and that he made mistakes due to the bad lighting conditions he was working under, but critics point out that this is impossible, as the doctored image added an entire plume of smoke, duplicated several buildings, and showed a repeating pattern indicating that one plume of smoke was "cloned" several times, over and over again.[21]

The repetition and indefinite duplication of images seems to have become a crucial political weapon. In June 2009 an article entitled "Someone in Iran isn't Good at Photoshop" denounced a widely circulating picture proving that Photoshopping was used to make the crowd at a pro-Ahmedinejad rally look much bigger.[22] Similarly, a few years before, during the 2004 presidential campaign, the Bush staff released a television ad that included a photo of a crowd of soldiers listening to a speech with a child in the foreground waving an American flag. A poster on the liberal Daily Kos weblog soon noticed that the image had evidently been faked, since the same faces were cloned over and over, reappearing in different places throughout the crowd. The ad was embarrassingly titled "Whatever It Takes." After the allegation of cloning faces to make the crowd look bigger started to circulate, the Bush campaign replaced the ad with a new version that did not include the doctored photo.[23]

But the continual repetition of the same unit is not the only possibility opened by Photoshop and pixelization techniques. Coloring is another crucial tool, particularly helpful when it comes to political correctness in a globalizing world. For instance, in the hope of emphasizing the diversity and pluralism of it enrollment, the University of Wisconsin at Madison manipulated a photograph on a brochure cover by inserting black students in a crowd of white football fans. To explain how this happened, university officials said that they spent a lot of time looking for pictures that would show the school's diversity, but had no luck. Photoshop came to their aid: they simply had to "paint it black" here and there.[24]

It is true that the doctoring of images for the sake of political correctness (or incorrectness) is no novelty as such. Rulers have always manipulated images. But what is new today is the degree to which images can be reworked though technologies that are widely (if not universally) diffused. While Stalin had to employ skilled technicians to make his political adversaries disappear from the pictures of the regime, today a single computer would suffice. This quantitative increase in the malleability of images is likely to determine a qualitative change whose final outcomes are difficult to predict. This could open the door to the nightmare of total manipulation, but also inaugurate a new era of the democratization of images.

An interesting example of the subversive use of such technologies is offered by the Internet meme called "Sarkozy was there." A meme is a joke on the Internet that is reproduced in various forms over and over again. The Sarkozy meme began in November 2009 after Nicolas Sarkozy posted a photo on Facebook of himself that shows him taking part in history by chipping away at the Berlin Wall in November 1989, saying that it was shot the very night that East German authorities surprised the world by announcing that their border with the West would be opened immediately. The problem is, as a subsequent search of available records has proven, he was not actually there. The photo was shot a week later.[25] This is no big novelty in itself, as politicians have always been eager to write history at their own discretion. What is new is the reaction that this event triggered: a new spectacle that subverted the dominant spectacle by using the very same means. Sarkozy's story of having been present in Berlin the night the Wall fell has inspired Photoshoppers to flood the Web with images showing him witnessing or taking part in a series of other famous moments in history: suddenly Sarkozy was jogging alongside President Kennedy's motorcade in Dallas in 1963, leading the French soccer team out for the World Cup final in Paris in 1998, dominating the Yalta Conference in 1945 (along with his son Jean), and observing the famous kiss photographed by Robert Doisneau in Paris in 1950.[26] In sum, he was shown to be "there" in his multifaceted imaginal being.

This example raises the question as to the possible options for fighting the effects of the increasing spectacularization of politics. If the spectacle has become a social relation from which no escape is possible, how can we fight it? Where can we find the resources for fighting the alienating and isolating effects of the spectacle, if the spectacle has become nothing less than society itself? The previous detour into Debord may be illuminating in this respect. Akin to the case of the Sarkozy meme, the specific way in which Debord and the Situationist International fought against the spectacular nature of contemporary capitalism was indeed through the spectacle itself. Precisely because the spectacle has become a relation that pervades all social relationships, we cannot escape from it, but what we can do is to fight the evil with its own weapons, answering the spectacle with another spectacle. Hence the emphasis on the tactic of *détournement*, recommended and practiced by Debord and the other members of the Situationist International. *Détournement* means that we cannot get out of the spectacle, but we can use preexisting elements of it in a new ensemble that subverts, destabilizes, *détourne* the dominant spectacular logic.

But the same technique is crucial to what we can call Rousseau's homeopathic method: his recommendation to fight a spectacle by injecting small quantities of the very same evil.[27] The homeopathic principle is something that Rousseau already alluded to in *First Discourse*,[28] but is even more explicitly elaborated in the *Preface to Narcissus*, where Rousseau, by then the acclaimed author of a devastating critique of the sciences and letters, had to defend himself against the charge of practicing precisely those fine arts that he criticized as mere—spectacular, we might add—"garlands of flowers covering our chains" (Rousseau 1997a:6). In the *Preface*, after dispelling the myth of a possible return to the original state of nature by saying that "there is nothing more contrary to my system than this absurd doctrine" (Rousseau 1997b:96), Rousseau defends his practicing the fine arts precisely as a way to fight those evils that they, together with the advent of modern society, have brought about. As he says: "it is now essential to use [those things that have done societies a great harm] against the harm they have done, as one does a *medication* or those noxious insects that have to be crushed on the bite [they give]" (Rousseau 1997b:105; emphasis mine). We have to crush the contaminating bite of the spectacle precisely on the bite itself, fight one poisoning substance with that very substance. This is a tactic that Rousseau, like Debord, not only recommended but also practiced, from the mise-en-scène of the character of a true philosopher that he began as soon as his role of public intellectual was established to the ongoing staging of the role of citizen of Geneva, the small virtuous republic where he was born, which he constantly opposed to great Parisian society (Carnevali 2004).

However, Rousseau is also well aware that there is not just one single recipe for putting the right spectacle onstage. As in any good homeopathic therapy, you have to find the medicine most appropriate for that particular subject. Even the very same illness must be cured with different remedies for different people, according to their temperament, history, and peculiar conditions. As in Debord's *détournement*, you have to reuse parts of the spectacle already going on in order to subvert it. So the spectacular garlands of the fine arts are in certain contexts particularly welcomed because, despite the fact that they may have fostered vices, they are helpful in keeping them from turning into crimes (Rousseau 1997b:103). This is because they coat vices with a kind of varnish that prevents the poison from being exuded quite so freely: "They [sciences and arts] destroy virtue, but preserve its public semblance, and this at least is a fine thing to do. They introduce politeness and propriety in its stead, and for the fear of appearing wicked they substitute the fear of appearing ridiculous" (103).

Science and the fine arts can thus actually be used to stage a spectacle that mitigates (if not subverts) the dominant spectacle. In Rousseau's view, in a very minimal way, in an already corrupted society the spectacle can at least distract men's wickedness and prevent them from spending their time in more dangerous pursuits (104). The spectacle thus works here as a palliative: a couple of hours in the theater may turn out to be hours subtracted from criminal activity, precisely like some extremely poisoning medications should be used as a sedative in the case of terminal illness.

But in small and virtuous cities like Geneva there is no reason to limit oneself to such an analgesic function. Here the homeopathic cure can actually aim for full recovery. That is why, in his view, one *should* not, but also *need* not build a theater there. Along with all the general negative side effects of such an enterprise (the slackening of work, the increase in expense, the introduction of a taste for luxury, etc.), Rousseau also makes the more fundamental remark that it is not the kind of spectacle appropriate for a republic. Instead of closed dark theaters where people have almost no interaction with one another, as in a "gloomy cavern," Rousseau recommends open-air public festivals where people can actually enjoy the pleasure of gathering and acting together (Rousseau 1960:125).[29] This is because it is in open-air festivals that, as Margaret Kohn observes, the chasm between individual and society is breached; it is here that intersubjectivity is fostered (Kohn 2008:471–472).

With regard to the question of what the object of such festivals should be, Rousseau has a rather striking answer: "Nothing if you please" (Rousseau 1960:120). Otherwise said, it is neither possible nor advisable to establish once and for all the specific ingredients of the homeopathic cure. On the contrary, writes Rousseau: "Let the spectators become an entertainment to themselves, make them actors themselves; do it so that each sees and loves himself in the others so that all will be better *united*" (120; emphasis mine).[30]

Notice in this passage how the same drive for recognition through the gaze of the other that Rousseau criticizes elsewhere plays a crucial and positive role instead.[31] Far from isolating us, it is by seeing and even loving ourselves in others that we can become better united. This, however, happens only in certain forms of spectacle, like those he is describing in this passage, where people are themselves actors in a play that is yet to be established, as Rousseau clearly suggests with his remark that there should be no preestablished object for such republican festivals.

The same opposition between closed spectacles and open-air festivals returns, for instance, in *Considerations on the Government of Poland*, where Rousseau makes a similar argument about the necessity of spectacles by observing that, if the creation of a virtuous republic is to succeed, "people should feel entertained in Poland more than in other countries, but not in the same way" (Rousseau 2009:186). In the case of Poland, however, spectacles seem to be orchestrated from above in order to generate a sort of patriotic intoxication that fosters attachment to the republic. This is very different from the openness of the spectacle without a prestablished object of the *Letter*, but, once again, a homeopathic reading can perhaps illuminate such a discrepancy: there are places where the political body is virtuous enough to trust the capacity of citizens to be actors and authors of their own spectacles, whereas in other cases the need may arise to give them a precise object and script.

In both cases, though, we can conclude with both Rousseau and Debord that it is only through the spectacle itself that we can overcome the isolating effects of the spectacle. This is because it is only here that we can learn to see ourselves in others. Precisely the spectacle that isolates us can bring us together and even unite us.[32] Having undermined the very possibility of a social bond with its alienating dynamics, the spectacle, when used in a homeopathic way, can actually unite us again and thus even foster democracy. That is the reason why Rousseau can reply to the question whether there should be entertainment in republics by saying there ought to be many, since it is only in their bosom that they can properly flourish (Rousseau 1960:125). Precisely in republics you need to be able to bring people together to fight the disaggregating effects of modern societies. Otherwise said, the poison here also becomes the cure.

To conclude on this point, we can say that the spectacle is the *pharmakon* of democracy in the Greek sense of the term: it is both poison and medicine. It is the spectacle that isolates us, but it is also the spectacle alone that can potentially subvert the alienating effects of the spectacular logic of modern society and thus contribute to that kind of togetherness that is a condition for the possibility of democracy. Otherwise said, the spectacle is the crucial ingredient of a homeopathic therapy that uses the evil against the evil itself, by formulating each time a specific medication adapted to the patient at stake. Should we conclude that homeopathy is the solution to the spectacularization and virtualization of politics?

In the *Preface to Narcissus* Rousseau (1997b:103) writes the following: "A man who has ruined his temperament by an injudicious use of medicines is forced to continue to rely on doctors in order to stay alive." Maybe this is also our present condition. Like that man, we, intoxicated by the spectacle of contemporary capitalism, have perhaps no other possibility of escape than trying to enact a different, hopefully less ridiculous, spectacle.

3

THE GLOBAL SPECTACLE

This society eliminates geographical distance only to reap distance internally in
the form of a spectacular separation.

GUY DEBORD, *The Society of the Spectacle*

We have seen in parts 1 and 2 that the concept of the imaginal can help us make
sense of a profound transformation in the nature of politics itself. If Weber could
still think of political power as being uniquely characterized by the possibility
of taking recourse to legitimate coercion, this possibility seems to be lost for us.
Politics is not (or no longer) a struggle for the distribution of power and the use
of legitimate coercion, but has become increasingly a struggle for people's imagination. Power has always depended on the imaginal. If power is the capacity to
influence another person and make him or her do what he or she would not have
done otherwise, then it is clear that the most effective power is the power that
can be felt without being theorized about. As a consequence, before the power to
exercise legitimate coercion, the power to construct a successful version of reality
is what guarantees political power per se. Today, however, this dependency has
reached a stage where the Weberian control over the means of physical coercion
is not only dependant upon but is actually overcome by the greater role played by
control over the means of interpretation. Otherwise stated, politics has become a
struggle for people's imagination (Bottici and Challand 2011).

In part 3 I illustrate this point by analyzing how contemporary imaginal politics displays itself in a search for legitimacy that includes the three ideal-typical
sources of legitimacy identified by Weber, but also goes beyond them. Together
with tradition, faith, and legal-rational grounds for the belief in the legitimacy of
authority, the conservative reproduction of life seems to have become a crucial

reservoir for claims to legitimacy. In the following chapters I will investigate those transformations by focusing on how, in a global society of the spectacle, reference to tradition tends to become mythical (chapter 7), while religions are resurrected in the public sphere (chapter 8), and how even human rights discourses have turned to the register of the spectacle (chapter 9).

7

The Politics of the Past

The Myth of the Clash of Civilizations

Die Geschichte ist Gegenstand einer Konstruktion, deren Ort nicht die homogene und leere Zeit sondern die von Jetztzeit erfüllte bildet.

WALTER BENJAMIN, *Über den Begriff der Geschichte*

The idea that history could ever be the simple reconstruction of how things have actually happened has been abandoned for a long time.[1] The past has always been at the service of the present. Friedrich Schlegel pointed to this when he observed that the "historian is a turned-back prophet" (Schlegel and Schlegel 1992:fragment 80). But if the past is always subject to the construction of an identity in the present, what is the difference between historical and purely mythical accounts of the past? If not even professional historians are immune from the temptation to subject the past to their vision of the future, what can we expect from professional politicians who are constantly in search of legitimacy?

The aim of this chapter is to argue that mythical and historical narratives are not necessarily the same thing, but that they tend to converge in contemporary societies. In a global society of the spectacle, references to "traditions" tend to assume mythical connotations. In this vein I will proceed in three steps. I will first explain what, in general, constitutes a mythical narrative and a political myth, in particular. I will then move on to explain how political myth relates to historical narratives, concluding finally with an analysis of the recent success of the myth about a clash between Islam and the West.

A myth is not a story that is given once and for all in a definitive form. Take, for example, the myth of Ulysses. Of the many variants of this myth, which is the true one? The one that sees him happily coming back home or that sees him swallowed up by the sea? It is implicit in the concept of a myth that there can be many legitimate variants of it. Indeed, properly speaking, a myth consists of the *process* of elaboration of the possible variants of a story. This is what Hans Blumenberg tried to convey with his concept of *Arbeit am Mythos* or "work on myth" (Blumenberg 1985). Following Blumenberg, by "work on myth" I mean here a process of elaboration of a single narrative core that stems from a need for *significance*. This need for significance evolves over time, and hence myth necessarily expresses itself through variants: in each context the same narrative pattern is reappropriated by and thus responds to different drives, needs, and exigencies. A narrative core either produces a variant that fulfills this task in the new context or it ceases to be a myth and becomes a simple narrative.

The term *significance* denotes a space between a "simple meaning" and what we can call an "ultimate meaning." Something can have a meaning and not have significance for us—although that which is significant must also have meaning in order to be named in the first place. Therefore, significance is something more than mere meaning. It operates in between what is consciously said about the world and what is unconsciously felt about it. At the same time, what is significant is not necessarily something that answers the ultimate questions about the meaning of life and the existence of an afterlife (hence myth and religion are not exactly the same thing either).[2]

The human need for significance is derived from the particular position of human beings within the world. Following Arnold Gehlen (1988), we can recover a famous Nietzschean expression and define human beings as the "always not yet determined animals." As Gehlen argues, human beings, in contrast to other animals, are not adapted to a specific environment and are therefore always *noch nicht festgestellt*. That is, whereas other animals have a fixed relationship with their environment—in the sense that they are adapted to it—human beings change the environment in which they live, and this puts them in a very peculiar relationship with their living conditions.

In the first place, this fact generates culture. As Blumenberg observed, when the prehuman creature was induced to avail itself of a bipedal posture and to leave the protection of a hidden way of life in the rainforest for the savannah, it exposed itself for the first time to the risks of a widened horizon of perception. This meant that the human creature was led to face the power of the unknown or "the absolutism of reality" (Blumenberg 1985:1:1). Being exposed to an always potentially different environment, human beings are subjected to a much higher number of stimulations from the outside world, from which they must seek relief, or *Entlastung* (Gehlen 1988). Culture and language are the means through which such a relief can be obtained. Second, the fact that human beings change their environment means that they entertain a problematizing relationship with their conditions of existence. Not only can they change them, but they also raise questions about them. As a consequence, human beings need meaning in order to master the unknown, but they also need significance in order to live in a world that is not indifferent to them.

The specific manner in which myth fights the indifference of the world is by inserting events into a narrative. Myth typically addresses the question "whence?" rather than "why?" As Kerényi has also pointed out, the function of myth is neither to provide a name for things, nor to explain them, but more specifically to "ground" them. According to him, the German language provided the exact word for this function: *begründen* (Kerényi and Jung 1963:6). The word *begründen*, which can be translated as "to ground" or "to substantiate," derives from the root *Grund*. *Grund* means both the English abstract noun *reason* and the concrete noun *ground*. Thus myths ground experience by telling stories about the origins of things and also where they are going.

Three elements are therefore central to the concept of myth: narrative, significance, and process. It is sufficient to have a sequence of events in order to have a narrative, but something more is needed to have a myth. A myth is a narrative that must respond to a need for significance that changes over time, and it is because it has to provide significance within changing circumstances that a myth is best understood as a process, as a "work on myth," rather than as an object.

What, then, is a specifically political myth? A political myth is the work on a common narrative that coagulates and thus grants significance to the political conditions and experiences of a social group. What makes a political myth out of a simple narrative is neither its claim to truth nor its content, as many have maintained.[3] For instance, there is nothing political per se in the idea that the world is about to disappear. Notwithstanding this, the narrative of the millennium, which stems from this idea, worked as a political myth—and as a powerful one in certain contexts.

Thus what makes a political myth out of a narrative are (1) the fact that it coagulates and reproduces significance, (2) that it is shared by a given group, and (3) that it can address the specifically political conditions in which a given group lives. A political myth must respond to a need for significance because otherwise it would be a mere narrative and not a myth; it must be shared because it needs to address the specifically political conditions of a social group. As we have seen in chapter 4, one can define politics in the more general sense of whatever pertains to the *polis*, to the decisions concerning the fate of a community or, *stricto sensu*, as a specific form of power that is characterized by the threat of recourse to legitimate coercion. In both cases politics concerns the life in common, and this is ultimately why a myth must be shared in order to be *political*.

The first consequence of this definition is that, to paraphrase Antonio Gramsci (1996:2:10, 41), political myths are not a "piece of paper." The work of a political myth cannot be reduced to the stories that we read in our books and archives. These are only *some* of the products of the work on myth. In order to establish whether a narrative is a political myth or not, we must look at not only its production but also its reception—at the way in which it is shared. It is the whole of production-reception-reproduction that constitutes the "work on myth."

The second consequence is that political myths are not learned once and for all, but are rather apprehended through a more or less conscious cumulative exposure to them. Significance locates itself between what is consciously learned and what is unconsciously felt. This also explains the condensational power of political myths, their capacity to be condensed into a few images or icons (see Flood 1996). By means of a synecdoche, any object or gesture—a painting, an image, a song, a film, or an advertisement—can recall the whole work on myth that lies behind it.

Just as myths are not objects but processes, icons are not self-contained objects, but rather operations of the mind. An icon does not exist in itself, but only for a(n) (un)consciousness that associates it with something else. In other words, an icon is a symbol. By symbol I do not simply mean signs, which, according to the etymology of the term, means pointing to what can be put together.[4] Symbols are not mere signs, but a special kind of sign: they refer to a hidden or undetermined reality.

This condensational capacity of myths explains why it is often difficult to analyze them. The work on a political myth is a process that can take place in the most diverse settings: speeches, arts (both visual and nonvisual), rituals, social practices, and so on. While all of them must be kept separate at the analytical level, mythical discourses are most often intermingled with other kinds of discourses: they tend, so to speak, to get lost within them. This brings us to the crucial issue of the relationship between mythical and historical narratives. In particular, if both are told from the standpoint of the present, should we then conclude that there is no difference between the two and that history is simply another form of mythmaking?

Some people have been tempted to argue this. In Robert Young's (Young 1990:7) view, for instance, the writing of history always implies a process of organizing events in a narrative plot, in a totality within which these events are conferred with meaning. In his view, writing history hardly differs from creating a myth.[5] As he puts it in the provocative title of his book, "history" is simply a "white mythology." The idea of "history," he claims, always reflects a totalizing mode of structuring events that is not only particularistic (because each society has its own specific way of organizing knowledge) but also mythological (because it is based on the exclusion of the other's perspective). Ultimately Young concludes that history should be seen as myth, as "the preposterous off-spring of a distorting egocentric illusion to which the children of a western Civilization have succumbed like the children of all other Civilizations and known primitive societies" (Young 1990:16, 19).

There are two problems with this theory. First, it works with a reductive concept of myth, used here simply in the polemical sense of "illusion." But it is misleading to speak of myth in general, and of political myths in particular, in terms of truth or falsity, since, as we have discussed, myths do not aim to describe the world as it is, but rather to create it. Even if they are illusions, they are self-fulfilling.[6] Second, it is a view that conflates myth and narrative. In the second chapter of his book, Young (1990) argues that the use of chronology—the code most often used by historians—creates the illusory impression of a uniform, continuous progression. Dates, he observes, tell us something only insofar as they are members of a class. This class may or may not correspond to other classes, such as periods, millennia, or ages; thus it always reflects a specific organization of an event (Young 1990:46). This narrative of uniform progression is, however, illusory and, in this sense, a myth.

Even if we accept the reductive definition of myth as illusion, the fact remains that myth and historical narrative cannot be unified on the basis of them being both distorting and biased. If a narrative is a series of events, then arguing that it is illusory because it superimposes a structure that they would otherwise lack on "real" events appears pointless. Certainly, a narrative involves selection as well as some form of organization. It presupposes a plot that structures events, conferring them with meaning as part of a whole. So Young is right in pointing out that a certain organization of events is taking place.

However, the point is that every "event" is always interpreted and thus presupposes a certain organization (even when it represents a break within it). No "pure" event is ever accessible to us. As the very etymology of the word indicates, an event is something that *e-venit*, that comes into being from a background of nonbecoming-events, which is, ultimately, the reason why history is based on oblivion as much as on memory (Stråth 2000). The point is, therefore, not to counterpoise "interpreted" and "noninterpreted" events, but rather to determine the degree to which these events have been organized. As Hayden White has shown in *The Content of the Form*, there cannot be content that has not already been organized in some form; different modes of writing history imply different forms and, therefore, also different degrees of organization (White 1987). Annals and chronicles—even statistics—all refer to events that have been organized in one way or another; yet not all these events have been organized (and therefore interpreted) in the same way and to the same degree.

Whereas myths in general and political myths in particular are always organized through a dramatic structure, the writing of history does not necessarily stage a drama; one may be part of the production and reception of a historical narrative without necessarily taking part in a play. This is not to say that a historical narrative cannot come to work as political myth. Although mythical and historical narratives often overlap, such as in the case of most nationalist *mythologems*, it is not always the case, which is why we should endeavor to differentiate the two.

It therefore comes as no surprise that mythical and historical narratives at times differ in their temporal perspectives. Both are narratives recounted from the standpoint of the present; although a myth may also be located outside historical time (such as most of Greek mythology for us today), a political myth may be projected into a future dimension (such as the myth of prosperity).[7] In other words, both history and myth may work as prophecies, but the fact that historians are "turned-back" prophets, to use Schlegel's expression, places further constraints on them. In the first place—nowadays at least—the historian will be asked to follow a method, whereas the very idea of a "mythical method" is senseless. A method implies that procedures can be followed by anybody with the same results, but no such possibility is offered in the case of myth. To put it bluntly, whereas historians are requested to refer to openly accessible and, in principle, verifiable evidences, political myths do not need footnotes. This is because, as we have discussed, the primary task of work on myth is to provide and coagulate significance for a given group and under given circumstances. Therefore, the work on a political myth is located between the conscious and the unconscious level.

But contemporary spectacularization and virtualization of politics has further increased what has been called the primacy effect of political myth (Flood 1996). By slipping into the social unconscious in the form of spectacles, political myths can deeply influence our basic and most fundamental perceptions of the world and thus escape the possibility of critical scrutiny. If political myths have always been difficult to analyze—since the work on significance can take place at a more or less conscious level—then the recent emergence of powerful new technologies has rendered the work on political myth less and less perceivable and more subtle. Indeed, through a peculiar intersection of the extraordinary and the banal, political myths have become the unperceived lenses through which we experience the world, and for this reason they tend to remain unquestioned (Bottici 2007:246–260).

All these features are shared by most contemporary political myths. Among them national political myths—such as the myth of the American Founding Fathers, that of the French Revolution, or that of the Italian "Resistance" against Nazi-Fascism—have been analyzed at length by social theorists.[8] What I want to do here is to illustrate these features of political myth through the analysis of a contemporary example that is particularly relevant for us insofar as it is a potentially global political myth: the myth of the clash between civilizations. Why is the idea of a "clash between civilizations" best analyzed as a political myth?

Surely the idea of a clash between civilizations is *also* something else—a scientific theory in the first place (Huntington 1996). But myth and theory can often be coupled, and if we limit ourselves to criticizing the notion of a clash of civilizations as if it were *only* a scientific theory, we would obscure where the power of this narrative actually lies. There is indeed a striking gap between the ways in which this narrative was received as a scientific theory and as a narrative through which people more or less unconsciously look at the world. When it was first proposed by Samuel Huntington in the 1990s, the idea of a clash of civilizations was strongly criticized as too simplistic and scientifically naive to render the complexities of world politics. Yet, particularly after September 11 and the terrorist attacks in Europe, this narrative became one of the most powerful and widespread worldviews.[9]

Different surveys of the ways in which these terrorist attacks have been framed in the U.S. and European media show that the idea of a clash between civilizations has been extremely influential.[10] After those tragic events, this narrative helped concentrate the emotional shock and provided significance to the political conditions of very different people across the globe. What were the reasons for such a success? How can a theory that has been so strongly criticized as too naive turn into a successful political myth?

In fact, Huntington merely named a political myth that was *already* in the making. To see this, one must not only focus on the production of such a myth but also on the whole process of its production-reception-reproduction. Only by looking at the whole work on myth can we understand how it is possible to criticize the idea of the clash as a scientific theory and still endorse it as a political myth. The reason it was easy for the media to frame the terrorist attacks as a clash between Islam and the West is that the work on this myth started long before

2001—a work that took place at both the conscious and unconscious level. As a result of this work, in the face of the terrorist attacks people were more keen to perceive "civilizations" clashing with each other (whatever one means by that term) rather than perceiving individual human beings acting out of a more or less complex set of motivations.

Intellectual discourses have played an important role in conveying aspects of the myth of the clash of civilizations. Even if the narrative of the clash between civilizations has been strongly criticized by some, components of this narrative have been circulating unquestioned in the literature for quite a while. Specialized literature on the Middle East has for a long time tended to portray the Muslim world as a radical "Other." The idea that Islam is a religion more violent than any other, or that it is fundamentally hostile to modernity, is part of a long tradition of what Edward Said named Orientalist discourses (Said 1978). The result is a Eurocentric and negatively biased representation of the Middle East in which Islam is portrayed as a fixed blueprint that determines an entire way of life for hundreds of millions of Muslims all over the world.

But the myth of a clash between Islam and the West is not only a "Western" political myth. The myth of the clash of civilizations is fed by an equally misleading representation of the West circulating in many Arab and Middle Eastern sources (see Bottici and Challand 2010). This points to a kind of Occidentalism—a reductive representation of the West that takes the East as its starting point. Intellectuals such as the Iranian Ali Shariati and Sayyid Muhammad Taleqani, or the Egyptian Sayyd Qutb depicted the West as idolatrous, materialist, and imperialist and counterpoised it to a spiritual East that follows the precepts of Islam. A dichotomy is thus established between the culture of Islam, at the service of God, and the culture of a new *jahiliyya* in the service of bodily needs (such as food, sex, and so on) that degrades human beings to the level of beasts.[11]

But intellectual discourses could never have produced a political myth without the work that took place at the unconscious level. The condensational capacity of a political myth is particularly evident in the power of the icons that are transmitted in the media. Iconic images slip into the social unconscious through a process of socialization that begins early in life. Recall from chapter 3 that the notion of a social unconscious differs from both the individual and the collective unconscious. Let me illustrate this concept through a specific icon. Consider the *Marianne voilée*, the image of the Marianne, the symbol of the French republic, wearing the Muslim veil, which first appeared on 26 October 1985 in the popular French newspaper *Figaro Magazine*.[12] This image is one of the most influential French icons of the myth of the clash of civilizations. When one looks at it what appears is only a woman with a naked breast, wearing a hijab. Yet, for a contemporary French person, the image evokes much more. Marianne, the beautiful woman with her breasts uncovered, is a symbol of the French republic as it emerged from the French Revolution; thus it recalls republican values such as freedom from domination, *laïcité*, and antitraditionalism. By contrast, in the contemporary French imaginary the veil recalls images of female submissiveness (if not direct oppression). There is therefore a dramatic contrast between tradition and oppression, on the one hand, and modernity and freedom, on the other. By looking at this image, sensations (the perception of forms, colors, signs, and so on) are transformed into particular feelings—feelings of incompatibility and threat.

This interpretation is reinforced by the context in which it first appeared. Published on the front page of an influential French magazine, the image accompanied a dossier on Arab immigration in France with the revealing title: "Will we still be French in thirty years?" The heading gives its accompanying image an apocalyptic tenor, suggesting the disappearance of French identity or its dissolution into Muslim traditions. This is an interesting example of the work of icons, because it clearly shows the ambivalence of political myth: the image of the veiled Marianne is revelatory of both the fascination and fear of "the others"—that is, those outsiders from an "incompatible civilization" that are immigrating into France—and it also illustrates Earl Hopper's point that, even when it is brought to consciousness and recognized as problematic, the unconscious is not considered with detachment and objectivity. Indeed, almost thirty years later, the French identity is still far from disappearing.

It is for this reason that I prefer to refer here to the concept of a *social* unconscious, as distinguished from both the individual and the collective unconscious. Particularly if we adopt a weak version of the social unconscious, we must conclude that it is not only formed through repression but also through the simple exposure to contents of which we are not aware.[13] It can *also* be the result of forms of repression, but it is not *necessarily* so. Indeed, it is now a common experience, well documented in the literature, that the human mind is able to consciously process only a certain amount of information at any given time, while other pieces of information necessarily have to remain in the background (Fromm 2001:98; see also Hopper 2003:127). This does not mean that they get lost: they are stored somewhere in the depth of our mind, ready to be mobilized when needed. And it is in this background that myths proliferate.

However, as we have also seen, the concept of the social unconscious also differs from Jung's collective unconscious. Although the concept is less contestable than it may prima facie appear in its many vulgarizations, the unconscious we refer to here is not universal because it is not the same for all human beings.[14] In my approach to political myth, I am not interested in looking for invariants in space and time, but rather for what is specific to each society. The example of the *Marianne voilée* is paradigmatic in this respect. One must not only be aware that the woman represented is called Marianne and that she is the symbol of the French republic, but must also have been exposed, more or less subconsciously, to the work of elaboration of those two symbols (Marianne and the veil) that took place in the specific French context to capture the full significance of the icon.

To sum up on this point, images such as the *Marianne voilée* are much more powerful purveyors of the myth of the clash between civilizations than any overt statement about it. Further examples of icons can be taken from the section "A Nation Challenged" that the *New York Times* launched immediately after September 11.[15] Articles appearing in this section had paranoid titles such as "Yes, This Is About Islam," "Barbarians at the Gates," "The Age of Muslim Wars," and "This Is a Religious War"; they were accompanied by pictures of religiously tainted atrocities, hate, and fanaticism. The last article mentioned here, for instance, was illustrated with pictures of atrocities from medieval Europe (Sullivan 2001).

An icon of the myth of the clash of civilizations that is particularly helpful in illustrating the change in the nature of the imaginal we are dealing with is one of the Danish caricature published on 30 September 2005 in the Danish newspaper *Jyllands-Posten*: that of the Prophet Mohammed with a fizzing bomb as a turban. Ostensibly a joke, it is nevertheless a telling one. As Freud, among others, observed, condensation is a typical mechanism at work in wit (Freud 1989). It is the brevity, the capacity to carry in such a condensed form a message that reveals resemblances among different things which gives us the specific pleasure of wit (Freud 1989:6–13, 29). And it is in its capacity to be a vehicle for the myth of the clash between Islam and the West that the evocative power of the "prophet-bomb" lies.

The Danish caricatures that mocked the Prophet Mohammed and the Muslim faith as violent and prone to fanaticism caused vivid reactions on the part of Muslims around the world. They did not mainly resent the publication of an image of the Prophet, which is forbidden in the Muslim faith, but rather the insulting portrayal of him. Notice here that the controversy was global precisely because it was conveyed by images: if it were not for the capacity of images to convey their message beyond but also before any linguistic barriers, the jokes of a remote Danish newspaper (written in a language notoriously difficult to decipher) could never have had the consequences that they had. Protests went from death threats, as they appeared on Web sites that mentioned Denmark as a terror target, to actual attacks, such as those that took place in Islamabad on June 2008, when a massive car bomb went off outside the Danish embassy, killing eight and injuring thirty-two (Lindekilde 2008). On the other hand, many Western newspapers reproduced the contested caricatures in the name of freedom of speech, engendering a true clash of images. In Italy, Roberto Calderoli, then minister for reforms and devolution and member of the Italian xenophobic party Lega Nord, appeared on Italian television in February 2006 with a T-shirt reproducing them, provoking outrage and further incidents.[16] Among all the twelve incriminated caricatures, that of the Prophet with a bomb in his turban remains the most contested and has rightly been defined as "iconic of the controversy" (Lindekilde 2008:2). One of the main reasons for this was its spectacular and virtual nature.

That image was circulated on the Web, where it was modified up to the point that it became difficult to establish its original author and features. One of the many versions of this icon, for example, is on a cartoon from a blog done in 2009.[17] The cartoon reproduces the contested icon of the Prophet with a bomb as a turban, but by drastically modifying it, inserting the face onto the body of a huge monster that eats babies and brings destruction everywhere, while (U.S.?) tanks and helicopters are trying to kill him. The caricature, which clearly has a slanderous intent, also proves our general point that myths (and icons) are not given once and for all. They are continuously evolving processes that express themselves through the proliferation of variants. The wit consists here both in the reversal of the Muslim invocation (*Allahu akbar*, or God is great) into the title of the cartoon as "Allah Snackbar," which appears next to exploding buildings, and in the association of kissing/eating. While eating one infant, the prophet-monster says, "What's wrong? You never seen a prophet kissing babies before?" suggesting that, with the excuse of "kissing" us, Islam is actually phagocytosing "us." The caption *Dar al-Harb* alludes to the traditional separation in Islam between the *Dar al-Islam*, which refers to the space where Islam is the dominant religion, and *Dar al-Harb*, where Islam is in peril. But here it is Islam that is the threat. The image thus synthesizes many of the icons of the evil Arab that circulate in the global society of the spectacles—the turban-headed, sinister-eyed, big-nosed Prophet, the essential carrier of a religion that is a bomb in itself. A war is declared on the West, and it is waged by a religion: Islam.

This spectacularization of the past tends to turn all historical narratives into a possible site for mythmaking. For example, references to medieval Crusades have recently become very common in both the West and the Middle East. The Crusades have become a crucial icon of the clash of civilizations, which is particularly interesting because it works on both sides in exactly the same way. The result is that, within a few years, the Crusades have been transformed from a historical event of interest to only a few specialized historians into a popular object of consumption. In the wake of 9/11, films, exhibitions, and publications devoted to them started to proliferate. The link between the medieval Crusades and the terrorist attacks was made patent by both intellectual discourses and politicians. Al-Qaeda material is full of references to a supposed crusade that the Western powers are leading in the Middle East at the service of Zionism (Kepel and Milell 2008). On the other side, *Foreign Affairs*, which in the past hosted a long series of critical responses to Huntington, launched a special issue just after 9/11, "Long War in the Making," with a leading article arguing that the real roots of the attacks on the Twin Towers lay in seventh-century Arabia, in the medieval Crusades, in the Mongol invasion, and the demise of the caliphate (Doran 2002:22–42).

This work did not fail to impact the discourse of politicians. President George W. Bush, for instance, often denied that a clash between civilizations was taking place, but still from the very beginning described the "war on terrorism" as a crusade. In this way, he implicitly suggested that it was about a clash between Islam and the West. We see here a perfect example of how a rejection of the paradigm of the clash between civilizations can go hand in hand with its unconscious endorsement. The result of such a work is that people act *as if* a clash between civilizations was taking place and, in doing so, make it real.

As Geisser also observed in his analysis of the sources of Islamophobia in France, French journalists tend to be very cautious in their statements and sometimes even explicitly deny the paradigm of the clash. The sources of Islamophobia are rather the continual insistence in the media on the need for more security and a parallel demonization of Muslims (Geisser 2003:25). The French media (similar to the American media) has developed a systematic, general discourse about Islam, which depicts it as an immutable and conflictual block. "Muslim" is represented in standardized ways—praying believers seen from the back, crying and threatening groups, veiled women, fanatical bearded men, and so on (24).

If we want to understand how is it possible to criticize the paradigm of the clash as a theory and still endorse it at a more or less unconscious level then we need the concept of political myth. All these icons are much more powerful precisely because they operate within the unconscious without it being possible to perceive, let alone critique them. Growing up in contemporary societies inundated by media stimuli, most people encounter an overwhelming number of myths that gradually grow into the social unconscious. Young children are exposed to a battery of more or less unconscious stimuli through comics, cartoons, films, and advertisements. A recent survey of the most popular American children's comics, such as *Superman, Spiderman,* and *Capitan America,* has shown that the icon of the "fanatic Muslim" has become one of the most powerful representations of the "threat." After the end of the Cold War, the role of the bad guys in these stories ceased to be played primarily by perfidious Eastern bloc spies and often assumed the features of Muslims, explicitly depicted as fanatical, mad terrorists (Frazzi 2004).

But the most inexhaustible and rich Western source of icons of the clash of civilizations are Hollywood films. In his survey of the role of Arabs in Hollywood films, Jack Shaheen has shown that, out of one thousand films that have Arab or Muslim characters, twelve were "positive" depictions, fifty-two "even-handed," and the rest of more than nine hundred were "negative" (Shaheen 2001). The most popular icons of the myth of the clash of civilizations that abound in such films are those of the barbaric bedouin, of the rich and stupid sheikh who wants to rape Western women, or, finally, that of the mad terrorist and airplane hijacker. This insistence on their "barbarism" and our "superiority" has the reassuring function of making us feel safe and preempting the need for criticism or critique of Western policies toward primarily Muslim states.

But, besides the implicit message of such icons (Arab = barbarism and threat), it is interesting to note their evolution and to examine how they can be understood from a psychoanalytical point of view. Let us take, for instance, the female counterpart of the mad fanatic terrorist, the veiled women that we have seen in the *Marianne voileé*. Traditionally, it was sexually provocative belly dancers that worked as the female counterparts of the male threat (i.e., the mad terrorist, the sheikh who wants to rape "our" women.) More recently, Arab females have been depicted not solely as submissive veiled women but also as potential terrorists themselves, as is the case in films such as *Black Sunday* (1977), *Death Before Dishonour,* and *Never Say Never Again* (1983). This change reflects the unconscious distress Western men felt toward the changing role of women in Western societies themselves in those years: by projecting the threat onto *another,* "barbaric" civilization, Western males are freed from the burden of recognizing their own distress vis-à-vis the emancipation of women in the West itself (Semmerling 2006:1–27).

At this point, it is interesting to explicitly apply the strong version of the social unconscious to explain how different variants of the "Muslim woman" help to produce a social unconscious in the way we have described. In recent years we witnessed new and striking alliances between emancipated Western feminists and conservative males who suddenly agreed in criticizing the subordination of the "Muslim woman." This strange convergence suggests that the icon of the female Muslim terrorist, together with that of the submissive veiled woman, represents a defense mechanism against facing the conflicts and struggles that still exist between men and women in contemporary Western societies themselves. The myth of the clash thus helps to project gender conflicts onto others and to idealize the collective self-image of belonging to the right part of the world, that is the part where "we" have already reached freedom and equality between sexes.[18]

In conclusion, an old but still persistent and insidious political myth inhabits our global society of the spectacle. People increasingly act *as if* a clash between Islam and the West is taking place, and, in so doing, they make it exist. As the passage quoted in the epigraph to the part 3 of this book suggests, Debord already understood that globalization, while geographically unifying the world, would at the same time have divided it again through some new spectacular division between us and them. Intellectual discourses, Hollywood films, children's comics, social practices, and—last but not least—politicians' actions have all been the sites for the elaboration of the myth of the clash of civilizations. The success of such a narrative shows that, in our contemporary societies, when imaginal politics sets out on its search for legitimacy in a more or less distant past, it all too easily turns this past into a myth. Reference to more or less invented traditions has always influenced the politics of the past. The difference is that today such politics has become imaginal more than ever.

The spectacular division between "us" and "them" is founded upon a peculiar map of the world. Behind the myth of a clash between Islam and the West there is a division of the world into conflictual blocks, opposing Islam and the West. But how can we possibly conceive of a clash between two such heterogeneous categories as a faith (Islam) and a purely geographical entity (the West)? In these concluding remarks, I would like to deal with this problem by disentangling the category of the West, while in the following chapter I will argue that the privileging of religion must be seen in the context of a new process of repositioning of religion in the public sphere.

The reason why one can possibly conceive of a clash between Islam and the West is that the latter is far from being just a geographical entity. As Raymond Williams pointed out some time ago, the term is overlaid with a long history of ambiguous usage (Williams 1988:333–334). It is a history that goes back at least to the west/east division of the Roman Empire, the east/ west division of the Christian Church, the definition of the "West" as Judeo-Christian and of the

"East" as Muslim, Hindu, or Buddhist, and finally to the postwar division of Europe into the capitalist West and the communist East (with the curiosity of Marxism, which began in what is by any definition Western Europe and yet is classified as an Eastern ideology). It is a long story and, what is more relevant, one in which politics largely overdetermines cultural geography (Williams 1988:334).

The West is thus not just a geographic direction: it is an imaginal being embroiled with cultural and political myths. Properly speaking, east and west are indeed only relative notions. In a sphere such as our globe there is no absolute East and West. When we speak of the West, we reproduce the reified gaze of the Europeans who first transformed the globe into a bidimensional map with Europe at its center during the heyday of European colonialism.[19] This gaze is what we call (with an oxymoron) a planisphere, something that is spherical but also a plane at the same time. And, precisely because it is a plane, we can organize it according to absolute coordinates. But why transform a sphere into a map and thus make of what are relative notions absolute ones? Who decides what is the center and where the boundaries are? Why look at the world as if it were a bidimensional map with the Americas as its extreme western boundary and Asia as the extreme East? Why not take the perspective of China, which calls "Western Asia" what we consider to be the "Middle East"?

The notion of the West is imbued with Eurocentrism, by which I mean here the attitude to make of Europe the observation point for looking at the entire globe.[20] Eurocentrism, in this technical sense of the term, envisions the globe from a single privileged point of view and maps the world in a cartography that centralizes Europe and its perspective. The West to Europe is assimilated to Europe itself, while the East is divided into "Near," "Middle," and "Far."[21] All this makes of Europe the arbiter of spatial order, just as the establishment of Greenwich Mean Time produces England as the regulating center of temporal measurement (Shoat and Stam 1994:2).

It is true that Eurocentrism first emerged as a discursive rationale for European colonialism—the process by which European powers reached positions of hegemony in much of the world. In this sense, it is the "colonizer's model of the world," as the title of Blaut's book reminds us (Blaut 1993). Yet Eurocentrism does not immediately mean colonialism or racism (Shoat and Stam 1994:2–4). Although colonialist and Eurocentric discourses are intimately intertwined, the terms point to two different things. While the former explicitly justifies colonialist practices, the latter embeds, takes for granted, and thus also normalizes the hierarchical power relations generated by colonialism and imperialism without necessarily even thematizing those issues directly. Although generated by the colonizing process, Eurocentrism's links to that process are obscured in a kind of buried epistemology (Shoat and Stam 1994:2–4).

Eurocentrism still permeates our perception of the world in a way we are often unable to recognize. People keep referring to "the West" or "Western civilization" or "Western tradition" without realizing that, properly speaking, they are nonsense—West of what? What is the center of this West that now comes to include, in certain understandings, Australia and Japan? Ultimately, there cannot be any West in a world that is spherical. We can perceive the West only because we have so much internalized the European planisphere that we look at the world as if it were a bidimensional entity with Europe as its center. But it is not. There cannot be any center in a rotating globe. We have come to perceive it only because the politics of the past has turned into the geography of our present. This, together with the repositioning of religion in the public sphere (to which we will now turn), can explain why so many people across the globe came to believe that a clash between Islam and the West is under way.

8

The Repositioning of Religion in the Public Sphere

Imaginal Consequences

This is why Moses, with his virtue and by divine command, introduced religion into the commonwealth, so that people would do its duty more from devotion than from fear.

BARUCH SPINOZA, *Theologico-Political Treatise*

In the previous chapter, we focused on the politics of the past as a way to assess changes in contemporary politics, with its search for legitimacy in a more or less invented tradition. In this chapter I want to focus instead on religion and faith from the point of view of the notion of the imaginal. In the last few years there has been a diffuse perception of a resurgence of religion in the public sphere; given that faith has always been one of the crucial sources of legitimacy, it is paramount to examine the way in which this change affects the nexus of politics and the imaginal.

In his reflections on the work of art in the age of its technical reproducibility, Benjamin provides a stimulating starting point for discussing the relationships between religion, politics, and the imaginal. Writing in the 1930s, when the consequences of the industrialization of image production began to manifest, he was in a perfect position to catch its radical novelty. As we have already mentioned, according to Benjamin, the possibility to reproduce an image in series—for example, in a photo or, even more so, in films—destroys the uniqueness of its being here and now, its *hic et nunc* (Benjamin 2002:23). By multiplying its reproduction, it substitutes a single image for an indefinite quantity of images, thereby destroying their authenticity together with the possibility of distinguishing between the original and the copy. In other words, what Benjamin calls aura, defined as "a strange tissue of space and time: the unique apparition of a distance, however near it may be" (104–105), disappears. This destruction, according to Benjamin, would bring with it the liquidation of the traditional value of images, resulting in a large-scale, radical questioning of all forms of traditions.

Benjamin stresses the ambivalent character of this process, which is also linked to the mass movements of the first half of the twentieth century; in his view, with the destruction of the aura also comes the potential for liberation from the chains of tradition. Has such a destruction actually taken place? Commenting on the possible positive consequences of the transformation he witnessed, Benjamin observed that the technology of reproduction detaches the reproduced object from the sphere of tradition: by replicating the work many times over, a mass existence is substituted for a unique existence. In his view, the result of this process should be the shattering of every form of tradition. Benjamin's reasoning is quite clear on this point: if tradition depends on the authenticity of things and if mass reproduction destroys authenticity, then it must also destroy tradition.

He thought that this was most evident in film. The social impact of film, particularly in its most positive form, has for him a "destructive, cathartic side," namely, "the liquidation of the value of tradition in the cultural heritage" (104). By commenting on the possible site for such a liquidation, he observed, "this phenomenon is most apparent in the great historical films. It is assimilating ever more advanced positions in its spread. When Abel Gance fervently proclaimed in 1927, 'Shakespeare, Rembrandt, Beethoven will make films. . . . All legends, all mythologies, and all myths, all founders of religions, indeed, all religions. . . . attend their celluloid resurrections, and the heroes are pressing at the gates,' he was inviting the reader, no doubt unaware, to witness a comprehensive liquidation" (104).

The sarcastic tone of the passage suggests that Benjamin was critical of Abel Gance. He wrote this passage between late December 1935 and the beginning of February 1936. Today, more than seventy years after Benjamin's prophecy, it seems as if Abel Gance was indeed right: what happened is precisely a resurrection of both myth and religion through films. The only difference is that more than a "celluloid" resurrection, concerning only film, what we are witnessing is a "virtual" resurrection embracing all new media. Even more striking is the fact that this resurrection does not mainly concern films watched in the private sphere, but invests the whole of the public sphere itself. In the latter, religion seems today to play a much greater role than foreseen by the theorists of so-called secularization—a notion more contested today than ever before.

Perhaps the expression *resurrection of religion* is misleading on a *sociological* level. According to some analysts, religion is rising on a global level, but still declining in advanced industrialized societies that can guarantee a certain level of existential security—with the only exception being the United States, where the absence of a social security system and continual immigration have kept religiosity at the same level since World War II (Norris and Inglehart 2004). Whether, and to what extent, the expression *resurrection of religion* is well grounded in sociological terms is a question to be dealt with through empirical studies on the topic.[1] What I want to do here is to use this expression in a *phenomenological* way to signal the fact that, even in industrialized, "secularized" societies, there is a widespread *perception* of an increased public role for religion. Debates such as those concerning the reference to Christian origins in the draft of the European Constitution, the threat to excommunicate Kerry supporters in the American presidential elections,[2] and the role of Islamic fundamentalism in the post-9/11 world are all signs that something has changed, if not in the substance of individual religious beliefs, at least in the perception of religion's public role.[3]

Note that even in developing countries the return of religion to the public sphere has been particularly evident: for some this is the result of the forced modernization of the 1950s and 1970s, whereas for others it is the consequence of the revival of local identities in contrast to values perceived as falsely universal.[4] Again, independent of the extent to which these societies have ever experienced a process of secularization, it is remarkable that in most of them people perceive a resurgence of religion in public life.

The aim of this chapter is to argue that in order to understand this transformation in the public role of religion we need to take into account the nexus between politics and the imaginal. The current resurrection of religion in the public sphere is linked to a transformation of imaginal politics, which has its roots in a twofold process: the reduction of politics to mere administration and the increased saturation of political life with spectacles. Otherwise stated, in an epoch when politics is said to be simply a question of "good governance"—of efficient administration within a neoliberal consensus—there is simultaneously a lack of political imagination that goes hand in hand with its hypertrophy through the media. In the following I will illustrate this paradox by discussing the interplay between the imaginal, politics, and religion and by focusing on a few contemporary examples.

As we have seen, according to Castoriadis, the human being, who is initially only a pure "representational/affective/unintentional flux," becomes a proper individual, that is, a social individual, only through a forced process of socialization to the imaginary significations of a society. This process starts very early, at least with the first contacts with language, and in particular the mother's language (Castoriadis 1987:303–304). Nevertheless, Castoriadis uses the expression *psyche* or *psychical monad* to stress the fact that, at its inception, it is an asocial and indeterminate being. In his psychoanalytical view, through the first encounters with language, the psyche is led to abandon its original objects in order to invest in socially instituted ones, those sanctioned by the social imaginary. As he emphatically puts it, it is only through the internalization of the world and the imaginary significations created by society that an individual is created out of a "little screaming monster" (Castoriadis 1991:148).

As we have already mentioned in chapter 2, Castoriadis recognizes that there are limits to the work of the social imaginary.[5] In the first place, this work must start from what it finds there already, be it the residual of previous social imaginaries, a minimal coherence of the imaginary significations, or the imperatives imposed by nature itself (for instance, any society defines in its own way the meaning of nourishment, but it must start from the need for food in the first place). Notwithstanding all these limits, the social imaginary has a capacity for virtual universal coverage so that any irruption of the raw world can immediately be treated as a sign of something; it can be interpreted away and thus exorcised. Even that which collides with this order can be subject to a symbolic processing: transgression of social rule can become an "illness," and completely alien societies that are fundamentally at odds with a given social imaginary can become "strangers," "savages," or even "impious" (Castoriadis 1991).

The major threat for the social imaginary nevertheless remains its own creativity. The social imaginary is said to be radical precisely because there cannot be individuals outside it, but also because it can always, potentially, question itself. The *instituting* social imaginary is at the same time always also *instituted* by individuals. There are no individuals outside it, but, likewise, no social imaginary can exist without the individuals that create, re-create, and sustain it. In such a particular relationship between a society that transcends the individuals that compose it and those very same individuals, we experience a unique relationship that cannot be reduced to a simple one such as that between the whole and its parts, even less between the universal and the particular (Castoriadis 1991:145).

Yet, as we have seen, there is a tension between the idea that there exists a unique relationship of mutual implication between society and individuals and Castoriadis's view of the psyche as a monad. He goes so far as to speak of an "absolute scission" between the instituting and instituted poles of the social imaginary: the psychical monad, on the one hand, and what he calls the social-historical, on the other (Castoriadis 1987). As we have already suggested, the idea of a monadic isolation of the psyche and that of heterogeneity between the psyche and society leads to an untenable metaphysical opposition (Habermas 1987:327). However, even within a psychoanalytical conception of the individual there is no need to maintain such heterogeneity. We are not monadic beings that become dependent on one another only through a violent socialization, but are rather dependent and independent at the same time from the very beginning.

As we have seen in part 1, the tension we have discussed is the sign of a deep philosophical problem. If we start from the idea that imagination is *in primis* an individual faculty, the problem emerges of determining the way in which it can be shaped by the social context. If we begin from the concept of the social imaginary understood as context, the problem is how to account for the free imagination of individuals. There are no easy ways out of this problem. For this reason, I have proposed that after a passage from a theory of imagination to a theory of the imaginary, we need to take a further step toward a theory of the imaginal. "Imaginal" simply means what is made of images (*imagines*) and as such it can be both the product of an individual faculty and of a social context, as well as the result of a complex, yet-to-be-determined interaction between the two. Furthermore, as we have seen, in contrast to the imaginary—conceived as the unreal and fictitious—the concept of the imaginal does not make any assumption as to the reality of the images that compose it. The concept of the imaginal therefore comes before the distinction between real and fictitious, because the latter makes sense only within a specific form of the imaginal. It is within this theory of the imaginal, which goes beyond any metaphysical opposition between the individual and the society, that some crucial insights into the relationship between politics and religion can be recovered.

In the first place, as Castoriadis observes, every social imaginary attempts to occult the instituted side of the society and one of the privileged ways to do so is through the attribution of the origins of social significations to an extrasocial source (Castoriadis 1991:153). By "extrasocial" he means external to the actual and living society, so that "extrasocial" sources can be gods, founding heroes, or even natural laws when they are presented as immune from human influence (Castoriadis 1997b:313–317). By contrast, according to Castoriadis, the possibility always exists for a society to recognize itself as the result of a process of self-institution. In this lies its autonomy.[6] I am autonomous if I am at the origins of what will be (*arche ton esomenon* as Aristotle used to say) and I know myself to be so (Castoriadis 1997b:329). Autonomy means that my discourse has to take the place of what is given as the discourse of the others.[7] This, as we will see, explains the tension between autonomy and religion, because the latter poses the origin of society in an extrasocial source, and it does so through a "revealed" discourse, which is, by definition, the discourse of an "Other."

It is certainly difficult, if not impossible, to provide a single definition of religion that reflects the complexity of the historically given forms of religiosity. For our purposes, however, it suffices to deal with the topic from the point of view of a theory of the imaginal. In this perspective, it is clear that politics and religion must be linked to one another because they both depend on the imaginal significations of the society within which they provide an answer to the question "what is the origin of society?" As a system of beliefs aimed at the elimination of contingency, religion plays a crucial role within the social imaginary, allowing Castoriadis, with Émile Durkheim, to conclude that religion is at the outset "identical" to society itself (Castoriadis 1997b:318). Religion is one and the same with society, but it is so because every society has to conceal its radical contingency, its being always *instituted* and *instituting*.

If it is true that religion identifies with society, the further question consists of asking "with what kind of society?" Castoriadis's answer is very clear: religion and society coincide in the case of heteronomous societies. In Castoriadis's words, "religion and the heteronomous institution of society are of identical essence. Both intend the same thing and do so by the same means. They do not intend merely the organization of society. They aim at giving *one and the same* signification to being, to the world, *and* to society. They *have to* mask the Chaos, and in particular the Chaos that is society itself. They mask it in falsely recognizing it, through its presentation/occultation, in furnishing it with an Image, a Figure, a Simulacrum" (Castoriadis 1997b:319–320).

In other words, both heteronomous societies and religion aim at the elimination of contingency, which is, by contrast, ineradicable in an autonomous society that recognizes itself as a process of self-creation and, therefore, as always open to the possibility of chaos. The price to be paid for autonomy is very high—society must face the possibility of chaos—and neither religion nor most known societies are ready to pay it. Therefore, good reasons exist for being skeptical vis-à-vis the possibility of fully realizing a truly autonomous society. Every society aims at its own self-preservation and thus tries to occult its own contingency in some way.

To conclude on this point, for Castoriadis the deep and systematic link between religion and heteronomy goes in both directions: all religions include the origin of institution in their system of beliefs and the (heteronomous) institution of society always situates its own origins in an extrasocial source. By occulting the possibility of total chaos through its system of beliefs, religion operates a sort of closure of the social imaginary. This holds particularly for the religions of the book, which transmit their revealed message through a written text. Saying "so it is written" amounts to saying "you cannot imagine it otherwise." Surely the message of the book can be interpreted differently, but the interpretation must stay within the boundaries of what is defined as the "sacred" history. An interpretation of the New Testament that denies the resurrection of Jesus Christ would immediately be stigmatized as heresy and, at best, could only generate another faith. Interpretations and commentaries, therefore, are more the means to preserve the revealed truth than to radically change it.

Herein lies the tension between democracy and religion. While the former coincides with an autonomous society, which acts as self-instituted and openly recognizes this fact, the latter situates its origins in a truth that has been revealed by an *other* relative to the society itself—and that is why the revealed truth must be preserved if the society is not to face the abyss of Chaos. One of the major consequences is the different evolutionary pace of religion and democracy.[8] While democracy follows the rhythm of the society itself, responding to needs gradually emerging within society, religious consciousness follows the evolutionary pace of a revelation that must be respected and preserved in the first place. Herein lies the discrepancy as well between the religious and juridical consciousness in many Western countries. An illuminating example is the different role of women, who remain in an inferior position in many ecclesiastical communities, although they have been recognized as possessing juridical (if not yet social) equality with the other sex.

How does the interplay of religion and political imagination change in the contemporary conditions of a mediatic and potentially global village? As we have mentioned, imaginal politics is nowadays characterized by a striking paradox. On the one hand, the reduction of politics to governance—to mere administration within a general neoliberal consensus—has brought about a decline in what philosophers used to call political imagination, understood here as the capacity to begin something new, to question the status quo by imagining that things may also be radically different from what they are.

Recall here that the World Bank introduced the concept of governance to the political vocabulary in the 1980s so as to denote its own policies in a juridical context that negates its right to exercise political functions. Thus the concept was originally coined to denote a form of authority that is not fully political: governance instead of a government. Since then the term has been extended to denote a particular networklike form of authority that situates itself above that of nation-states.[9] As such, the concept has been associated with the crisis of nation-states and the traditional sites of democracy in preference to transnational and supranational bodies that escape the existing mechanisms of representative democracy[10]—what to many appeared to be nothing less then the "end" of politics itself (Boggs 2000).

In a context in which the sites of decision making increasingly break away from democratic constraints, the capacity to question the status quo by elaborating alternative images of the new seems to have dried up. If the power to make decisions effectively binding is—or appears to be—located so far way, there seems to be no reason to put imagination to work to imagine alternative political scenarios. The slogan "another world is possible," which was coined in Seattle in 1999 and reappears occasionally on the scenes of social movements, is for many just one of the ill-fated attempts to rekindle political imagination.

Governance does not only mean a multilayered system of authority. It also implies an increased role for expertise and knowledge. Together with physical force, new modes of exercising political power appear: first, the threat of exclusion from the benefits of governance itself and, second, the central role of experts. One has only to think of the huge amount of "gray literature" produced by institutions such as the World Bank, the International Monetary Fund, and all the expert committees to realize the extent to which governance relies on knowledge and expertise. This, in its turn, goes hand in hand with the expansion of the scope of political power that increasingly includes issues such as health, well-being, and even sex changes that characterize politics after the biopolitical turn described in chapter 4. Although an eighteenth-century commentator was still able to point to the sex of individuals as an example of an issue that escapes the possibility of being ruled by political power, this is no longer possible. In an epoch where biotechnologies are now able to penetrate the deepest mechanisms of life, in which politics has become biopolitics, nature seems to have become unable to set limits on political power. It may be worth remembering a famous aphorism concerning the natural limits to power that Albert Venn Dicey borrowed from an eighteenth-century writer and made famous, which reads as follows: "It is a fundamental principle with English lawyers, that a Parliament can do everything but make a woman a man, and a man a woman." (Dicey 1959:43). In our biopolitical condition this is no longer the case.[11]

To sum up the different threads of the argument until now: the emergence (and fortune) of the concept of governance points to profound changes in the nature of politics. These include, on the one hand, its reduction to mere technique within highly specialized fields and, on the other hand, the widening scope of competence of political power, which has come to invest areas that were traditionally thought to have been outside its scope. After the biopolitical turn, political power came to include not just issues such as sex changes but also issues of the good life and even the good death. And, in dealing with such issues, it was inevitably meant to meet religion.

Paradoxically, then, the crisis of what philosophers called political imagination goes hand in hand with its hypertrophy. If we consider the issue from the point of view of a theory of the imaginal, which looks at the change in the nature of images rather than at those of the faculty that produces them, we cannot but register both the quantitative and the qualitative changes described in chapter 6. As we have seen, if we think of what politics meant before the large-scale diffusion of the media, we can clearly perceive the exponential increase in the number of images that enter contemporary politics. It is hard to imagine politics outside the continual flux of images that enter the homes of millions of spectators around the globe every day. The quantitative increase is such as to produce a qualitative change as well. Competition among images is so high that a selection must be made, and the criterion for choosing is clear: only those images able to capture people's imagination are newsworthy events. The mass media tends to transform images into *media events* The latter is the expression coined by Elihu Katz and Daniel Dayan to refer to a social, political, or religious event that can be transformed into a television event thanks to its spectacular and exceptional potential (Katz and Dayan 1992). The result of such a transformation is that images are no longer what mediate our being in the world, but have become an end in themselves, such that the spectacle of politics prevails over its content. And it is within such spectacular images that ultimate questions of life and death find a fertile terrain.

We have already mentioned some of the effects of the spectacularization of politics, elections being one privileged example. The spectacle that accompanies electoral campaigns occults the fact that it is not there that the real battle takes place. First, candidates with a chance of succeeding quite often have very similar programs. Second, the crucial decisions are made elsewhere, in sites that escape the traditional mechanisms of democracy. In the end, the real political battle is between those who have a role in the spectacle and those who are left out—that is, between those political options that are acceptable within the political imaginary and those that have to remain outside.

As we have seen, along with a quantitative change, we are also witnessing a qualitative one that directly affects the nature of images. Benjamin already registered a qualitative change in the nature of images when he observed that, as a consequence of their technical reproducibility, images had lost their aura. But he looked mainly at the transformations induced by photography and cinema, whereas today we have reached a further stage. While both photography and cinema maintained a link with the *hic et nunc* so that one could still distinguish between original and fake, between an authentic image and a photomontage, all this is lost with virtual images. Images are not only *reproducible* in series but also *modifiable* up to a point where it no longer makes sense to distinguish between original and fake. There is no original "here and now" and therefore no authenticity to be preserved. Virtual images are not objects created once and for all, but processes. There is no act of original creation, but only processes of perpetual maintenance.

It is perhaps too early to determine the ultimate consequences of this process, although we have already mentioned its democratic potential. However, there are also more alarming consequences that we need to consider. If virtual images are never-ending processes, then there is nothing that can orient us with regard to their reality. *Virtual* images have by definition an uncertain status of reality. They remain, so to speak, suspended. Hence the need to look at them from the point of view of a theory of the imaginal, which does not make any assumption as to their reality or unreality. Many of the pathologies of political imagination in our epoch are due to this fact: images present themselves as real, although we have no criteria with which to establish their reality.

The impact of such a transformation on the link between religion and politics is twofold. Put simply, we can speak of a politicization of religion that goes hand in hand with its mediatization. Caught in the vicelike grip of spectacle, on the one hand, and the reduction to governance and mere technique, on the other, politics is increasingly unable to provide resources of meaning. Hence the request for a greater role of religion in the public sphere: the latter, with its vocation of eliminating contingency through its system of beliefs, is an endless reservoir of meaning, capable, potentially, of covering over any appearance of chaos. This generates a crisis of the secular model, according to which politics and religion must be separated: this model works only if politics and religion can rely on resources of meaning that are comparable. If politics drains away, it is inevitable that we look for meaning elsewhere.

The problem is that once we have opened the doors to the public role of religion, it is very difficult to set an effective limit on it, let alone close it. Solutions such as Habermas's, which distinguish between an informal part of the public sphere, where religious arguments are admitted, and a formal decision-oriented one, where they have to be "translated" into secular arguments (Habermas 2006), work at best from the point of view of "the reasonable," but not from that of the "imaginal." Once religious contents make a considerable entry into the collective and potentially global social imaginary, it is very difficult to circumscribe them by law.

In the first place, this is because the law, and in particular democratic law, is still, to a large extent, anchored by state boundaries, while the public sphere is now, if not global, at least transnational in scope. In the second place, and what is more important, once religious content is given political significance and inserted in the public sphere it risks exploding beyond any distinction between formal and informal parts of the public sphere. The imaginal does not respect the subtle distinctions made by reason about what is more or less formal and therefore triggers a mechanism in which public reason is powerless.

Consider the way in which 9/11 impacted the global imaginary. The attack on the Twin Towers not only brought onto the scene new political scenarios but also triggered reactive mechanisms of identification with one's own more or less invented tradition, thus fueling the idea of there being a clash between Islam and the West. The result, as we have seen in the previous chapter, is that the latter has become one of the most powerful political myths of our time. We have also seen the underlying reasons why an increasing number of people around the globe started to believe that a clash between Islam and the West is taking place (see also Bottici and Challand 2010). I would like here to note only briefly that nobody in the face of the bombs blown up by Christian Identity in Oklahoma City in 1995, or in Atlanta in 1996, spoke of a clash between Christianity and the federal state, whereas a significant percentage of journalists and the global media did not hesitate to interpret 9/11 as a clash between Islam and the West. The result of the working of this myth is that people no longer perceive the deeds of single individual human beings, acting out of a more or less complex series of motives, but entire civilizations clashing with each other. And insofar as an entire Islamic civilization is perceived as a threat, it is inevitable for Western citizens to perceive a need to go out in search of their alleged Christian identity.

But what are the reasons for the success of Islamic fundamentalism—provided that this is an appropriate label for the actions of groups such as Al-Qaeda?[12] Surely, fundamentalism is an extreme example, but precisely because of its extreme character it is best suited to illustrate the intertwining of religion and imaginal politics characterizing our current predicament.[13] The rise of fundamentalism must not be understood as a residual atavism in a globalizing world or as a simple reaction against globalization. As Olivier Roy (2010) has recently noted, religions also entered the global market. We cannot separate the present resurgence of religion in the public sphere from an analysis of the new markets of religion, which have grown increasingly global as well. Indeed, it has become possible to convert to any religion, independently of where one is physically located and one's relative cultural background. This is because religions have cut any essential link with local culture and thus have become standardized into what Roy (2011) termed "McDonald religions." But precisely because religions sell the same product everywhere in an increasingly competitive global market, they tend to become fundamentalist: instead of drawing their force from their belonging to a local culture, they take it from the unique imperative of faith—"you just have to believe" (Roy 2010:187–215, Roy 2011).

Since they have become an integral part of the global society of the spectacle that, as Debord suggests in the passage quoted in the epigraph to part 3, eliminates geographical distance only to increase it internally in the form of a spectacular separation, the repositioning of religion in the public sphere is the privileged place to observe the current transformations of the nexus of politics and the imaginal. Communion of politics and religion is fueled by those very transformations in a way that tends to escape a purely rationalist approach to the issue. Let me illustrate the point by turning to a couple of examples.

Whoever starts to investigate the nature of Al-Qaeda by exploring its internal logic and grammar cannot fail to register a first striking characteristic. The most tangible proof of the existence of this group is a body of writings and images that circulate on the Web and on television. Al-Qaeda has first and foremost a mediatic existence, so much so that journalists investigating its nature and specificity have coined the expression *Jihad via the media*.[14] According to Gilles Kepel, the reasons for the success of Al-Qaeda—which can be translated literally as "the base" (also in the sense of electronic database) and "the norm"—is a loose and rambling ideology devoted wholly to the media from which it draws its power. It is indeed in the virtual space of television and the Internet that Al-Qaeda fights its battle and quite often wins the competition against more moderate and coherent ideologies.[15]

Both in the propaganda and the actions of Al-Qaeda we find all the transformations of the imaginal I have described: the prevalence of the spectacle over the content and virtuality of images together with the loss of their authenticity. Let us start with an analysis of the propaganda. Al-Qaeda's propaganda consists of a more or less coherent set of writings and images, circulating on the Internet, satellite channels, and digital media, in the form of videotapes and DVDs. All this material—brief and simple doctrinal messages, often read by turban-clad ideologists; spiritual testaments of young martyrs, filmed just a few seconds before their suicide attacks—largely plays on the register of people's emotions, as all good spectacles do. The ideological content remains relatively simple: in addition to faith in Allah and the duty to respect the five pillars of Islam, they also add the duty of jihad. The latter is portrayed in the mythical terms of the original struggle of Islam against a protean enemy, now depicted as the atheist, infidel (*kafir*), apostate (*murtadd*), etc. The many references to the medieval epoch, as well as the use of the hegira calendar and ancient place names, are aimed at reviving the founding myth of an original battle. History thus becomes the eternal return of the same, the endless repetition of sacred history: the coming of Islam brought about through the fight against the infidel.

It is, therefore, a very simple and loose religious ideology, which even contains striking contradictions. For instance, fighting in the name of God is presented at times as an individual duty that must be fulfilled by each and every Muslim (*fard'ayn*) and at times as a broad collective duty (*fard kifaya*) performed by a minority in the name of the entire community. Thanks to such a loose ideology, Al-Qaeda has managed to attract the consent of a wide rage of followers.[16] Rational coherence does not matter when you can enjoy a strong imaginal appeal.

Together with the prevalence of the spectacle over the content of propaganda, we can also note the clearly virtual nature of the images involved. One of the first characteristics that will strike whoever looks at the multifaceted body of Al-Qaeda propaganda is the frequent impossibility of establishing the author of the material. Not even written text can be univocally attributed to a single author. The only guarantee of the authenticity of images and texts is most of the time the anonymous Webmaster, who attributes the texts to one or another ideologist. This holds even more for images: whether the testaments of martyrs just about to blow themselves up are real is often impossible to determine. Even less often are we able to identify the authors of such images. Precisely because it remains suspended between reality and spectacle, Al-Qaeda's propaganda did not fail to attract proselytes and meet with general acceptance among nonmilitants. Playing on continual references to the tragedies of Iraq and Palestine—true catalyzers of consent in certain countries—Al-Qaeda's discourse managed to appear as a moment of redemption after many years of political deadlock.[17]

Let us now look at the actions done by, or at least attributed to, Al-Qaeda. Here too we can observe the prevalence of the spectacle over content. The attacks almost never have an intrinsic value, but only a symbolic one. The targets, too, do not have a value in and of themselves, but rather for what they represent. The actions, and in particular simultaneous actions, which follow the virtual logic of endless reproducibility, have the same mass-media logic: they take place at highly symbolic places and times; they use metonyms (a synagogue to mean Israel), synecdoche (claims are always in the name of the whole of Islam), and symbols (burning its flag to declare war on the United States). All this is not simply well suited to the media, but feeds on them, because it could not exist without them: it is consubstantial to their essence.

Far from being a mere residual of atavism, a regression vis-à-vis an accelerated modernization, Al-Qaeda is a product of modernity and its acceleration.[18] It is thanks to the media and the unification of the global mediatic space that the concept of *ummah*, for instance, has left the books of theologians to become a living reality for millions of Muslims around the globe (Challand 2011a). And not by chance, have some authors who focus on Muslim politics gone on to claim that politics has become a struggle for people's imaginations (ibid.).

Think for instance of the role of television. The new satellite channels, such as Al Jazeera, worked as a kind of sound box for the spectacular actions of Al-Qaeda. There is an objective alliance between a movement that has no consistency other than the one provided by the images and a few peripheral media that aim at increasing the audience at any cost. Bin Laden, like Al-Zarqawi, another media star, learned the rules of the new channel's aggressive and hypermodern journalistic style: short films or advertisements, with brief speeches, easy to place in prime time, and carefully thought out staging lacking in sophistication—all in order to increase the reality effect.

Once again, the prevalence of spectacle goes hand in hand with the uncertain status of the reality of images. The virtuality and spectacularity of images imply a loss of the link with the "here and now" that guarantees the possibility of establishing their authenticity. Suspended between reality and spectacle, the actions of Al-Qaeda, which often follow the virtual logic of simultaneous multiplication, are difficult to attribute to a definite author. It is not by chance that at first sight, in the face of the images of the collapsing Twin Towers, many spectators around the globe wondered whether it was real or simply another special effect. It also does not come as a surprise to learn that immediately after 9/11 videotapes representing the towers in flames accompanied by scenes from Hollywood films went on sale on the Chinese market: it was as if the real event, the huge towers collapsing on thousands of people, was not enough and only the Hollywood imagination could render the proportions of the catastrophe.[19]

But fundamentalism is not the prerogative of Islam alone. Evangelical preachers who became famous precisely through their use of modern mass media present the most widely known case of the mediatization and politicization of religion (Pace 2007:166). The phenomenon of the so-called electronic church began in the United States at the end of the 1970s, in the aftermath of the Vietnam War, in a country in search of its new identity. By reaching people directly by phone or through television, evangelical preachers base their discourses on the infallibility of the Bible and the mutual dependency of politics and religion (De Kerckhove 1990). The growing influence of this movement from the 1970s onward gave rise to what has been called the video-Christian civilization (De Kerckhove 1990).

It is through the media that evangelical fundamentalists wage their wars against abortion, demand the exclusion of Darwinism from school curricula, argue for the introduction of systematic preaching in schools, etc. The means for collective mobilization is the religious performance of television anchors who transmit moving messages by making use of spectacle—people crying, live miracles, etc. The result is that, already in 1989, spectators already amounted to 60 million Americans each month (Pace 2007:166).

Once again, here we find the signs of the transformation of the imaginal we have analyzed. We find it, first, in the systematic use of spectacular and virtual images. Evangelical fundamentalists make constant use of spectacular images and often images that possess an uncertain status of reality (think of live miracles).[20] It is true that fundamentalists remain a minority (and an extreme one at that), and that they cannot be taken as representative of the variegated forms of politicization of religion today. Still, precisely because they are extreme cases, the two examples of Islamic and evangelical fundamentalism demonstrate, in a conspicuous form, the transformations I am talking about. They work, so to speak, as magnifying glasses. If we move on, after, to analyzing less extremist forms of religiosity, it will not be difficult to find similar processes taking place.

The reason for this is easy to see: religious movements and associations, which do not want to abandon the possibility of mobilization offered by the new media, must still come to terms with the logic of the mass media. The latter rely on the spectacularization imposed by the "golden rule" of the audience, according to which we can speak only of what can capture people's imagination. The mass media tend to value and give visibility to forms of religiosity that produce media events—that is, events that contain a potential for spectacle and exceptionality.

Take as an example the travels of John Paul II. The television treated them as a series of performances by a telegenic star, insisting more on the image of the exceptional character of the pope—always able to overcome difficulties and attract huge crowds—than on the religious message itself (Pace 2007:165). As Gustavo Guizzardi (1986) observed in his analysis of the media coverage of these travels, the charisma of John Paul II was specifically mediatic because it could not have existed without the media. The latter were the first and real followers of Pope Wojtyla, because his charisma was constructed through them and vis-à-vis them. Wojtyla was such a pope precisely owing to his capacity to produce images capable of moving a medium that is by nature as cynical as television (Guizzardi 1986). Every gesture of Wojtyla—his travels in difficult conditions, the appearances at Saint Peter's with his trembling hands kissing the ground—was a media event. The last one was his exit from the stage: the Gospel opened on his coffin, the pages fluttering in the wind, the same wind that had been one of the crucial scenic elements of his television performances. And during the final media event, just a few days afterwards, images of the dead pope's first miracles started to circulate.[21]

There seems to be something intrinsic to religion that makes it easily subsumable to mass-media logic. The latter relies on the two fundamental ingredients of personality cult and spectacle, and religion can easily provide the two. Religion has always included both these ingredients: charismatic characters and extraordinary events. It is such homogeneity between the language of the media and that of religion that creates a vicious circle, which explains the nature of many forms of the politicization of religion today. Religions are given a crucial choice: they can come to an agreement with the mass media, and thus become a mass-media commodity, or remain below the line of visibility that only the media can guarantee and try to survive in the cleavages of society (Pace 2007:164). Some of the contemporary forms of religiosity choose the latter road, but they then have to face the possibility of complete oblivion.

Before concluding this chapter, let me note that the resurgence of religion in the public sphere during a biopolitical epoch cannot be understood outside a more general process of questioning the distinction between "private" and "public"—a distinction that has been central to the Western philosophical tradition. Already, in the 1980s, Norberto Bobbio (1985:16–17) observed that the great dichotomy of public/private is tackled in the contemporary world by the double process of privatization of the public and publicization of the private. In his view, the latter found its most concrete expression in the state welfare policies and more generally in any policy of public intervention on the economy (16–17). As an example of the opposite process of "privatization of the public," he mentioned the emergence of contractual relationships—typical of the private sphere—in public formal affairs such as trade unions' labor contracts and contracts between different parties for the coalitions of government (16–17). Another example we may add is so-called Islamic finance, the set of financial regulations governing economic exchanges that are defined on the bases of Islamic principles. Even if such practices emerged in Muslim-majority countries (Saudi Arabia, in particular, after the economic boom generated by the increase of oil prices in the 1970s), it is now widely practiced by the world's largest corporate banking resorts; this

Islamization of the market does not create any sense of disagreement in public debates.[22]

Today we have reached a further stage in both such processes because the privatization of public affairs has coincided with an increased influence of the public within the private sphere. It is revealing that issues that at one time were considered exemplary of a sphere that cannot be ruled by state power—such as changing the sex of individuals—is now subject to a great deal of legislation. The possibility of intervention in the ultimate questions of life and death possessed by the state and other formal apparatuses today is incomparably greater than in the past. This is what in chapter 4 we tried to convey with the expression *biopolitical turn*, which has been accompanied by a series of words (such as *bioethics, biolaw, bioterrorism,* etc.) pointing to the new centrality of life itself. In an age when the political is conceived in terms of contractual relations once limited to the private sphere and when, by contrast, typically private issues such as the sex of individuals are regulated through the instrument of law, it seems to be difficult to maintain the public versus private dichotomy. The questioning of such a dichotomy is, therefore, not only limited to Western societies, but rather a process linked to political and economic globalization, on the one hand, and to the new possibilities of intervention in private life opened by biotechnologies, on the other.

There certainly are no univocal or easy recipes to break with the circle created by the mediatization and politicization of religion. For the reasons I have tried to illustrate in this chapter, they cannot but reinforce each other. In an epoch where politics oscillates between being simple administration and empty spectacle, religion is deemed to acquire an increasingly greater role in the public sphere.

This creates however a crucial philosophical-political dilemma: is it possible to reconcile such an increased role of religion with Castoriadis's project of autonomy? As I have suggested here, reconciling such a project with the new role of religion in the public sphere is easier from the point of view of the reasonable than from that of the imaginal. Why this is so is easy to see: the imaginal is much more insidious and pervasive than the reasonable and can, therefore, be dealt with less easily through law. Once religious contents have been massively inserted in the imaginal, it cannot be limited to the sole "informal" part of the public sphere, as in Habermas's solution. Religious contents risk exploding within it, invading both its informal and formal parts.

In a context in which religion has an increasingly public role, it is much easier to answer the question "how can I be autonomous?" in the sense of the reasonable (to give oneself one's own law) than to answer the more complex "how can I be at the origin of what will be and know myself to be so?" in the sense of the imaginal. In dealing with such a question, we cannot neglect the danger that threatens contemporary politics: if the latter, taken between the Scylla of reduction to mere technique, on the one hand, and the Charybdis of empty spectacle, on the other, decides to unconditionally open the doors to religious resources, it risks being phagocytosed. In the contemporary political condition, the risk is, therefore, not so much that religion is becoming a "conversation-stopper,"[23] but rather that it is turning into an "inflamer of political imagination," something that can rekindle political imagination but that may also burn it out.

9

Imagining Human Rights

Gender, Race, and Class

Le droit est la plus puissante des écoles de l'imagination.
JEAN GIRAUDOUX, *La guerre de Troie n'aura pas lieu*

We live in an epoch of accelerated changes that often generate striking paradoxes. Human rights are one of them. The language of human rights is used by the mighty of the world, but also abounds in the mouths of the wretched of the earth. Notwithstanding its massive use, the emancipative potential of the language of rights has not diminished. To put it bluntly, they are simultaneously a means both for the *ideological* justification of the status quo and for its *utopian* subversion. If we agree with Karl Mannheim (1966) that utopia differs from ideology—the former breaks the bonds of the existing social order, whereas the latter aims to preserve it—then we cannot but conclude that the paradox of human rights consists precisely in this: they are both a means for ideology and for utopia, for the preservation of the status quo and for its disintegration.

The main argument of this chapter is that in order to account for such a paradox we need to consider not just the power of the reasonable but also that of the imaginal. While most philosophical reflections on human rights look at them from the point of view of reason and the reasonable, I want to show how fruitful it can be to take the point of view of imagination and the imaginal. Contemporary philosophy neglects and, at times, even seems to ignore this fundamental fact: our capacity to form images plays an important role in both the justification of human rights and their enforcement. Behind the supposed humanity of human rights, there is often a very specific image of humanity on the basis of which we provide a rational justification for them. Similarly, it is by virtue of such a capacity to form images, and thus also to represent what is not immediately present, that we are often led to enforce them. And, as we will see, it is often a certain image of gender, race, or class that we have in mind when humanity is invoked.

I will proceed in two main steps. After recalling the main feature of the concept of the imaginal, I will move on to show how the imaginal enters the three major strategies of justifications of human rights, when we conceive them as "human," as "rights," and as "rational." An often unexpected and unaccounted guest, the imaginal is frequently there, close to reason and the reasonable. Subsequently, I will show that the imaginal is also the force that compels us to enforce human rights, to put ourselves in the shoes of others and imagine a world that is different from the one we are currently living in.

One of the reasons why contemporary political philosophy is ill equipped to make sense of the paradox of human rights is its primary focus on reason and rationality. As I have argued elsewhere, together with an analysis of the conditions for public reason, political philosophy also needs to elaborate those for public imagination.[1] While some (although few) have already dealt with human rights from the point of view of imagination or of the imaginary, what I want to do here is to look at them through the prism of the imaginal.[2] Through this radical change of perspective, from the "reasonable" to the "imaginal," a new point of departure can be developed to tackle the paradox from which we started.

As we have seen, the imaginal denotes what is made of images (*imagines*); as such, it can be both the product of an individual faculty and of a social context, as well as the result of a complex, yet to be determined interaction between the two. Furthermore, in contrast to the term *imaginary*—which primarily refers to what exists in fancy, has no real existence, and is therefore opposed to *real* or *actual* (Simpson and Wiener 1989:2:668)—the concept of the imaginal does not make any assumption about the reality of the images that compose it. The definition of what is real is not an a priori of human understanding, but something that has continuously changed over the centuries; we should, therefore, leave the issue of the "reality" of the imaginal open. This is particularly crucial for an inquiry into human rights. Characterizing human rights as "imaginary" means suggesting that they are "unreal," thus making a determination from the beginning about their status of reality.[3] On the contrary, the category of the "imaginal" leaves the issue open.

Let us now see how the concept of the imaginal can thus throw light on the paradox of human rights. The concept of human rights implies both the emergence of the concept of rights, understood as subjective entitlements, and that of the humanity as its horizon of application. In European modernity the two, notoriously, went together. The first declarations of human rights are indeed imbued with the Enlightenment's belief in the equality of human beings as bearers of natural rights.[4] However, analytically speaking, the two concepts are separated. Clearly, there can be "rights" that are not "human," but conferred on the basis of other entitlements such as citizenship.

On the analytic level, we can therefore distinguish between two major strategies of justification of human rights: the first says that "human rights" are justified because they are "rights" (by which I mean here "legal rights"), whereas the second grounds their legitimacy on their being specifically "human." The first goes back to legal positivism, or the idea that rights are such insofar as they are part of a juridical system. The second stems from the natural law tradition, which justifies human rights as fundamental rights that are granted to every human being by their very humanity and are therefore impervious to the oscillations of political power.

Many have criticized the idea of an alleged human nature as a crucially flawed, metaphysical hypostatization. Is there a human nature that goes beyond the cultural differences and anthropological transformations produced by social and historical changes? Is not so-called human nature the product of cultural, material, and historical transformations? All these perplexities have recently led to a third strategy for the justification of human rights. In this view, human rights are justified because they are "rational" either because these rights would be chosen by any rational contractor as fair (Rawls 1999) or because they are discursively justified (Habermas 2001; Forst 2007).

There can indeed be many different variants of the aforementioned strategies of justification; a lot has been said and written about them. What I want to do here is to show the role that the imaginal plays within them. Let us start from the first one: human rights as "human." All examples of this strategy rely by definition on a certain image of humanity. However, the latter has, surprisingly, proved to be particularly variable in different contexts and epochs. Even within the same context, the image of humanity presupposed may vary considerably, hence the usefulness of focusing on the concept of the imaginal, which accounts for the possibility that, even within a rather monolithic social imaginary, the power of individual imagination emerges.

Let me illustrate this point by comparing two declarations of human rights that have been written in the same context, i.e., during the French Revolution: the first is the famous French Declaration of the Rights of Man and the Citizen (1789) and the second is much less renowned, Olympe de Gouges's Declaration of the Rights of Woman and the Citizen (1791). Tellingly, only the first was adopted by the National Assembly, which refused to accept de Gouges's alternative declaration (she was instead sentenced to death). De Gouges's Declaration reproduces article by article the more famous 1789 Declaration, but extends all those rights to women, on the basis of the observation that there is nothing in human nature itself that justifies the exclusion of women from the exercise of civil and political rights that are granted to men (preamble).

De Gouges's Declaration is particularly crucial for us. In the first place, this is because with her alternative declaration she deconstructed the implicit gender bias of the apparently universal 1789 Declaration and thus also showed the power of the imaginal in sustaining a certain ideology; those who drafted the 1789 "universal" declaration spoke about humanity, but it was the image of white males that they had in mind and that led them to devise juridical mechanisms to exclude women. On the contrary, de Gouges's message to the National Assembly was very clear: you are proclaiming the rights that pertain to every human being by virtue of their birth, but in fact you are imagining only white males. With her alternative declaration, which concludes with a postscript against slavery and discrimination on the basis of race, she also shows the utopian and critical potential of the concept of the imaginal. Indeed, once you start to investigate the role that unspoken images play in triggering discrimination, it is easy to extend such a critique beyond gender and perceive other classes and groups that are being equally discriminated against, such as slaves and blacks.[5]

In sum, the images of humanity that are presupposed by the two declarations are diametrically opposed: both spoke about humanity, but the first one envisions a humanity made of white adult males, while the second entails a much broader conception in which women and slaves are also included. Both declarations used the concept of humanity to justify the existence of inviolable rights, but the authors of the 1789 Declaration imagined women and slaves as ultimately less "human." Born from the utopian spirit of the revolution, the 1789 Declaration turned into the ideological means for perpetrating the domination of white males.

A positivist lawyer may here contend that de Gouges's Declaration is not a real declaration of rights because those rights were not "legal," that is, they were not formally recognized by a juridical body. Indeed, one had to wait until the Universal Declaration of Human Rights (1948) to see women's rights become rights in this sense. But we are here dealing with another strategy of justification that considers rights as full rights only insofar as they are part of a legal system.[6] Let us now move to this second strategy, with an eye to the role of the imaginal.

Every justification of the concept of subjective "rights" presupposes either their intrinsic legitimacy or, more indirectly, the legitimacy of the power that has sanctioned them. As Bobbio observed, what is specific to the concept of right is the possibility of taking recourse to coercion to obtain respect for it (Bobbio 1990:312). But coercion that is not legitimate could never provide "rights" with their specific normative core. Without legitimacy, the justification of rights amounts to validation of mere force. The crucial question thus becomes: what is the source of the legitimacy of rights?

Historically speaking, the sources of legitimacy of rights have been innumerable. If we take Weber's three ideal-typical bases for the belief in legitimacy, we see that all of them rely on the imaginal (Weber 1978:1, 36–38, 212ff.). As has been argued, it is not by chance that the notion of "images of the world" (*Weltbild*) plays a crucial (although often unrecognized) role in Weber's thinking (D'Andrea 2009). In the case of charismatic authority, as we have seen, people obey a command because they have faith in the sacred or heroic image of the person exercising it. But the imaginal is also crucial in traditional authority because no tradition can be respected without imagining it at the same time. One needs to imagine a certain continuity in space and time, and therefore something that is not immediately present, to perceive a "tradition." Finally, the imaginal is also important for legal-rational authority. Even in this case, belief in the legality of institutions derives from a certain image of what law must be like—an exemplary law.[7] Historically speaking, law has always had its peculiar politics of images, because it is through such a use of images that legitimacy is conferred upon the system of rights as well as the political authority emanating them (Douzinas and Nead 1999). To conclude on this point, even in a positivistic view that grounds legitimacy in the system of rights itself, there is space for the work of the imaginal, because there still needs to be a belief in the legitimacy of the authority emanating them. To these three sources, as we have seen, we must add the conservative reproduction of life, which is all the more dependent on the imaginal, since in a society of the spectacle no bare life is accessible to us outside the flux of images that convey it.

Let us now move to the third strategy: the idea that human rights are justified because they are "rational." There are today many different variants of this strategy, and not all of them accord the same role to the imaginal.[8] But let me focus on John Rawls's justification of human rights, which has been particularly influential in recent debates about international justice. For our purposes, it is significant that in his theory the imaginal plays an unrecognized but important role. Human rights are not justified on the basis of a comprehensive view of human nature, nor on a mere positivistic view of human rights as legal rights, but rather on their being reasonable.

As Rawls (1999) argues in *The Law of Peoples*, respect for human rights ranks among the principles that the rational representatives of peoples would chose if they were put in the hypothetical original position of not knowing their specific position in the world. It is Rawls's famous device of a "veil of ignorance," according to which all information about representatives and the people they represent must be unknown in the moment of the choice in order to guarantee its fairness (Rawls 1999).[9] The idea of an original position and of a social contract is a device that Rawls has extended from domestic society (where they justify a liberal conception of justice) to the international one. Notwithstanding significant differences between the two (the most important being that the domestic original position is made of individuals, whereas the international one is made of representatives of peoples), in both cases they are models of representation, of what we would regard as fair conditions under which the parties (rational representatives of free, equal, and reasonable citizens in the first case and of liberal peoples in the second) are to specify the basic principles regulating domestic and international society (Rawls 1999).

Rawls's original position with its veil of ignorance has been interpreted in many different ways. For some, it is a thought experiment notable for its hypothetical nature (Ackerman 1994:368), while for others it is an allegory (Ricoeur 1992:231) or even a myth, given its fictitious character and its reference to the idea of origins with all its evocative power (La Caze 2002:94–118).[10] In all these cases it is hard to deny its imaginal character: even if we think that the original position and the veil of ignorance are meant to be rational devices, it is nevertheless patent that they rely on the evocative power of an image, that is, of a representation that can also be visualized: a veil lying on the eyes of people gathered to decide on matters of common affairs.

In her feminist analysis, Marguerite La Caze (11) distinguishes between three main functions that images can perform within philosophical texts: (1) to express a philosophical point, (2) to persuade and provide support for a particular view, and (3) to structure and frame the debate so that certain solutions are possible and radically alternative options excluded. In her view, the original position and the veil of ignorance perform all of these functions: they are a way of dramatizing "impartiality" and thus giving expression to a central tenet of liberalism, while also providing support for it and excluding alternative options, such as feminist ones, which ask for the specific interests of women to be recognized as such rather than put "under a veil of ignorance" (108).[11]

La Caze's main point of criticism is that the original position is not a guarantee for adequate representation of women's interests. For their male companions, imagining they could be in the women's place (the veil of ignorance) does not necessarily help them to identify women's rational interests. This is just as likely to lead them to merely identifying what their interests would be if they were in the women's position. The example she makes is that of a male advertising executive who has to decide whether his ads are sexist or offensive to women. In order to do so, he performs a mental experiment similar to Rawls's veil of ignorance: "would I accept this advertisement if I were a woman?" So he imagines himself in the position of the woman in that ad and thinks about how he would feel if represented by that image; since he does not feel offended, he thinks it is right to proceed with the ad (112). However, what he imagines as "rationally acceptable" may well not be so for a person of a different sex or of a different cultural background.[12] It is the very assumption that gender differences can be put under the veil of ignorance that makes Rawls's procedure not so reasonable for La Caze's feminist perspective. To assume that gender differences can be handled in a rational way when put under the veil of ignorance, rather than taking them explicitly into account, is a way to turn the utopia of a just society into the ideology of a society dominated by men.

One may or may not agree with La Caze's criticism, but her argument—that imagining ourselves in the others' shoes is not yet a guarantee that those shoes, in the end, will not be more ours than theirs—should be taken into account. It also proves our more general point that Rawls's strategy of justification relies on the evocative power of images. If this holds true for the general contractarian philosophical apparatus that he sets up, it will hold for both its domestic and its international applications.

Moreover, the role of the imaginal in Rawls's justification of human rights also emerges if we look more carefully at the specific list of rights he proposes. We have until now mainly looked at the concept of human rights as if they were a monolithic category, as if everybody agreed on their specific content, but this is far from being the case. And, as I will now try to show, it is also in the specific choice of human rights that the power of the imaginal emerges. It is the specific image of humanity people have in mind that leads one to choose certain rights as specifically more human or rational over others. In the case of Rawls's argument, he clearly builds his catalogue of rights by selecting only some of the rights listed in the Universal Declaration of Human Rights of 1948.[13] The whole group of rights listed in Articles 19 through 30 is not included within human rights. Some of them, such as the right to social security (Article 22) and the right to equal pay for equal work (Article 23), are explicitly denied that status because they seem to presuppose specific types of institutions, although in fact not all of them do. What is the basis for excluding them? Why are certain rights more "human" than others? Rawls's peculiar selection of human rights reflects a precise choice of what it means to be human, and thus, again, a specific image of humanity itself, one that may be more or less conscious. Some rights appear to be more universally "human" and therefore more "rational" according to the image of humanity that we have in mind. It is again the power of the imaginal that emerges—a power that strongly influences us, but of which we are often unaware or, to be more precise, that so powerfully influences us because we are unaware of it.

It is symptomatic that even an author such as Alessandro Ferrara (who criticizes Rawls for not adequately supporting his selective choice of specific human rights) does not explicitly recognize the power of the imaginal within his own strategy of justifying human rights.[14] In *The Force of the Example* Ferrara (2008) vindicates the power of the example as an alternative to Rawlsian, principle-based public reason. Yet, as he makes clear at many points, his strategy for engaging in a fully fledged justification of human rights can only proceed from a consensus of the peoples of the planet that is formed solely via public reason (see, for instance, Ferrara 2008:9, 137–139).[15]

In this view, human rights are justified because a fulfillment of human identity requires that they should be respected (138–139). Ferrara recognizes that he provides a context-dependent view of what it means to be a human being (137), but he tries to turn this view into a strength rather than a weakness. Just as exemplary works of art are able to raise potentially universal consent by remaining particular, so the Western view of human rights, if articulated in an exemplary way, may be inspiration for others in different situations (139).[16]

Even in this view the imaginal plays a central role. This clearly emerges when Ferrara observes that the Universal Declaration of Human Rights covers too broad a spectrum because it includes too much, even rights such as the "right to leisure and rest." Why, one might observe, should this not be recognized as a *human* right? Even within a "Western" view of human rights, why should this not be recognized as a fundamental right toward the fulfillment of human identity? Behind the criticism of such an inclusion of the right to leisure and rest, there is again an implicit image of humanity—in this case, one whose identity can be fulfilled without leisure and rest.

To sum up, we have seen that the imaginal often plays an important role in all three major strategies for justifying human rights. When we argue that they are "human," "rights," or "rational" we often have a specific image in mind. Let us see why these are so important, not just in philosophical arguments that justify human rights but also as a source of motivation for their enforcement. The application of human rights depends on the imaginal, both when we are mere spectators of their violations and when we are directly involved in them. Let us start from the first scenario. We are a spectator to human rights violations when we are called to be impartial spectators of them, when we compassionately participate in the suffering that these violations imply, or when we feel some distant pity.

Even as impartial spectators we often rely on the imaginal. As Arendt observed, it is thanks to our capacity to imagine that we are able to transcend our own peculiar conditions and put ourselves in the shoes of others (Arendt 1982:72).[17] It is this capacity to strip ourselves of our peculiarities and assume an "enlarged mentality" that enables us to assume the point of view of others (72). Arendt sketches this view in her political reading of Kant's *Critique of Judgment*. Judgment differs from taste insofar as, while the latter is inevitably linked to our emotions, since it is the "faculty of judging a priori the communicability of feelings that are bound up with a representation" (72), the faculty of judgment introduces distance. We speak of judgment and not of taste because judgment, by means of representation, establishes the proper distance, the remoteness or uninvolvedness that is requisite for approbation and disapprobation, for evaluating something in its proper worth. Otherwise said, by removing the object, one has created the conditions for impartiality (67).

Arendt looks at the power of imagination as the faculty to represent what is absent (66). In this way, she concentrates on only one aspect of the imaginal: images of what is absent that, precisely because of this absence allow for the creation of distance. By contrast, a theory of the imaginal does not make any assumption about the status of the reality of images and must therefore account for both possibilities: images of absent but also images of present objects. In this latter scenario, and particularly when the objects of our imagining are in some sense "close" to us, we are less likely to avoid an emotional involvement and reach the distance of which Arendt speaks.

This can happen when the images are of an object that is present, as when we directly observe somebody's sufferings or remember it immediately after seeing it. If we have just seen a child starving, we are not likely to feel the remoteness that is the requisite for impartiality, but are in general directly affected by the image. Yet we can also feel "close" to a fictitious image, as occurs when reading literature. In this case, we know that the situation represented is not real, but this is nevertheless able to move our passions since we feel emotionally close to it. We have moved here to a second scenario, wherein we are compassionate spectators of human rights violations.

According to some, we should speak of our capacity for *empathy*, which literally means feeling the same as the suffering person. Nussbaum, for example, argues that literature is an important way to cultivate humanity because through it we are trained to imagine what it is like to be in another person's place (Nussbaum 1997). In her view, this form of empathy requires a sense of one's own vulnerability. Human beings are needy, incomplete creatures who are, in many ways, dependent on circumstances beyond their control for the possibility of well-being. And, as she argues, people do not fully grasp that fact until they can imagine suffering vividly to themselves and feel pain at imagining it (91). The vivid images of suffering that literature provides are one of the chief means for doing so.

With an argument very close to the one put forth by Nussbaum (1997) in *Cultivating Humanity*, but more focused on human rights, Van Peer (1995) explores the potential of literature to enlarge our own sense of humanity. Literature nourishes our capacity to imagine because, as Aristotle famously argued, it describes not what has happened, but a kind of thing that might happen. Therefore, literature can liberate us from the encapsulated world we live in and open up new horizons beyond the culture we have grown up in. In comparison with other sources of images, the advantage of literature is precisely that it achieves this by depicting tangible human characters in such a vivid and lively manner as to engage the passions of every sensible reader (Van Peer 1995:283).

Enforcing human rights frequently depends on the force of images that affect us emotionally.[18] Thanks to such power, the notion of humanity has been enlarged to the point where it is now. As Van Peer (1995) shows in his analysis of English and French literature, works such as Dickens's *Hard Times* or Victor Hugo's *Le dernier jour d'un condamné* have deeply contributed to the extension of what had been perceived to be the boundaries of humanity. Together with gender and race, class has also been another factor in dehumanization. It hardly needs to be demonstrated that factory workers barely qualified for the category "human" during the times of the early Industrial Revolution. What happens in such a situation is a sort of self-fulfilling prophecy: because poor workers, due to their exploitation, do not look like civilized humans, they are not regarded as human and hence are more easily refused rights. As a result, they continue to differ in their appearance from established groups (Van Peer 1995). Novels such as those I have mentioned contributed to breaking a vicious circle by showing the humanity of those social classes that were excluded not just from the exercise of rights but also from the parallel image of full humanity.

Comparable effects of enlargement of the sense of humanity through literary images have been observed, for instance, concerning African Americans in the United States: to enlarge people's sense of humanity by showing the suffering of black people is what Van Peer named the *Uncle Tom* effect, after the title of the famous novel by Stowe, which itself played a crucial role in fueling the abolitionist cause (287). The same holds for women, not just in the United States, but in most Western countries (287). Novels such as *Moll Flanders, Madame Bovary,* and *Anna Karenina* deeply contributed to contesting the dominant imaginal significations and thus diffusing a culture of women's rights. Feminist critical theorists such María Pía Lara have focused on the importance of women's narratives in the public sphere. Feminist narratives (both novels and biographies) have been a viable way to enlarge our moral textures and thus open the path for the emancipation of women in the public sphere (Lara 1998).

The power of literature to augment our sense of humanity has a double root. The first is the disclosive capacity of language (Lara 2011). When Simone de Beauvoir (1953) called women "the second sex" and observed that "on nait pas femme: on le deviant," she not only disentangled the hidden prejudices of our male-oriented culture, but she also further disclosed new spaces for social critique. In a similar vein, the feminist slogan of the 1960s and 1970s, "the personal is political," worked to criticize existing mechanism of female segregation in the private sphere and also to reveal new fields for action in the public sphere.

But one of the most perspicuous analyses of the feminist capacity to use the disclosive power of language comes from a man, Richard Rorty. He did so by commenting on a sentence by Catharine MacKinnon (2000:43), "being a woman is not yet a name for a way of being human." Rorty (1998a:203) observes that injustices may not be perceived as injustices "until somebody invents a previously unplayed role," that is, "not only new words, but also creative misuses of language"—familiar words used in ways that initially sound crazy.[19] Rorty (1998b:205) concludes, "MacKinnon's central point, as I read her, is that "woman" is not yet the name of a way of being a human—not yet the name of a moral identity, but, at most, the name of a disability."

The other element that confers upon literature the power to shape our sense of humanity and justice are narratives. Narratives are redemptive of suffering because, as Arendt (1968a:104) put it, "all sorrows can be borne if you put them into a story or tell a story about them." However, they are also transformative, insofar as they are the means to negotiate, in a public sphere, the recognition of one's own suffering and identity (Lara 1998:69–80). Feminist narratives, both novels and autobiographies, played and still do play a crucial role in this sense, but they do so thanks to the way in which they can question established images. If it is true that the imaginal, as we have defined it, is primordial in that it cannot be reduced to linguistic descriptions, we must nevertheless add that narratives, precisely for their evocative power, are one of the chief vehicles for conveying certain images as well as for contesting dominant ones.

This does not mean that narratives are always the means for the emancipation of women; narratives can perpetuate their oppression, as has frequently been the case throughout the centuries. In her analysis of fairy tales, for instance, Sherry B. Ortner observed that in many well-known fairy tales females are systematically denied real agency. One has to think only of the role of heroines such as Snow White or Cinderella to have a sense of what a lack of agency means in this context: while the former is frozen under a magic spell, the latter has to wait for Prince Charming to find her shoes to exit her destiny as a servant. Reconstructing her experience with fairy tales, Ortner wrote the following:

> I once spent time analyzing Grimm's *Fairy Tales*, with an interest in seeing the ways in which female agency was constructed differently from male agency, the ways in which heroines were different from heroes. I suppose I expected to find usual binaries: passive/active, weak/strong, timorous/brave, etc. What I had not quite expected to see was a recognition in the tales that female characters had to be *made* passive, weak, timorous, that is, a recognition that agency in girls had to be *unmade*. Most of Grimm's heroines are in the mode of what the folklorist Propp calls "victim heroes"; although they are protagonists, the action of the story is moved along by virtue of bad things happening to them, rather than their initiating actions in the case of the majority of male heroes. Thus non-agency, passivity, is to some extent built into most of them from the outset. Yet in many cases these victim heroines take the roles of active agency in the early parts of the story. Though their initial misfortunes may have happened to them through outside agency, they sometimes seize the action and carry it along themselves, becoming—briefly—heroines in the active questing sense usually reserved for male heroes.

> (Ortner 1996:9)

Ortner's remarks are particularly relevant here because they point out the ambivalent role that images of womankind can play in literary texts. The imaginal can be both a means for denying agency to women, but it can also be the tool for fully recognizing their humanity. Both have historically been the case. Women's emancipation had to go through a stage in which they were imaginatively shown to possess characteristics that were largely denied them in daily life. As Lara observes, "narrating evil" is a school of our moral imagination, a learning exercise in which we are led to put ourselves in the shoes of others and feel compassion for their suffering, thereby extending the image of humanity beyond existing borders (Lara 2007).

But there is a third possibility between an impartial judgment and compassionate participation in other people's sufferings. This third scenario consists of situations when the image of the suffering of others is not accompanied by a sense of close compassion or empathy. This is what Luc Boltanski (1999) called a "politics of pity." Pity differs from compassion because it implies a difference between human beings that suffer and those who do not suffer. In Boltasnki's view, the whole contemporary discourse about humanitarian intervention and the promotion of human rights in Western countries is more based on pity than compassion. This is because our relationship to suffering is filtered by the media, which introduces a distance between those who feel pity and those that are the objects of it. But pity depends on the imaginal as much as compassion does, as Boltanski makes clear at many points in his work. We need images of suffering to feel pity, and the contemporary politics of pity is undergoing a huge crisis precisely as a consequence of the excess of images our media transmits every day. The spectacle of suffering is so continuous that our capacities both for compassionate reaction and for genuine pity are anesthetized.

But the enforcing of human rights also relies on the imaginal when it takes recourse to images of what the world would be like if they were enforced. Many authors have emphasized the strong utopian appeal of human rights. Utopian thinking does not necessarily rely on images. If by utopia we mean, along with Mannheim, a form of thinking that is incongruous with the status quo (Mannheim 1966), then utopias are simply counterfactual thinking, and in this sense they are not always imaginal. But when it comes to the enforcing of human rights in a global society of the spectacle, it is often the smile of a little starving child or some other pictorial representation of a better world that spurs us to action.

Many authors have insisted on the capacity to create alternatives to the status quo as a specifically human capacity. The philosopher who has most systematically reflected on this is perhaps Ernst Bloch (1986b). In his monumental *The Principle of Hope* Bloch presents a phenomenology of hope by showing that human consciousness is primarily an anticipating consciousness, that is, a consciousness projected toward the "not-yet."[20] Our capacity to create alternative images is particularly evident in utopias, that is, in images of "good-places" (*eu-topoi*) that are "no-places" (*ou-topoi*; Bottici 2010b). It is not by chance that the philosopher who most systematically reflected on the importance of the "not-yet," the anticipating consciousness, is also the one who most vigorously pointed out the utopian potential of human rights. By reconstructing the origins of human rights within a natural law tradition that begins with Epicurus and the Stoics, Bloch (1986a:xviii) argued that human rights express the "forward-pressing, not-yet-determined nature of human beings." In doing so, Bloch (1986b:3:§44) observes that the language of human rights is based on images of a fulfilled moment, on those "guiding images" of what it is like to become a proper human being.[21] And if this was true at the time Bloch was writing, i.e., immediately after World War II, this is even more so today as a consequence of the spectacularization and virtualization of politics as described in this book.

Thus the enforcing of human rights depends on the imaginal, both because it depends on our capacity to put ourselves in others' shoes and also because we need to form images of alternatives to the current state of affairs in order to apply them. In other words, we need to be able to have hope in a better future to possess alternative guiding images of it. In sum, not only when we formulate abstract philosophical justifications for human rights do we often rely on images, but first and foremost when we are urged to enforce them. Both when we are emotionally overwhelmed by empathy and when we exercise the function of distant spectators or of benevolent dispensers of a politics of pity, the power of the imaginal comes to light.

In conclusion, let us return to the paradox of human rights with which we began. It is because they are so often dependent on the imaginal that human rights can be both a source of ideology and utopia. The imaginal can indeed be both the result of a social context dominated by images of the world that are aimed at its preservation as well as of the free power of individuals to create alternative images. As we have seen, the 1789 Declaration reflected an ideological image of humanity that was restricted to white males, while de Gouges's alternative Declaration disclosed the full humanity of women and slaves; whereas the former sustained the dominant ideology of a male-dominated society, the latter opened the path for the utopia of a much broader humanity.

Recovering the utopian potential of human rights is thus possible, but implies being fully aware of this ambivalent power of the imaginal. Thanks to it, certain human beings have been perceived (and still are perceived) as more human than others. We may indeed believe that, in the epoch of globalization, the image of "humanity" has now reached its incontestable boundaries—those dictated by the simple fact of being born a human being. But this is far from being the case. As MacKinnon (2000) reminds us, there are still many voids in international human rights legislation for women, so much so that it is still possible to raise the question "are women human?"

But women are not the only ones who suffer from the deprivation of such a full image of humanity. Guantánamo detainees or illegal immigrants are also deprived of their full humanity and therefore of their full enjoyment of human rights. Like factory workers at the dawn of the Industrial Revolution, they are often deprived of even the most basic human rights because they are deprived of their full status as humans. A symbol of such human rights violations are prisons like Guantánamo, or the innumerable detention centers all over Europe, where illegal immigrants are kept by force and from which they have no right to exit.[22] The media campaign that depicts aliens as a danger to public security occults the vicious circle of exclusion: the fewer rights they are recognized as possessing, the more likely they are to find themselves in dehumaninzing conditions. It is a self-fulfilling prophecy: they are neglected rights because they are not perceived as fully human and, as a consequence of this deprivation, they are likely to continue to differ in their image from established groups. For these people, applying human rights means, in the first place, breaking such a vicious circle and reestablishing an image of full humanity. The imaginal is what impedes our perception of their full humanity, but it can also be the vehicle to reestablish it.

The problem of human rights is not, as some have argued, that utopia is dead. The issue at stake is no longer, as the herald of the end of utopias said, to envisage just bigger pieces of cake for everyone, but to design different ingredients for a different cake.[23] And to do so we need utopias, alternative images of the world that are at the same time "no-places" and "good-places." The problem is, rather, that of a deep transformation of the imaginal in the present conditions of a global society of spectacle. As we have seen, the imaginal went through both a quantitative and a qualitative transformation. As a consequence of the first, we are now so image-saturated that a perverse search for always more spectacular images has become inevitable. The number of spectacles of human rights violations is so overwhelming that both our capacity to feel empathy as actors and pity as spectators has been annihilated. The spectacle is so excessive and so continuous that our capacity for a passionate reaction is anesthetized. But victims meet their ultimate dehumanization when, on top of their suffering, they must carry the burden of boring us.

To this we should also add a certain cynical skepticism that results from the hypertrophy of the imaginal described in the course of this book. As we have seen, together with the quantitative transformation, we have also witnessed a qualitative change—one that directly concerns the nature of images. Virtual images have, by definition, a suspended status of reality. Many of the images that circulate on our computer screens raise our suspicion and incredulity. As Boltanski (1999) noted, the crisis of pity is linked to the fact that the distance is always greater, not just from the object of the image, but also from the narrator, so that we have no criteria to establish their authenticity. The spectacle of human rights violations has the paradoxical effect of rendering them more distant rather than closer to us. As we have seen in chapter 6, the paradox of the spectacle is precisely that it separates us in the moment that it brings us together.

An example taken from Italian political events illustrates this ambivalence. The right to free medical care is said to be a fundamental human right by the Italian Constitution, and all residents on Italian soil have, until recently, benefited from it.[24] In February 2009 the Italian government made two contrasting decisions. On the one hand, it tried to pass an executive order to prevent doctors from fulfilling the desire of the parents of a woman in a desperate vegetative condition of separating her body from the machines that had kept her alive for seventeen years.[25] Medical assistance—so the argument went—is a fundamental human right that cannot be denied any human being, not even bodies that are in a vegetative condition. Recall here that one of the major sources of legitimacy for contemporary imaginal politics is indeed the conservative reproduction of life, which explains the relentlessness of Italian politicians in that regard.

At the same time, the government discussed a series of laws on immigration (the so-called security package) that invited doctors to report illegal immigrants who ask their medical advice. The law amounts to negating the right to medical assistance insofar as immigrants without a valid residency permit risk deportation by asking for medical care. Both decisions were accompanied by huge media campaigns. The first depicted the woman who was nothing more than a vegetative body with images from her life before entering into the vegetative condition; these images, circulating through the media, depicted a beautiful and lively teen the government was now trying to protect from cruel parents and doctors who were willing to kill her. The second campaign, never explicitly associated with the former, pictured immigrants as criminals, thieves, and rapists. Through the imaginal, a vegetative body is given humanity, while millions of immigrants are simultaneously denied it. The imaginal lies at the heart of this paradox: the same people are not only able to impose the right to medical care on those who do not want to take recourse to it but also to take it away from others who most desperately need it. The right to life is sacred, but, in the end, the life of some is more sacred than that of others.

Let me conclude with a quotation from Primo Levi's *Se questo è un uomo (If This Is a Man)*. In the 1976 appendix to a book that describes the dehumanization Levi suffered in a Nazi concentration camp, he observes that in the Germany of Hitler there was a particular habit of silence: those who knew did not talk, and those who did not know raised no questions. In this way, the German citizens defended their ignorance: closing their mouths, eyes, and ears, they could construct the illusion of not knowing and thus not being accomplices. "The world we westerners live in today," writes Primo Levi, "has many shortcomings and dangers, but in one respect at least presents a significant advantage over the world of yesterday: everybody may instantly know everything about everything. . . . It is very easy: listen to the radio of your country or of any other country if you like, or go to the kiosk and choose the newspaper you prefer" (Levi 2005:159; translation mine). Or, we may add, just turn on your computer. Not only can we know, but knowing has never been easier—even easier than in 1976, at the time Levi was writing. We know. Therefore we have no excuse, unless, perhaps, that we know too much.

THE FREEDOM OF EQUALS
A Conclusion and a New Beginning

Wo aber Gefahr ist, wächst:
Das Rettende auch
J. C. F. HÖLDERLIN, *Patmos*

We are all on the same boat,
and the boat is sinking
OCCUPY WALL STREET SLOGAN

We have seen in this book that politics has always been imaginal. The technical transformations of contemporary capitalism have tightened the link between politics and the imaginal to such a degree that we can no longer ignore this fact. We have reached a critical threshold: the quantitative and qualitative changes to the imaginal are such that images are no longer what mediate our doing politics, but that which risks doing politics in our stead.

If Hölderlin is right in the passage quoted above, that where there is a danger the rescue grows as well, a question emerges: what are the available paths for dealing with the transformations described in this book? A first strategy consists in a critical examination of the power of the imaginal itself. Contemporary political philosophy, focused as it is on the conditions for public reason and the reasonable, has, to a large extent, overlooked discussing public imagination and the imaginal. A reorientation of the priorities of critical theory is needed if we are to avoid the risk of losing control of the imaginal. This book is meant to be a contribution in that direction.

The second strategy is instead more imaginative and calls upon us to imagine things differently. If, at the beginning of the nineties, Fukuyama could still earn worldwide celebrity by stating that we have trouble imagining a world that is radically better than the liberal and capitalistic one we live in (Fukuyama 1992), at the beginning of the new millennium, in an epoch of the alleged clash of civilizations and economic crisis, it is hard to still believe in false prophecies about the end of history. We not only need a bigger piece of cake for everyone, but also different ingredients for a different cake. And the evocative power of new images of the world is a useful starting point for designing a different recipe.

As we have seen over the course of this book, reactivating imagination and producing new images is made particularly difficult by the fact that we are image saturated. However, we should remember that new possibilities can also emerge in the "reorientation" of existing ones. As Buck-Morss puts it, reorientation may be the revolution of our times (Buck-Morss 2011). What I want to do in these concluding remarks is recover an old image, that of humanity as a boat, and explore the way in which it has been reoriented in recent times. In particular, I will try to show that such an image embodies a conception of freedom particularly suited to face the challenges of our epoch. From the new global movements of the early 2000s to the Arab revolts of 2011 and the Occupy Wall Street movement, which has recently spread all over the United States, a certain image of freedom, understood as a freedom of equals, has emerged. It is a peculiar understanding of freedom, where two traditions of thought that have often gone together, but also at times drastically departed from one another, anarchism and Marxism, converge. It is in an image of freedom that draws from both these traditions that we can find a conclusion, but also a new beginning for our imaginal politics.

In 1967 Italian anarchist Belgrado Pedrini wrote a poem that depicts a miserable galleon, manned by slaves, deprived of freedom. Days and nights pass and nothing changes until someone starts to incite her fellow slaves to revolt by pointing out that they have nothing to lose and everything to gain from the rebellion:

Siamo la ciurma anemica	We are the anemic crew
d'una galera infame	of an infamous galley
su cui ratta la morte	on which quick death
miete per lenta fame.	cuts down slowly as we grow hungry.
Mai orizzonti limpidi	Never do clear horizons
schiude la nostra aurora	open up our dawn
e sulla tolda squallida	and on the squalid deck
urla la scolta ognora.	cries the guard all day long.
I nostri dì si involano	Our days pass as we sail
fra fetide carene,	through fetid careens,
siam magri smunti schiavi	we are thin and pale slaves
stretti in ferro catene.	bound together by iron chains.

Sorge sul mar la luna	The moon rises above the sea
ruotan le stelle in cielo	stars revolve in the sky at night
ma sulle nostre luci	but, for us, a funeral veil
steso è un funereo velo.	lies draped over our lights.
Torme di schiavi adusti	Swarms of scorched slaves
chini a gemer sul remo	bent to groan over the oar,
spezziam queste catene	let us break these chains
o chini a remar morremo!	or we will die bent to row!
Cos'è gementi schiavi	Tell me, groaning slaves,
questo remar remare?	why do we row just to row?
Meglio morir tra i flutti	Better to die among the waves
sul biancheggiar del mare.	on a sea of whitening foam.
Remiam finché la nave	Let us row until the ship
si schianti sui frangenti,	dashes against the reef,
alte le rossonere	raise the black and red
fra il sibilar dei venti!	upon the whistling breeze!
E sia pietosa coltrice	And let the frothy wave
l'onda spumosa e ria	be a pitiful place to lay
ma sorga un dì sui martiri	but let the sun of anarchy
il sol dell'anarchia.	rise o'er the martyrs one day.
Su schiavi all'armi all'armi!	Rise, slaves, to arms, to arms!
L'onda gorgoglia e sale	Oh, gurgling waves and brine
tuoni baleni e fulmini	thunder and lightening clash
sul galeon fatale.	above the fateful galleon.
Su schiavi all'armi, all'armi!	Rise, slaves, to arms, to arms!
Pugnam col braccio forte!	Let us strike with all our strength
Giuriam giuriam giustizia!	Justice, we swear, justice!
O libertà o morte!	Give us liberty or give us death!

(Pedrini 2001a:69; translation mine)

The image of the galleon conveys a crucial political message. In contrast with the biblical ark of Noah, this is a galleon where 99 percent of its travelers are slaves.

If you are on their side, you do not have anything to lose from the revolt. On the contrary, you have all to gain, as slaves are the overwhelming majority that makes the galleon work. This is because, as the rowers on the same galleon, we are so dependent on one another that it becomes impossible to be free alone. Even the master will constantly be threatened by the slavery of others, because he depends on them. There is no intermediate option: we are either all free or all slaves.

Pedrini's biography is not dissimilar to that of many anarchists who lived through the troubled years of the Italian fascist regime.[1] Hounded for his anti-fascism, he was finally imprisoned for the death of a fascist policeman in a clash between a group of anarchists and the fascist secret police (Pedrini 2001b). A few years later, he was liberated by the partisans and fought in the Resistance against the fascists and the Nazi army. After the end of the war, the newly constituted Italian republic recognized the importance of this fight, but still put him back in jail. He remained there for thirty years, notwithstanding the numerous international campaigns for his liberation. Why?

For the Italian state, Pedrini was a criminal, a normal murderer. The fact that he had killed the policeman because he was a fascist, who was just about to shoot him and his comrades, did not matter. His true crime, it would seem, was being an anarchist. Like many of his anarchist comrades he had to be banned because he was truly subversive of the status quo. The fact that the ministry of justice was in the hands of the communist Palmiro Togliatti did not help; hostility between communists and anarchists was, at the time, perhaps even stronger than that between communists and fascists.

However, it is precisely in Pedrini's galleon that we find the symbol of a peculiar view of freedom that, so I will argue, represents the platform for the convergence of anarchism and Marxism. Pedrini's image tells us two important things: first, we are all in the same boat and, second, the freedom of every individual strictly depends on that of all others. You cannot be free alone, because freedom can only be realized as a freedom of equals. With this expression I do not mean that we have to be free *and* equals, but that no one can be free unless we are all equally so.[2]

There is, I will contend, a significant convergence between Marxism and anarchism in that they both conceive of freedom in this way. There are some historical antecedents to this view, in that various philosophers conceived of equality as a precondition for freedom. But the contribution of classical anarchist thinkers to this view is all too often neglected, even within contemporary critical theory. This is all the more striking, since it seems to be a particularly timely view. What is distinctive of the anarchist tradition is indeed its global vocation, its capacity to think of the freedom of equals outside any national framework: either all human beings living on this planet are equally free, or they are equally slaves. Equals, as we will see, are not the members of a specific community, but rather all the individuals on this planet—a view that has become particularly timely in an epoch when the modern image of a world divided into nation-states has begun to crumble. After exploring the meaning of this conception of freedom and distinguishing it from that of autonomy, I will argue that today's social, economic, and political conditions render this view particularly timely and thus call for overcoming the historical divisions between anarchism and Marxism. The ban on the black and red flag that led Pedrini to prison is still there, but perhaps the time has come to lift it.

At the beginning was freedom. It is commonplace to say that freedom is the crucial issue for anarchism, so much so that some have claimed that this word summarizes the essence of the entire anarchist doctrine and credo. There are good reasons to argue that freedom is also the crucial problem for Marx, who, from his very early writings, is concerned with the conditions for human emancipation. Indeed, the entire path of his thought could be described as a reflection on the conditions for freedom, understood first as a more general human emancipation and, later on, as freedom from exploitation in light of his theory of surplus value.[3] I will first illustrate this view of freedom and distinguish it from that of freedom as autonomy; then I will show that Marxism and anarchism can provide each other the antidote to their possible degeneration.

Why is freedom so fundamental to these movements and, moreover, what is this freedom? Max Stirner's phrase is helpful. In *The Ego and Its Own*, Stirner (1990) observes that most theories of society pursue the following issue: "What is the essence of man? What is its nature?" As such, they either expressly begin with such a question or take it as their implicit starting point. However, he notes, the true question is not *what* is the human being, but rather *who*: and the answer is that "I," in my uniqueness, am the human being. In other words, we should not start with an abstract theory about a presumed essence or (which is equivalent) the nature of the human being, but with the simple fact that "I" am, here and now, in my uniqueness. Otherwise said, there is no other possible beginning because, as an answer to the "who?" question, "I've set my cause on nothing" ("Ich hab' mein' Sach' auf nichts gestellt"; Stirner 1990:41, 351).

It may appear paradoxical to start with a quotation from Stirner, an author who has been very much criticized within both Marxism and anarchism for his strong individualism. But it is nevertheless a helpful starting point to think about the centrality of freedom: freedom is at the beginning, because at the beginning there is the "who?" question, and its answer—the being endowed with the capacity to say "I am." The ego is at the beginning as activity, as the capacity to move and speak, and here lies the roots of its capacity to be free. And yet, if this interpretation is correct, and the being who says "I am" cannot but be a being endowed with language, then it follows that Stirner's deduction of a radical individualism, which depicts a continual war between the individual and society, is contradictory. The individual cannot be at "total war" with society, as Stirner claims, because the individual is, to a large extent, its own product.

The ability to speak presupposes language and hence a plurality of "egos" because language can never be learned without such a plurality. An entirely asocial being, such as the one that Stirner depicts, would be a speechless being. So if Stirner is right in identifying this primordial activity of consciousness, as the starting point for thinking about freedom, he is nevertheless wrong in deducing from it a radical egoism. His individualism, which he presents as a rigorous logical deduction, may then well be the historically identifiable egoism of the then emerging European bourgeoisie, as Karl Marx and Friedrich Engels suggest in their "The German Ideology" (Marx and Engels 1976:1, 3). To use another Marxian expression, we can say that the very idea of an individual separated from all other individuals is a "Robinsonade" (Marx 1978d:221), a fantastic desert island, which is nothing but the imaginary representation of the concrete economic development of a specific epoch.

But such an isolated and unrelated individual cannot exist, in the first place because the mere possibility to speak presupposes a being endowed with language. The human being does not become social at a discrete point in time and for the sake of particular purposes, but she is so from the very beginning. We do not create society but are, rather, created by it. In one of his lectures on anarchy, Mikhail Bakunin (1996:28) illustrates this point through the example of an infant endowed with the most brilliant faculties. If thrown in a desert at a very young age, such a being will perish or else survive but become a brute, deprived of speech, and all the other traits that we usually associate with humanity. Together with speech, she will also be lacking in the development of proper thinking, because there cannot be any thought without words. While it is true that one may also reflect through images, in order to *articulate* a complex thought one needs words, words that can only be learned by interacting with other human beings.

This view lies at the heart of Bakunin's idea that you can be free only if everybody else is free (Bakunin 1996, 2000). Otherwise stated, freedom can only be a freedom of equals. If this view appears paradoxical, this is because we have so internalized the ideological construction of the human being as an independent individual that we have difficulties representing freedom as a relation, rather than as a property with which separate individuals are endowed. Let me illustrate this view in more detail.

According to Bakunin, because human beings are so dependent on one another, you cannot be free in isolation, but only through the web of reciprocal interdependence. Although quite refined in its developments, the view is not far from a commonsense understanding of the term *freedom*. Freedom, in Bakunin's view, consists "in the right to obey nobody other than myself and to determine my acts in conformity with my convictions, mediated through the equally free consciousness of everybody" (1996:81). Freedom is, therefore, the capacity to do what I want, to act in conformity with my convictions, but—and here is the refinement—in order to know what my own convictions are, I need the mediation of the "equally free consciousness of everybody." This is a view of freedom that resonates with typically Hegelian themes; however, as will be clear later on, it is a view that Bakunin will bring far from Hegel (and the Hegelians) by extending it to humanity as whole, a whole that transcends social, political and even historical borders.

We can clearly see how such a view differs from the mainstream liberal view of freedom as self-determination as well. According to Bakunin, there is no such thing as an isolated self that can determine her/himself independently of other human beings. This is a point where Marx and Bakunin, with their Hegelian background, patently converge (and the list could be extended to many other exponents of both traditions). According to such a view, social contract theories are wrong, not just because they assume that society is not coeval with human beings but also because they take the single individual, separated from all others, as the starting point of their inquiry. As Marx acutely observes, this image of the individual as a discrete being is an ideological construction, because primitive human beings are far from being the free independent beings depicted by social contract theorists: the freedom they attribute to the individual in the supposed state of nature is in fact that very freedom constructed by members of modern civil society and thus not the freedom of the beginning of history, but rather that of its bourgeois phase (Marx 1978d:222).

In response to the social contract theorists—today all too often in vogue—both Marx and Bakunin argue that the human being is determined by her position within society. In a passage that echoes contemporary theorists of the technologies of the self (such as Michel Foucault),[4] Bakunin (2000:85) observes that it is not individuals who create society, but the society that, so to speak, "individualizes itself in every individual." Bakunin is well aware that freedom as self-determination is empty if there is no such thing as a "self" that can autonomously choose. The crucial point of freedom, then, is not simply doing what I want, but rather being sure that what I believe to be the fruit of my free choice actually is. If I am led by the circumstances of my life to believe that my servitude is either immutable or even desirable, there is no way I can be free. It is the dilemma of voluntary servitude, and therefore of the techniques through which compliant subjects are created, that has been at the center of anarchist thinking for a long time.[5]

In Bakunin's view, human beings are determined by both material and representational social factors. When still in the womb of their mother, every human being is already determined by a high number of geographical, climatic, and economic factors that constitute the material nature of their social condition (86). In addition to this series of material factors, which Marx investigated in far greater detail, Bakunin also mentions a series of beliefs, ideas, and representations that are equally crucial. Again, in an extremely timely passage, Bakunin observes that every generation finds a whole ready-made world of ideas, images, and sentiments that it inherits from previous epochs (87).[6] They do not present themselves to the newborn as a system of ideas, since children would not be able to apprehend them in this form. Rather, such a world of ideas imposes itself as a world of "personified facts," made concrete in the persons and things that surround them, as a world that speaks to their senses early on through whatever they see and hear (87).[7] Put in more contemporary words, we can say with Castoriadis (1987) that individuals are at the same time instituting and instituted by society: society does not exist without the individuals that constantly create and re-create it, but, at the same time, individuals exist only as a product of society itself.

But if individuals are at the same time instituting and instituted, if, to use Bakunin's phrase, individuals are nothing but the society that individualizes itself in them, then you cannot be free unless everybody else is free—hence also the importance of the notion of recognition in Bakunin: "For the individual to be free means to be recognized, considered and treated as such by another individual, and by all the individuals that surrounds him" (Bakunin 2000:92; translation mine). To recognize freedom, you need the mediation of the imaginary significations of society. Freedom implies recognition, to be recognized and to recognize the other as free.[8] Masters who do not recognize the freedom of their slaves are—for this very reason—also not free. In this way, they contribute to perpetuating the image of slavery within the society of which they are a part, and this very slavery will come back to them, in one form or another. As Errico Malatesta, puts it, by quoting Bakunin,

> No man can achieve his own emancipation without at the same time working for the emancipation of all men around him. My freedom is the freedom of all since I am not truly free in thought and in fact, except when my freedom and my rights are confirmed and approved in the freedom and rights of all men who are my equals. It matters to me very much what other men are, because however independent I may appear to be or think I am, because of my social position, were I Pope, Tzar, Emperor or even Prime Minister, I remain always the product of what the humblest among them are: if they are ignorant, poor, slaves, my existence is determined by their slavery. I, an enlightened or intelligent man am, for instance—in the event—rendered stupid by their stupidity; as a courageous man I am enslaved by their slavery; as a rich man I tremble before their poverty; as a privileged person I blanch at their justice. I who want to be free cannot be because all the men around me do not yet want to be free, and consequently they become tools of oppression against me.
>
> (Malatesta 2001:23)

This is a very radical idea of freedom, but one that, if read in light of recent developments, is more timely today than ever before. In sum, freedom is inevitably a freedom of equals, because I cannot be free if everybody else around me is not free, or, which is the same thing, if I do not have both the material and cognitive means to realize my freedom. We are imbued with the customs, ideas, and images that dominate our society. Human beings are not independent selves who, like billiard balls, collide with each other on a green baize table. They are bodies that are instituting and instituted by the society in which they live. There are two main consequences that follow from such a view.

The first is that, however abstract this view may appear, it can only be realized in a very concrete way. Not by chance, Bakunin (2000:91; translation mine) calls it a "materialist conception of freedom" and opposes it to the idealistic one. If freedom is to be realized not just by a separate self (which does not exist), but through society as a whole, it follows that an entire reorganization of society is necessary for its realization. For Bakunin, this implies a restructuring of society from below, according to the principle of free association and federation (96). But why is this so? Free federalism follows from a view of freedom articulated in three moments. First, Bakunin says, there is the positive, social moment that consists in the development of all human faculties and potentialities through education and material well-being—all things that can be acquired only through the psychic and intellectual work of the whole society (82). This is a view very close to Marx's positive conception of freedom, according to which freedom does not consist in the negative capacity to avoid this or that, but in the positive power to develop our potential.[9] The basic idea is that abstract civil and political rights are empty words if we do not have the material and the intellectual means to exercise them.

The second moment for the realization of free federalism is instead more negative: Bakunin calls it "the moment of the revolt" (82; translation mine). It is the revolt against every authority, human or divine. First and foremost, it is a revolt against God, because, in Bakunin's words, "as long as we have a master in the sky, we will not be free on earth" (82). At times Bakunin seems to have a very traditional idea of God, but I think we can extend his thought to all forms of transcendent authority. If we believe that we owe a divine authority unconditional obedience, we are necessarily slaves to it, as well as to its intermediaries, such as ministers, prophets, or messiahs (82). That is why Bakunin strongly criticized nationalism as a new form of "political theology": by presenting the "nation" as a transcendent being, to which obedience is due just because it is our supposed "fatherland," nationalists such as Giuseppe Mazzini have replaced a God in the sky with another one on earth (Bakunin 1974). We begin here to see why Bakunin's notion of freedom so strongly differs from any Hegelian understanding of it: far from celebrating the nation-state as the culminating point of ethical life, Bakunin calls for its elimination as a pernicious form of political theology.

The revolt against God and transcendent authority must indeed be combined with revolt against specifically human authority. Here Bakunin introduces a fine distinction between the legal and formal authority of the state and what he calls the "tyranny of the society" (Bakunin 1974). The revolt against the first is easier because the enemy can straightforwardly be identified, but the revolt against the second is much more complicated because, to a large extent, we are its products. Society, as we have seen, exercises its tyranny through customs, traditions, sentiments, prejudices, and habits on both our material and intellectual life. Part of its influence is natural and we cannot escape it (Bakunin 2000:84); however, part of it is not. Bakunin seems to believe that education and scientific knowledge are sufficient to this end, but I believe that we have grounds today to be more skeptical. Knowledge is not enough. Knowledge does not liberate from power, because it is itself power. The production of scientific knowledge is no exception to the tyranny of society, because, as Foucault has shown us, it may even be the chief means for the domestication of revolt and the creation of compliant subjects.[10] Natural and social sciences, such as chemistry, demography, and sociology, have all proved to be potential means to discipline and domesticate human beings rather than to liberate them.

Where to start then? Where to get liberation from the subtle tyranny that society exercises through its customs, traditions, and sentiments? Here, I believe, enters the more radical interpretation of federalism. The old anarchist motto "multiply your associations and be free" can indeed be seen as a multiplication of both the political, but also the social and imaginal ties one is subjected to. By entering into contact with different images and expanding one's knowledge of different regimes of truth, it is possible to find a moment of friction where the tyranny of society breaks down. As I will try to show, it is here that, particularly today, the possibility of freedom lies.

Before I do so, let me briefly illustrate the second main consequence of this conception of freedom as a freedom of equals. Recovering this view today is an implicit invitation to go beyond freedom understood as autonomy. There are many possible definitions of autonomy, but the most important (because it is the most influential) is that which goes back to its etymology: *autonomy* literally means *autos* and *nomos*, to give the law to oneself. From this original meaning, and through the influence of philosophers such as Rousseau and Kant, the term came to mean self-determination more generally, as if every determination would be a subjection to law (which, I believe, is far from being the case). I cannot enter into the details of the historical path of the concept of autonomy, but let me just briefly mention the deep influence that it has exercised, until very recently, on liberal and democratic thought.[11]

Of course, the concept of autonomy has not been immune to criticism. The most obvious is that it presupposes a "self" that actually gives a law to herself. As we have already suggested, this assumption is far from being unquestioned. Furthermore, the idea of a separate self is an assumption that inevitably leads to what we may call a "limitative view of freedom." If we believe that human beings are self-enclosed selves, endowed with autonomy, the problem necessarily becomes that of restricting such autonomy in order to make space for the autonomy of others. Like billiard balls colliding on a green baize table, the freedoms of individuals must eventually conflict with one another, and the problem inevitably becomes that of limiting them. By contrast, if we assume that we are the product of the society we live in, a different perspective emerges: the problem is no longer how to *limit* freedom, but rather how to *enhance* it. In other words, the imperative is no longer "limit freedom, so that everybody can enjoy it," but rather "create it, because it may not be there yet."

Different authors have tried to address the problem of autonomy. Radical thinkers such as Castoriadis in France and the Workerists in Italy have, for instance, tried to solve the dilemma by arguing that autonomy is also a social enterprise. The latter argued for the autonomy of the proletariat, showing that agency is immanent to its spontaneous action and does not need the guiding role of the party.[12] On the other side, Castoriadis, as we have seen, articulated the project of autonomy in relation to the problem of the imaginary significations within which we all are socialized (Castoriadis 1987). In his view, you are autonomous if you are at the origins of what will be (*arche ton esomenon* as Aristotle used to say) and you know yourself to be so (Castoriadis 1987:479). Autonomy means that your discourse has to take the place of what is given as the discourse of the others—a view that, similar to Bakunin's, stresses the importance of the cognitive means for the realization of freedom.

These interventions have certainly brought the discussion on the problem of autonomy much further than where modern liberal thinking had left it. However, as I will now try to argue, focusing on autonomy alone is misleading. Autonomy may also be an important condition for freedom, but it is only one part of it. You cannot be free without being autonomous, but being autonomous does not automatically mean being free. This particularly emerges if we consider that the contrary of *autonomy* is *heteronomy*, a condition where one is given the law by somebody else, whereas the opposite of *freedom* is *domination*, something that can occur in ways *other* than simply being given the law by somebody else.[13] The tyranny of society can take place in many different ways that go well beyond lawgiving and include even self-oppression and voluntary servitude. In sum, freedom and autonomy, from a conceptual perspective, only partially overlap. For those who are skeptical of analytic philosophical distinctions, just consider common language. I can say that my child is very autonomous because she can dress herself, eat, and walk on her own, but by no means does this amount to her freedom.

To sum up, to be autonomous does not yet mean to be free. But this is not just an issue of semantics. It is a question of conceptual clarity that has crucial consequences for the practice of freedom. For instance, many autonomist movements gave rise to utopian communities, based on the principle of autonomy understood as the main road to the realization of freedom. Let us admit for the moment that one could still realize completely autonomous communities in our globalizing world. The question is, "are the people living in such communities really free?" My impression is that they are (possibly) autonomous in the sense of being (materially) independent from the outside, but they are by no means free and perhaps not even self-determined. If you live in a self-imposed ghetto, separated from the rest of the world, you are not free because you cannot live where you want, nor are you self-determined inasmuch as your choice to live in that particular community is imposed by some external factors.

Thinkers such as Paul Goodman may, therefore, be right in saying that autonomy is a necessary step for freedom. In his view, this is because the problem with oppressed people lusting for freedom is that, if they manage to break free, they do not know what to do with such freedom (Goodman 2009:331). Not having been autonomous, they do not know how to go about it and usually learn it too late. New managers will have taken over, and they may or may not be benevolent and imbued with the ideals of revolution, but they will never be in a hurry to abdicate. Autonomy is therefore, so to speak, an important school for freedom. Yet it still remains only one part of it. The critics of the concept of freedom, like Goodman, who argue that freedom is a cumbersome metaphysical concept, are perhaps right. Autonomy is much thinner and therefore at least apparently easier to realize. However, such critics are also mistaken in that they do not realize it is a burden we have to take on if we want to avoid the self-imposed ghetto of autonomy.

I have tried to illustrate why Marxism and anarchism converge in the idea that freedom can only be a freedom of equals. What I want to do in the remaining is argue that a marriage between Marxism and anarchism is particularly beneficial in that, in each other, they can find a reciprocal antidote to their possible degenerations, as contemporary social movements have shown. First, anarchism finds in Marxism a good antidote to prevent a possible individualist twist on its absolutization of freedom. It is a fact that the radical praise of freedom that characterizes anarchism in its historical manifestations has declined in both directions: the individual and the social. According to the former, freedom is mainly the freedom of the individual, whereas, according to the latter, which we have analyzed here through Bakunin, freedom can be attained only collectively.[14]

The point is not only that, historically speaking, an individualist interpretation of anarchism has proven to be possible. Much more radically, individualism is a temptation that is always present within anarchism. We began by considering Stirner's advocacy of a radical egoism, but many other examples may be added. One only has to think of anarcho-capitalism, which, particularly in the United States, combines an emphasis on freedom with advocacy for the unrestricted development of capitalism.[15] One may simply dismiss these positions as fallacious Robinsonades, but the point remains that they are still influential because they align with the prevailing individualist assumptions that underpin our societies.

In light of the difficulties encountered in promoting the realization of the freedom of equals on a large scale, leftists may easily fall into the individualist temptation and limit their fight for the realization of spaces of autonomy in small self-enclosed communities. This, I believe, is the risk that many autonomist movements have fallen into in the past without realizing that the creation of autonomous communities may well turn into a form of individualism on a large scale. The creation of such self-enclosed spaces is usually justified on the basis of the argument that they prefigure what a free society might look like, but they risk prefiguring nothing but what society actually is: individuals, singular or collective, pursuing their own interests in isolation.

Marxism provides a powerful antidote for this possible degeneration. Marx's critique of Robinsonades can be extended at all levels to concretely support the idea that either we are all free or all equally slaves. The reason Marxism is better equipped than traditional anarchism to make this point (as we have seen, Bakunin equally supported the idea of freedom as freedom of equals) is that it more emphatically focused on the economic conditions for the realization of such a freedom. Few intellectuals have embarked on such an extensive analysis of the concrete economic conditions for the realization of freedom as did Marx. His critique of utopian socialism (and, more generally, the idea that to describe an ideal state of things will automatically engender change simply because of its intrinsic intellectual value) is a powerful reminder of the dangers of any abstract metaphysics of freedom. By envisaging utopian communities on the sole basis of the fanatic belief in the miraculous effects of one's theory, one risks ending up in a reactionary position, unable to keep pace with the current state of the world.[16]

I cannot enter here into a detailed reading of Marx's analysis of capitalism and modernity. To be sure, there are parts of it that are outdated—in particular as a result of the novelties brought about by post-Fordism and flexible capitalism.[17] Let me simply point out what I believe are the most timely aspects of Marx's work. In the first place, there is the analysis of capitalism's capacity to overcome all sorts of political barriers. We live in an epoch where there is so much talk about globalization and the crisis of the nation-state vis-à-vis the capacity of the economy to go beyond national boundaries, but this is something that nobody predicted more acutely and precisely than Marx. In many places in his work he talks about capitalism's capacity to transcend national boundaries. Consider, for example, the following passage from the "Manifesto of the Communist Party," which he wrote with Engels:

The bourgeoisie has through its exploitation of the world market given a cosmopolitan character to production and consumption in every country. . . . In the place of old wants, satisfied by the productions of the country, we find new wants, requiring for their satisfaction the products of distant lands and climes. In place of the old local and national seclusion and self-sufficiency, we have intercourse in every direction, universal interdependence of nations. And as in material, so also in intellectual production. The intellectual creations of individual nations become common property. National one-sidedness and narrow-mindedness become more and more impossible, and from the numerous national and local literatures, there arises a world literature.

(Marx and Engels 1978:477–478)

In a time when there is so much talk about the novelty of globalization that, so many argue, calls for a new form of cosmopolitanism, it is worth returning to this passage. Here Marx and Engels clearly point to the "cosmopolitan character" of capitalistic production and consumption, to the fact that with the heavy artillery of the "cheap prices of its commodities" capitalism will batter down all Chinese walls (8), so that in place of the old local and national self-sufficiency we have "intercourse in every direction" on both the material and cognitive level (477). One cannot but be struck by the timeliness of these remarks. It has become something like a commonplace to say that we live in a globalizing world, where material and cultural boundaries are being challenged from different sides. I think only the historical amnesia of a generation of scholars that, after 1989, has too quickly become militantly "ex-Marxist" can explain how it is possible to talk so much about globalization without ever mentioning the author who most emphatically and accurately predicted it more than a century ago.

Marx's economic analysis gave further support to the concept of freedom of equals as well with his pathbreaking analysis of commodity fetishism (Marx 1976:163–177). If Bakunin is right in saying that freedom has to be a freedom of equals because from the beginning we are subjected to the tyranny of a society that imposes its material and representational significations on our minds and bodies, then it is precisely from the possible commodification of such significations that we have to start. Perhaps only the visionary Guy Debord (1994) has sufficiently underlined this point with his idea of a society of the spectacle.[18] As we have seen, Debord recovered Marx's fundamental insight about commodity fetishism and brought it to a further level, arguing that "in societies dominated by modern conditions of production, life is presented as an immense accumulation of *spectacles*" (thesis 1). We live in a society of spectacles that rests on the commodification of the imaginal, within which all of us are socialized. The global spectacle we live in is imbued with commodity fetishism to the point that even our bodies are constituted by it.

However, it is not only anarchism that needs Marxism if a freedom of equals is to be realized. Anarchism plays an equally crucial role because it contains the antidote for a possible statist and authoritarian degeneration of Marxism. Marx remained vague about the path to the realization of freedom. If it is clear that, according to him, the freedom of equals can only be obtained through a radical revolution that subverts the capitalist system of production, the ways to bring about such a revolution remain open to dispute and change considerably in his various works. Whereas Marx is ambiguous on this point and in some places does not hesitate to speak of a "dictatorship of the proletariat" as a necessary transition period from a capitalist to a communist society,[19] Bakunin is crystal clear: if freedom is the end, freedom must also be the means to realize that end. As Bakunin (2000:98), and Malatesta (2001:52) after him, put it, to endanger freedom under the pretext of protecting it—be it through the dictatorship of the proletariat or an avant-garde party that could authoritatively lead the masses to the revolution—is dangerous nonsense that cannot but ultimately destroy freedom itself.

Incidentally, this insight will lead to Bakunin's expulsion from the International Workingmen's Association, then dominated by Marx and the German social democrats. If Marx was ambiguous in his writings, he was much less so in calling for Bakunin's ban on the basis of his unorthodox views.[20] However, the experience of the Soviet Union showed that Bakunin was right when he criticized the idea of a dictatorship of the proletariat, along with any other authoritarian attempt to realize the freedom of equals. There is not just one absolute truth about the road to revolution; thus no avant-garde party, no matter how well versed in theory it might be, can ever explain to the masses how they should liberate themselves (Bakunin 1872). If you restrict freedom, albeit temporarily, with the pretext of preparing for its realization, you cannot help but end up destroying it. As a consequence, any workers' state, be it a dictatorship of the proletariat or not, cannot but reproduce the same logic of every state, where a minority of bureaucrats rule over the majority of people, i.e., authoritarianism (Bakunin 1872). To conclude this point, anarchism not only provides the antidote to the statist degeneration of Marxism, but it can, more generally, prevent the authoritarian trap into which any attempt to realize the freedom of equals can fall. This is an antidote that communists of all sorts need, since, as Proudhon pointed out very clearly, communism can well be realized through the principle of authority itself (Proudhon 2001:125–133).[21] Anarchism, by contrast, cannot.

One of the reasons why anarchism contains an antidote is that anarchist thinkers work with a more variegated notion of domination that emphasizes the power of noneconomic forms of exploitation. Hence also its happier marriage with feminism: if the relationship between Marxism and feminism has been

characterized overall as a problematic one, in which the same logic of domination going on between the two sexes has been reproduced between them (Arruzza 2010; Sargent 1981), the relationship between feminism and anarchism
seems to be a much more convivial encounter. Historically, the two have con-
verged so often that some have argued that anarchism is by definition feminism
(Brown 1990; Kornegger 2009 [1975]). The point is not simply to register the
historical fact that, from Michail Bakunin to Emma Goldman, and with the only
exception of Proudhon, anarchism and feminism often went hand in hand. This
historical fact signals a deeper theoretical affinity. You can be a Marxist without
being a feminist, but you cannot be an anarchist without being a feminist. If anarchism is a philosophy that opposes all hierarchies, including those that cannot
be reduced to economic exploitation, it has to oppose the subjection of women
too, for otherwise it is incoherent with its own principles. Within the conception
of freedom we have highlighted, where I cannot be free unless everyone else is
equally free, the subjection of women cannot be reduced to something that concerns only a part of society: a patriarchal society will be fundamentally oppressive for both sexes, precisely because I cannot be free on my own.

If it is true that, anarchism is by definition feminism, does the opposite hold?
Can there be feminists who are not anarchists? It is true that, historically speaking, many feminist movements have not been anarchist. However, some feminists
claimed that feminism, and in particular the second-wave feminism of the 1970s,
was anarchist in its deep structure and aspirations. According to Peggy Kornegger
(2009), for instance, radical feminists of this period were unconscious anarchists
both in their theories and their practices. The structure of women's groups (e.g.,
consciousness-raising groups), with their emphasis on small groups as the basic
organizational unit, on "the personal is political," and on spontaneous direct action, bore a striking resemblance to typically anarchistic forms of organization
(494). But even more striking is the conceptual convergence with the conception
of freedom that I have described. For instance, Kornegger also emphasizes that
"liberation is not an insular experience" because it can only occur in conjunction
with all other human beings (496), which is another way of saying that freedom
cannot but be a freedom of equals.

This also means that one cannot fight patriarchy without fighting all other
forms of hierarchy, be they economic or political. As Kornegger (493) again puts
it, "feminism does not mean female corporate power or a woman president: it
means no corporate power and no president." In this view, therefore, feminism
does not mean that women should take the place occupied by men; rather, the
point is to radically subvert the logic of domination where sexism, economic ex-

ploitation, and political oppression reciprocally reinforce one another, although with different forms in different contexts.

This holds even more so today, in a globalizing world where different forms of oppression and exploitation, whether based on gender, race, or class, sustain each other. Perhaps the greatest contribution of third-wave feminism is that it pointed toward the need for a multifaceted analysis of domination, with its emphasis on postcolonialism and intersectionality (Chanter 2006:90-111). For if, by feminism, we understand simply the fight for formal equality between men and women, we risk creating new forms of oppression. We take the risk that equality between men and women will only signify that women must take positions once reserved for white bourgeois males, thus further reinforcing mechanisms of oppression rather than subverting them. For instance, if we take the emancipation of white women to simply mean entering the public sphere on an equal footing with males, this, in turn, may simply imply that somebody else has to replace these women in their households. But for the immigrant woman who replaces the white housewife in providing domestic care, this is not liberation: she simply exits her household in order to enter into another one as a waged laborer. The emancipation of some (white) women risks therefore meaning the oppression of other (immigrant, black, or southern) women if feminism does not aim at dissolving all forms of hierarchy, whether they are entrenched in gender, class, or racial oppression.

To conclude on this point, maybe feminism has not always been historically anarchist, but it should be so because it should aim at subverting all forms of hierarchies, whether sexist, economic, or political. Feminism, today more than in the past, cannot simply mean women rulers or women capitalists: it means no rulers and no capitalism, because you cannot defeat one form of domination without fighting all the others.[22] This means that the conception of freedom highlighted earlier is not only a black and red one, as Pedrini suggested in his poem. If a marriage between black and red, Marxism and anarchism has to take place, both partners will have to be dressed in pink.

This encounter is not simply a demand of theoretical reason. It is not just a marriage that *ought* to take place if the freedom of equals is to be realized. It is something that is inherent to the changes we are witnessing and that, for the sake of brevity, we can summarize under the name of globalization. In simplest terms, there is only one freedom because the world has become one. Globalization does not only mean that there are processes that objectively unify the globe but also, and foremost, that we have come to recognize this fact. In a minimal sense, this has always been the case, because we have always inhabited one and the same planet. What is different today is that we have to recognize this, because it is no longer possible to adopt an exit strategy. We have always been in the same boat; the difference is that now we cannot fail to perceive it.

Let me briefly illustrate what I mean by this. As we have seen, globalization is a set of processes that shifts the spatial form of human organization and activity to transcontinental and interregional patterns of activity, interactions, and exercises of power (see Held et al. 1999). As such, the concept of globalization points to the stretching and deepening of social relations and institutions across space and time. Fluxes from the local to the global and vice versa have unified the planet. The world has become one at all levels: economic, political, military, and cultural. Together with economic globalization comes political globalization: they are inseparable, from many points of view. A promoter of economic and financial globalization, the nation-state seems to be one of its most illustrious victims. To be sure, states are far from vanishing, but they are certainly challenged by a dispersion of sovereignty both above and below them (Strange 1996).

Perhaps the crisis of the nation-state system is most evident in the domain of security. It is in this field where the modern state, at least since Thomas Hobbes, has traditionally, although surreptitiously, drawn the strongest justification for its existence; hence here one can best measure the degree of the crisis. Human beings, so the modern argument went, are led to cede their unconditional freedom to a sovereign power to enhance their individual security.[23] Even admitting that this has ever been the case (and I would deny that it has), it no longer holds true. The state is today patently incapable of guaranteeing the security of it citizens, not only vis-à-vis attacks with nuclear, bacteriological, or other nonconventional weapons but also, and perhaps most important, vis-à-vis ecological and other kinds of man-made global challenges (Cerutti 2007). No single state could ever arrest an epidemiological attack or even simply counteract global warming's effects. Hence sovereignty is dispersed through what some have termed *multilayered global governance* (see Held et al. 1999) and what Negri and Hardt instead termed *empire*.[24]

All this points to the fact that, whether we want it or not, an anarchist turn has already begun. This dispersion of state sovereignty both below and above nation-states closely resembles what anarchists for centuries called federalism. Indeed, if it is true that there is a historical amnesia about Marx's prediction of globalization, there is an even more striking form of amnesia over the contribution of classical anarchists in depicting what a postsovereignty world might look like. Titles such as *The Anarchical Society* (by Hedley Bull), *The End of Sovereignty?* (by Jim Falk and Joseph Camilleri) or even *The Global Covenant* (by David Held) could well have been envisaged by classical anarchists.[25] But they are all books by political thinkers trying to make sense of what is happening in the world, with little awareness of how helpful classical anarchism could be in this enterprise. Conversely, there are many passages in classical anarchist thinkers that could well have been written by one of the contemporary theorists of globalization. Consider the following by Malatesta: "Today the immense development of production, the growth of those requirements that can only be satisfied by the participation of large numbers of people in all countries, the means of communication, with travel becoming a commonplace, science, literature, businesses and even wars, all have drawn mankind into an ever tighter single body whose constituent parts, united among themselves, can only find fulfilment and freedom to develop through the well-being of the other constituent parts as well as of the whole" (Malatesta 2001:24). Malatesta's idea that the development of production, the increase of needs that can only be satisfied through the concourse of everybody, the new means of communication, the habit of traveling, science, literature, and even wars themselves, are tightening humanity into a single body whose parts can only find their freedom in the health of the other parts and of the whole itself—such an idea could well be used as a description for what globalization amounts to today (24). Yet this was instead Malatesta's definition of anarchy. This shows how strong the ban on anarchism still is: anarchy is already there, but it cannot yet be named.

This is, however, only one side of the story. If it is true that an anarchist turn has already begun, we must immediately add that it is far from going in the right direction. Globalization does not only mean a horizontal extension of the chains of interdependence. It also implies an intensification of vertical ones. Power is not only dispersed below and above nation-states, it has also penetrated into the deepest mechanisms of life: in a word, it has become biopower. As we have seen, the biopolitical transformation Hardt and Negri integrated into their concept of empire (Hardt and Negri 2000) was first diagnosed by Foucault, who traced it back to the intimate constitution of modernity. Foucault's major intuition is the idea that while traditionally sovereign power was mainly the power to inflict death, in modernity it becomes a power that is aimed at inciting, promoting, articulating, and, in a word, disciplining life itself. The two poles of such biopower are the body of the individual and the body of the population, whereas the means through which it is exercised are various disciplines such as medicine, biology, statistics, demography, and the science of police.[26] But today biopolitical transformations seem to go beyond Foucault's analysis: they now invest not only modes of governance but also economic production in that it is the whole of our subjectivity that is invested in post-Fordist capitalism (Bazzicalupo 2006).

Today's governance is global both in its spatial dimension and in its inner nature. The fact that people felt the need for a new word (*governance* or *governamentality* instead of *government*) is due to the fact that the thing itself has changed. No longer the centralized, vertical power of the modern nation-state, governance denotes a reticular and decentralized form of power that is enriched by the pervasiveness furnished by new biopolitical technologies. It is a transformation that can offer possibilities for liberation, but also open the path to the most horrible servitude. Power can today more than ever control the deepest mechanism(s) of life, as well as the way in which we imagine it.

Today's governance is global because it governs our bodies as much as it disciplines our minds. The stretching and deepening of the social chains of interdependence also mean the stretching and deepening of the imaginal chains that potentially connect the entire globe. We think globally because the globe has become the horizon of our perception of the world, but also because our images are increasingly intermingled. This is what I have tried to convey with the idea of a global spectacle. The spectacle is not only a set of images but also, and primarily, a social relationship between people mediated through images (Debord 1994:thesis 4). But this means that the way in which we relate to others is mediated by the images we have internalized from a commoditized social imaginary.

Just consider what politics has become and what it used to be. As we have seen, the activity we usually denote with this term is inconceivable without the continual flux of images that enter our screens every day (chapters 5 and 6). The competition among images, like that among every other commodity, is so steep that the golden rule of the audience imposes itself, hence the increasing spectacularization of politics. In one respect, however, Debord was wrong. Similar to Marx before him, he thought it was possible to counterpoise the spectacle with the reality of things (see, for instance, Debord 1994:thesis 7). In our epoch, images have instead become ongoing processes so that there is no longer the possibility of distinguishing between the original and a fake. In other words, the society of the spectacle has become global in the double sense that it has stretched its boundaries to embrace the entire globe, but also in that it has invaded all spheres of life so that one can no longer say where the spectacle ends and real life begins (chapter 6).

Within this scenario, Bakunin's idea that you cannot be free unless everybody else around you is free is more timely than ever. If our being increasingly depends on what other people imagine we are, then it is clear that freedom can only be realized as a freedom of equals. There is no intermediate possibility: we are either all slaves or all free. The new global movements that have emerged worldwide in the last twenty years have shown this very clearly. Note that I use the term *new global* and not *no global*. The reasons why the worldwide media have called a movement that is the result of and even advocates globalization no global is because they looked at it from the point of view of neoliberal ideology itself. The idea behind this is that neoliberalism is one and the same thing as globalization, so that whoever criticizes neoliberalism with its dogma that "there are no alternatives" is immediately stigmatized as a critic of globalization itself. With their direct actions on the occasion of the G8 and other summits, the new global movements of the beginning of the 2000s may not have changed the course of those specific political meetings, but they have certainly changed the spectacle that was staged by them. Equally, the Occupy movement that began explicitly as the symbolic occupation of a space that is in itself only a symbol—Wall Street— has managed to bring a different script onstage.

The organization and the actions of such new global movements perfectly respond to the challenges of our epoch.[27] This is not only because many of their militants merge elements of Marxism and anarchism—the two traditions of thought from which we derived the idea of freedom as freedom of equals. Most of the time, activists creatively combine elements from the Marxist and anarchist tradition with ecological and feminist claims without even being aware of their provenance (Corradi 2013). However, it does not appear an exaggeration to say that "anarchism is at the heart of the movement, its soul; the source of most of what's new and hopeful about it" (Graeber 2002:62). By this I do not mean that its activists openly recognize themselves as "anarchist"—which is far from being the case, as many have noted (Juris 2009). I mean that the intimate logic of its functioning is anarchical in its essence, since it responds to the principle of free federation and association.

As is well known, the new global movements lack any central authority, a single charismatic leader or even a fully fledged program determined once and for all. However, this does not mean that activists do not know what they want, as observers locked into traditional terms of hierarchical politics may think. It means that they are movements that grew up according to a networking logic that strictly follows the emerging needs and affinities of the people. Its organization is nonhierarchical, its coordination decentralized, and its decision making shaped by an attempt to reinvent new forms of direct democracy (thus favoring strategies for consensus building rather than majority rule). In brief, it works according to what anarchists have for a long time called free federalism.

The new global movements that began in the early 2000s seemed to many to have died soon after 9/11. But this is far from being the case. The reactionary turn that followed 9/11 made those movements go dormant, but their legacy has continued to work in a more or less subterranean fashion during the past decade.[28] Whether there is any direct connection between them or not, it is a fact that the spontaneous rebellions that began in the spring of 2011 in the Arab region follow the same logic that we have seen at work in the new global movements of the early 2000s. It is perhaps too early to say where this will lead, whether the revolutions will produce permanent changes in the deepest structure of those societies or whether new dictators will take the place of old ones. But one thing is sure: these revolutions have changed the spectacle of politics and disclosed new political imaginaries by dismantling regimes ossified by decades of authoritarianism (Challand 2011b), and they have done so through the same modality we have seen at work for some time in other regions of the world, from Seattle to Genoa: horizontal networks that have no single central leader or vertical forms of organization and which are thus, strictly speaking, *an-archical*.

The same holds for the Occupy Wall Street movement that began in the fall 2011 in New York City and quickly expanded to the whole United States and even outside of it. After the "Arab spring" came the "American fall," as one of the slogans circulating among New York City critics of financial capitalism said. The idea behind the occupation of a square in the Wall Street district is indeed that of staging a different spectacle of what is going on every day: it is a symbolic occupation (because it took place with tents and words rather than armies and tankers), but—most important—it is a symbolic occupation of a symbol, since it is well known that it is in the immaterial space of the Web that financial transactions take place and not within the closed walls of Wall Street.[29] At the moment of this writing it is not yet clear what the destiny of the Occupy movement will be within and outside the United States. One thing is certain though. It has reactivated the political imagination worldwide and it has done so by reorienting an old image: as the slogan quoted at the beginning warns us—not only "we are all on the same boat" but also be wary because "the boat is sinking."

Bringing together the different threads of the argument, we can say that globalization has become reflexive. People act in the world and think about their actions with the entire globe as their horizon of experience. Activists networking from one side of the globe to the other, migrants crossing (legally or illegally) borders, and even political institutions above and below nation-states, they all proclaim one and the same thing: networks are better than hierarchies. Otherwise said, globalization has demonstrated what modern political thought has always been reluctant to recognize: an anarchic order is not only possible but also desirable.

As we have seen, this is only one side of the story. If it is true that an anarchist turn has already begun, it is still far from going in the right direction. A freedom of equals has more chances today than ever, but it is still far from being realized. Capitalism's omnivorous capacity to overcome every challenge by incorporating its inner logic is the main threat. When the social movements of the 1960s criticized Fordist capitalism for its totalitarian logic that aimed at producing one-dimensional men, capitalism replied by becoming fluid, multidimensional, horizontal, post-Fordist. In other words, it incorporated the logic of its opponents. This has been capitalism's strategy of survival, but this time it may prove lethal for it, because there have emerged new and unprecedented possibilities for radical political action.

In conclusion, let me recall Pedrini's poem with which we began. It is not by chance that this image of a galleon has kept recurring within the new global movement. The reason why people find it inspiring these days is that it perfectly expresses the view of freedom outlined before: one is the world, one must be freedom, because we are all on the same boat. In a world in which the fate of a few islands depends on the behavior of industries on the other side of the globe, in which a nuclear explosion in Japan can have effects worldwide, in which the planet has become a global society of spectacle, you cannot be autonomous without being free or, equivalently, you cannot be free on your own. This is a radical view of freedom, but one that is timelier today than ever before. History itself has reversed the liberal motto "your freedom ends where that of the others begins" into its opposite: "your freedom can begin only with that of everybody else."

NOTES

INTRODUCTION

1. By new global movements, I mean social movements that go from the so-called no-global movement to the recent Occupy. Notice, however, that *no-global movement* is a misleading term because the social movements that lined up under the slogan "another world is possible" are movements in favor of globalization and not against it. Corporate media have used the label *no-global* because they are determined in their perspective by neoliberal ideology, which assumes that criticism of the neoliberal dogmas of free trade and deregulation amounts to a critique of globalization itself. As an accurate analysis of these programs and the ideas that circulate among them shows, this is far from being the case. On this point, see Graeber (2002).

2. See chapter 7. For a more detailed analysis of the myth of the clash of civilizations in both Western and Arab Middle Eastern sources, see Bottici and Challand (2010).

3. On this point, together with Debord (1994), see also the classical Benjamin (2002).

4. For a discussion of the way in which the concept of reality changes from one context to another, see also Castoriadis (1987:chapter 4). In his view, reality does not define what is imaginary, but rather every social imaginary defines what must count as real or unreal in every context.

5. Spinoza (*Ethics* II P6) explicitly says, "by reality and perfection I understand the same" (*per realitatem et perfectionem idem intelligo*). As I have argued elsewhere, this view allows him to endorse a different attitude toward imagination, one that fully acknowledges its crucial cognitive, moral, and political role (Bottici 2012).

6. On Kant's ambivalent treatment of imagination, see chapter 1.

7. In fact, Habermas is in no better situation. Castoriadis starts with monadic isolation, and then the problem becomes establishing how communication is possible; Habermas starts with the fact of communication, but then the problem is how this relates to the unconscious. On this point see Whitebook (1989).

8. For a discussion of the notion of images, see chapter 3.

9. See Habermas (1992:149–204) and Mead (1967).

10. I am grateful to an anonymous reviewer for pushing me to elaborate on this difference.

11. See the *Oxford English Dictionary*.

12. On this point, see Steele (2005), who, however, focuses only on history, and Butler, Laclau, and Žižek (2000), who, on the contrary, focus on the category of hegemony. More recent examples are Lara (2007) and Ferrara (2008), but none of these works is devoted to a systematic analysis of the nexus of politics and imagination.

13. Among those who have recently developed Arendt's insights, see Lara (2007) and Ferrara (2008). While the latter focuses on the importance of examples in a political theory of reflective judgment, the former develops a theory of reflective judgment by focusing on narratives and storytelling.

14. See, for instance, Lacan (1999:vols. 1 and 2). The distinction between the three orders, Imaginary, Real, and Symbolic, returns in different places in the text. For a mapping of these places, see Lacan (1999:1:541).

15. See for instance Žižek (1999a, 1999b, 2006).

IMAGINING

1. In the past I have applied this strategy to myth, which is one of the products of imagination (Bottici 2007).

2. In his interpretation of Nietzsche, Deleuze strongly emphasizes this point. See in particular Deleuze (2006).

3. Owen (2010) rightly emphasizes that destabilization of our confidence in a given perspective is the aim of any critical genealogy.

1. FROM *PHANTASIA* TO IMAGINATION

1. In contrast to the philologists of Nietzsche's time, today philology can rely on computer technologies like the *Thesaurus Linguae Graecae*, which enables scholars to search instantaneously for all the occurrences of a word within the entire corpus of Greek literature. There are reasons to suspect that this will progressively change the nature of philology itself, in particular its pace. Nevertheless, even today, philology still remains the art of the "goldsmith of words" as it still requires extensive and delicate work.

2. Among them, it may be worth mentioning Xenophanes, fragment 49; Empedocles, fragments 81, 108; and Protagoras, fragments 1, 15.

3. I have further developed this point in Bottici (2007:20–43).

4. I will use the original term *phantasia* because the corresponding contemporary terms *imagination* and *fantasy* could be misleading for reasons that will become clear later on.

5. According to Kearney (1988:87–99), Plato's general metaphysics inevitably led him to a generally negative verdict with respect to the imagination and image making, particularly as these concepts were treated in the *Republic*. Besides the fact that Kearney himself later recognizes the paradox of Plato's extensive recourse to images for the pursuit of truth (99), he seems to conflate three different things, for which Ancient Greek had three different names: *phantasma, eikon,* and *eidolon*. While *phantasma* had the general meaning of "appearance" or "presentation," *eikon* (from which *icon* derives) means the artistic support of images, whereas *eidolon* is the term corresponding to the current term *idol*. Plato's general metaphysics leads him to be wary of the *materiality* of images and image making in general, but not necessarily toward *phantasmata* and *phantasia*, the faculty that produces them.

6. As Watson (1988:6–8) observes, a similar view emerges from the *Theaetetus* (260d–264a).

7. Most English translators render the Greek *eidos* with "form" because the term *idea*, since Descartes, came to denote mental content alone whereas, in Plato's view, ideas are what are most real (Bottici 2007:40–43, 62–81). Since this shift in the concept of reality itself is precisely what is at stake in this genealogy, I prefer to use the term *idea*, which is the closest to the Greek *eidos* and its root—id, which recalls the verb to see (*orao*). This translation is standard in other European languages, such as Italian, French, and German, all of which use the word (*idea, idée, Idee*).

8. Watson strongly emphasizes the cognitive value of Plato's *phantasia* (see Watson 1988:1–12), whereas, as we have seen in note 5, Kearney (1988:87–99) emphasizes much more Plato's ambivalence toward imagination.

9. According to Dillon (1986:55) and Nikulin (2002:174), the Aristotelian treatment of imagination is nothing but an elaboration of Plato's account. Castoriadis (1997c) instead underlines the distance between the two.

10. On this point, Castoriadis (1997c) observes that rendering *phantasmata* with images is both "unfaithful and highly interpretative." I will try to maintain a balance between both in the course of the text precisely to signal the distance existing between our common notion of images and Aristotle's notion of *phantasmata*.

11. Indeed, it is here that the term tends to recur. *Thesaurus Linguae Greacae* gives forty entries, a substantial number considering that the term recurs only eleven times in *De*

Motu Animalium, the other typical *locus aristotelicus* for a discussion of *phantasia.* Always in quantitative terms, it may be helpful to observe here that the term recurs only seven times in all of Plato's writings, confirming both Aristotle's greater interest in the topic and Plato's reluctance to treat it; see *Thesaurus Linguae Greacae* (accessed on 13 March 2010).

12. These include sensibles that are specific to every sense, such as the color and form for sight, the flavor for taste, etc., others that are common such as mass and movement, and finally others which are so just by contingency (*De Anima* 428b 18–30).

13. When we are overwhelmed by a sensation, we do not clearly perceive the role of *phantasia,* but it is active, and its activity reverberates as well when sensation has ceased, as when we remember something that has taken place (*De Memoria* 450a 12) and, in sleep, through the visions that we have in dreams (461aff.).

14. Aristotle's theory of *phantasia* has been the object of a lively debate (Camassa 1986; Cattanei 2008; Nussbaum and Rorty 1992; Nikulin 2002; Schofield 1978; Watson 1988). According to some interpreters, even the passage from *De Anima* that we have commented upon would be full of inconsistencies and, moreover, it would contrast with the account of imagination given in other places such as the *De Motu Animalium,* when the emphasis is not on the production of images but on the association with *phainesthai* (Camassa 1986:35). Among such interpreters see, for instance, Freudenthal (1863:53), whereas on the *De Motu Animalium* see, in particular, Nussbaum (1978).

15. Both Nussbaum (1986:277–279) and Cattanei (2008) insist on this point.

16. On "deliberative imagination," see Cattanei (2008). Note that we are so accustomed to speaking about deliberative reason that the concept of "deliberative imagination" appears as bizarre to our ears. This embarrassment is signalled by the fact that we usually feel the need to put "deliberative imagination" within inverted commas, whereas very few would today put "deliberative reason" within them.

17. In an epoch when there is so much talk about deliberative reason and deliberation in general, the neglect of imagination's role in deliberation in recent debates is striking. A noteworthy exception is Nussbaum (1978).

18. For a discussion of this point, see Camassa (1986:23–24). As Camassa (25) observes, it is only very late and very rarely that the term *phantasia* was used in the sense of the contemporary term imagination, that is, as a creative faculty. Nikulin (2002:174) also agrees that Aristotle does not really elaborate the notion of productive imagination (a notion that Nikulin attributes to Philostratus), although he leaves room for the distinction between productive and reproductive imagination.

19. Nussbaum (1978:223) also insists on the need to understand Aristotle's notion of *phantasia* in connection with the verb *phainesthai.*

20. As Watson (1988:14) observes, this gap is probably one of the reasons why so many interpreters considered Aristotle's theory of *phantasia* to be full of inconsistencies: the translation of the term with "imagination" has frequently led to unnecessary confusion. On this point see also Castoriadis (1997c:216) and Nussbaum (1978:221–273). Nussbaum rightly points to the fact that we must understand *phantasia* in its link with the verb *phainesthai*, but her discussion of what she calls the "image-view of *phantasia*" seems to be misleading because of the differences between Aristotle's *phantasmata* and our own notion of image.

21. Those who want to follow this path may begin with Fattori and Bianchi (1986); Cocking (1991); Ferraris (1996); Fleury (2006); Friese (2001); Kurotschka Luzenberger (2008); and Vattimo (1999b).

22. According to Cocking (1984:47), the nodal point was Augustine, who used both the transliterated word *phantasia* and the word *imaginatio*. This dual language continued in the European vernaculars, where *imaginatio* became the important serious activity, and *fancy* (the contraction of *fantasy*) the light, airy playful activity of the mind in its freedom. However, the distinction was never fixed and rarely respected in philosophical usage until, through Paracelsus, Boehme, Schelling, and Coleridge, it became commonplace in the aesthetic theories of European Romanticism.

23. On Bacon's view of imagination, see Cocking (1984).

24. Maguire (2006:17–59) criticizes the reading that emerges from this fragment by saying that Pascal had a more nuanced view of imagination. Still, it can hardly be denied that what emerges in this fragment is a rather negative view of imagination. Among those who classify Pascal as a critic of imagination, see Robinson and Rundell (1994:120) and Cocking (1984:265).

25. Hobbes, who uses the terms *imagination* and *fancy* almost interchangeably, is in this respect still a premodern author, very much indebted to Aristotle (see in particular *Leviathan*, part 1, chapters 1, 2). Similarly, Spinoza presents a conception of imagination that retains much of its premodern connotations (see for instance *Ethics* II P40 S). Not by chance, he also understands reality in the old sense of perfection (*Ethics* II D6). On the link between Spinoza's understanding of imagination and his notion of reality, see Bottici (2012).

26. On this point, philosophers as different as Blumenberg (1983) and Habermas (1987) seem to converge.

27. In some cases such as this one, I do not interpolate feminine pronouns in the text, since I want to signal the fact that in most of the texts analyzed here the subject of modernity is written in a masculine form. Not to feminize the text must therefore be taken as a way to signal the problem rather than to obliterate it.

28. This clearly emerges from Hobbes's *Leviathan,* particularly in part 4, where he criticizes the kingdom of darkness (*Leviathan,* part 4, chapter 45). Spinoza makes a similar argument in his *Theological-Political Treatise,* where he criticizes the political use of superstitious beliefs, while in his *Ethics* he explicitly affirms that imagination is the sole source of errors, although he admits that imagination is not always false (*Ethics* II, P41). I have analyzed Spinoza's ambivalent conception of imagination more extensively in Bottici (2012).

29. Before modern times, the term art (*ars*) covered a very wide range of meaning, including everything that had to do with the application of general principles to a certain domain. In the Middle Ages, *artes* included dialectic (i.e., philosophy) together with grammar, rhetoric, arithmetic, geometry, astronomy, and music. Subsequently, the meaning of the term has been restricted to the fine arts.

30. The most important exception to this view is Vico's concept of *universali fantastici* (Vico 1999). Vico recognized the cognitive function of imagination in its nexus with poetry, but this view remained marginal at least until Romanticism. For a discussion of the modern authors that recognize the cognitive role of imagination, see Maguire (2006).

31. Castoriadis (1997c) insists on the similarity between this view and Aristotle's account of *phantasia,* so much so that he even speaks of an Aristotelian schematism.

32. Despite the fact that the title *Critique of Pure Reason* may surreptitiously suggest that Kant wanted to simply criticize the idea of a pureness of reason, this is in fact far from being the case. If it is true that the engines of Kant's criticism are the antinomies of pure reason, then we should conclude that his philosophy as a whole is aimed at placing a limit on the legitimate use of reason precisely in order to guarantee its pureness. As becomes increasingly clear in the second critique—whose title was originally intended to be *Critique of Pure Practical Reason*—the aim of Kant's philosophical enterprise is to show what pure reason can do (within its own limits), but in particular to make sure that there can be something like a "pure practical reason"—that is, that reason in its purity can be practical (Kant 1997:3)

33. Heidegger's interpretation of this point has been particularly influential in the past century. Nevertheless, it is important to note with Castoriadis a striking paradox in Heidegger: if it is true that no further traces of the question of imagination will be found in any of Heidegger's subsequent writings, then Heidegger, like Kant, seems to recoil equally from the "bottomless abyss" opened by the discovery of transcendental imagination (Castoriadis 1997c:215–216).

34. For a detailed analysis of the degree to which judgments of taste are judgments without knowledge, see Bernstein (1992).

35. In this respect, not surprisingly, in her reading of Kant's notion of imagination, Arendt (1982:80) gives it the name of *nous*, the term that had been used for centuries to denote the more intuitive side of the faculty of the intellect.

36. Žižek (1999b:34–35) strongly emphasizes this point in his critique of Kant's notion of transcendental imagination.

37. To Bacon, Galilei, and Pascal, one should add Descartes. According to Nikulin's reading, Descartes's treatment of imagination exhibits a similar ambivalence: although Descartes accords to imagination a crucial cognitive role in his early writings—particularly with respect to geometry—he tends to retreat from this perspective in his more mature writings (particularly in the *Meditations*) by diminishing its cognitive function (Nikulin 2002:187–230, in particular). See also Sepper (1989), who goes so far as to speak of an "eclipse of imagination" in Descartes.

38. In my genealogical approach to myth, I have focused on the sacred logos's negative attitude toward myth. In the case of imagination, which is a broader concept, the rejection is not as clear because imagination is not, like myth, immediately condemned as polytheist. For Christendom's attitude toward myth, see Bottici (2007:chapter 2).

39. Note that such is not the case in other European languages. Italian scholars, for example, almost always translate *eidos* as "idea" in order to keep the term as close as possible to the Greek original. See also note 8 on this point.

40. Despite the fact that, as Courtine (1992b:189) demonstrated, Kant is the origin of today's hegemonic conception of reality (*Augangspunkt für die heute vorherrschende Bedeutung*), Kant's treatment of the notion of reality and realism is a much more complex topic (see for instance also Abbagnano 1961:713–717; Courtine 1992a; Hoffmann et al. 1992).

41. For a commentary of this inversion, see also Courtine (1992b:191).

2. FROM IMAGINATION TO THE IMAGINARY AND BEYOND?

1. See, for instance, his four-volume analysis of *mythologiques* (Lévi-Strauss 1969, 1973, 1978, 1981).

2. According to Castoriadis (1997c), in the Aristotelian text we can perceive two different accounts of *phantasia*: one, much more conventional, that reduces the term to a combinatory activity dependent on sensation and another, emerging in *De Anima*, that emphasizes instead the radical character of imagination—the fact that it is an originary creative faculty that cannot be reduced to anything else.

3. See Lacan (1999:vols. 1 and 2). The distinction between the three orders, Imaginary, Real, and Symbolic, returns in different places of the text. For a mapping of these, see Lacan (1:541). The major difference between Lacan's early writings and his

post-1950s works is perhaps that, as a consequence of his structuralist turn, he stops inquiring about the origins of the mirror phase in terms of the premature birth of human beings (Tarizzo 2009:46). He, nevertheless, never reneges on his early discovery of the mirror phase.

4. The same holds for those authors who have been inspired by him, such as Žižek (1999a, b, 2006).

5. See Lacan (1999:1:348).

6. See Anderson (1991); Hays (2009); Maza (2005); Zavala (1992); and Zwicker (2006)—to name but a few.

7. As I have argued elsewhere, once we start looking at the world as divided into discrete cultures or civilizations, which interact with one another as if they were individuals, we risk nurturing the myth of the clash of civilizations, even when apparently criticizing it, as happens in theories of the dialogue of civilizations (Bottici 2007:227-246, Bottici and Challand 2010:chapter 5.)

8. I am referring here to the critique of the "specter haunting multiculturalism" identified by Richard Bernstein (2010), who argues that such a specter is the thesis of the incommensurability between cultures.

9. I have discussed this at length in Bottici (2007:chapter 4). But notice that the emphasis there was on the notion of language games, whereas here I am concerned with the imaginary and thus with what is prelinguistic.

10. See, for instance, Coulter (1999) and Von Savigny (1991).

11. According to Lentin (2005), for instance, the very notion of culture has replaced the no longer politically correct notion of race, but culture still plays the same role, so much so that a politics of multiculturalism can easily open the way to a form of racism.

12. Stavrakakis (2002) emphasizes, for instance, the similarities between Castoriadis and Lacan, in that they both allow us to think creativity and innovation, despite the divergences of their trajectories.

13. The paradigm of multiple modernities or multiple civilizations runs a similar risk. For a critique of this paradigm, see Bottici and Challand (2010:111-138).

14. On the notion of multiple modernities, see, for instance, Eisenstadt (2002).

15. Husserl assigns to imagination a cognitive, an ethical, and even a methodological role for phenomenology. On the different aspects of Husserl's theory of imagination and fantasy, see Ghiron (2001, 2002); Baptist (2008); and Volonté (1997).

16. For an analysis of this passage, see, in particular, Ghiron (2002), according to whom §43 of Husserl's *Idee* (Husserl 1976) provides a radical critique of the theory of mental images.

17. The puzzlement in the face of the issue of the unreality of fantasy generates his view of the consciousness operating in fantasy as a "double ego," that is, as one that keeps presence and absence, object and unreality at the same time (Husserl 1980:349–350, 467–468; see also Baptist 2008:157).

18. The same holds for Jean-Paul Sartre's influential theory of imagination, which developed Husserl's phenomenology in an existentialist direction by underlining the strict link between imagination and freedom (Sartre 1940; in particular see his conclusion). As Sartre (358) points out, it is because we can imagine things, that is, pose objects as real but yet unreal, that we can also be free (358). Freedom is the condition of imagination, inasmuch as "in order to imagine, consciousness must be free vis-à-vis all particular realities and this freedom must be a 'being-in-the-world' which is at the same time constitution and negation of the world" (*constitution et néantisation du monde*; 357). Hence, imagination is for Sartre purely imaginary, as the title of his most influential book on imagination suggests (Sartre 1940). As a form of double negation, "constitution and negation of the world," imagination poses the object as absent. Thus, once again, imagination is associated with the ambit of an absence. On Sartre's phenomenology of imagination, see Cumming (1992); Breeur (2006); and also Flynn (1992).

19. For instance, Nussbaum (1995:xvi) openly states, "My own preferred version of the ethical stance derived from Aristotle, but everything I say here could be accommodated by a Kantianism modified so as to give the emotions a carefully demarcated cognitive role."

20. This is, for instance, the perspective that emerges from one of the most beautiful Marxian texts on the problem, *The Eighteenth Brumaire of Louis Bonaparte* (Marx 1969) with its recurrent opposition between imagination and the reality of facts. I have further developed this interpretation in Bottici (2007:190–200).

21. Habermas is equally problematic in this regard, albeit for the opposite reason. Castoriadis starts with the monadic isolation of the subject, and then the problem becomes how to establish the possibility of communication; Habermas starts with communication, but then the problem is how this relates to the unconscious. On this point see Whitebook (1989).

3. TOWARD A THEORY OF THE IMAGINAL

1. I have used this concept in Bottici (2009b, 2011a, 2011b).

2. In this respect, the notion of imaginal has some similarities with Karl Popper's concept of a World-3, understood as a world between that of physical objects and that of mental states (Popper 1978). The major difference though is the focus on images,

as distinct from all the general abstract objects that are included in Popper's World-3, ranging from myths and songs to scientific theories (144).

3. Together with the term *imaginal,* consider other new expressions, such as *visual culture* (Mirzoeff 1998) or *pictorial turn* (Mitchell 2005), all of which point to the new role that images play in our lives.

4. On the link between Kant and Corbin, see the insistence by, for instance, Wunenburger (2006).

5. On the French side of the debate, see in particular Fleury (2006) and Wunenburger (2006). On the Italian side, see Piro (2008) and Chiodi (2010).

6. Wunenburger also distinguishes the concept of imaginal from both imagery, that is images simply aimed at communication, and the imaginary, in the strict sense of the term of what is associated with the unreal (Wunenburger 2001:79).

7. Examples of such an approach include Armstrong (1968:291–303) and Dennett (1986:132–146).

8. For examples of this attempt to bring images back into discussions about the imagination, see the philosophical work of Kind (2001) or the psychology developed by Kosslyn, Thompson, and Ganis (2006) in their *The Case for Mental Imagery.*

9. This is registered even by sympathetic writers such as Kosslyn, Thompson, and Ganis (see in particular Kosslyn, Thompson, and Ganis 2006:4–5).

10. Despite the fact that, as we have seen in the previous chapter, Freud is ambivalent toward imagination, Hillman's interpretation of this famous passage of Freud seems a bit ungenerous. If, by this passage, Freud really meant that consciousness should occupy the entire place of the unconscious, then psychoanalysis would end up in its own annihilation.

11. In an essay comparing Castoriadis and Freud, Whitebook (1989:230) observes that Freud's notion of fantasy formation is much more rooted in the biological-corporeal and therefore much less spontaneous than it is for Castoriadis. Both Whitebook and Castoriadis seem, therefore, to agree in their critique of Freud's approach to images and imagination.

12. Unfortunately, despite having considered alternative terms such as position/presentation or even *phantasma,* Castoriadis decides to follow Freud's usage, which leads to the same confusion that he had so acutely diagnosed in Freud (Castoriadis 1987:400). Yet, as we have seen in chapter 2, he is at least able to go beyond the first dilemma of the genealogy of imagination through his notion of radical social imaginary. As Urribarri (2002) pointed out, the introduction of the notion of radical imagination/radical imaginary is Castoriadis's greatest contribution to psychoanalysis.

13. This is a usage that Wittgenstein employs in the *Tractatus* when he observes, "a picture presents a situation in a logical space, the existence and non-existence of a

state of affairs" (Wittgenstein 1922:8; 2.11). Since pictures are "models of reality" (2.12), propositions can be said to be pictures (21, 4.021).

14. This very broad understanding of images is common in psychotherapy (see, for instance, Singer 2002). See also Kosslyn, Thompson, and Ganis (2000).

15. Note, however, that empirical research in the field of visual perception has long since been emphasizing that we normally see both more and less of what the retinal stimulation affords (for a succinct discussion of this point, see Mack 2011).

16. What makes something visualizable is very much debated in the literature. Mitchell (2005) points to the importance of considering pictures as living beings and thus invites us to look at what they want, while Kulvicki (2006) makes a list of four structural properties of pictures. For my purposes, it is sufficient to point toward the two minimal conditions of variation in shape and color as the most important features of pictures. As a result, with unconscious images that are visualizable but not visualized, variations in shape are more approximate, but such is still a crucial element: if we dream of a little fish or of a gigantic one, the difference is crucial. The same holds for colors.

17. In my analysis of the way in which myth operates within the social unconscious, we have indeed observed this fact many times (see in particular Bottici and Challand 2010). See also below Hopper's definition of the social unconscious.

18. As Laplanche and Pontalis (1992:196) observe, the notion of *imago* and that of complex are very close. This emerges already in *Wandlungen und Symbole der Libido* (1911) where Jung distinguished between the maternal, paternal, and fraternal imagos.

19. It may be worth remembering here that Hillman has been director of the Carl Gustav Jung Institute for more than ten years.

20. I am not sure that Lacan would agree with my interpretation of this sentence, in the first place because *imagos* are in his view always alienating (Lacan 1999:181) and secondly because the term *imago* disappears from his writings from the 1950s onward (Evans 1996:95–96), that is, after the so-called structuralist turn with its emphasis on language.

21. This is something on which people such as Jung, Hillman, or Castoriadis would all agree. On the contrary, philosophers such as Habermas who have put language at the very center of their philosophy would probably disagree. As Whitebook (1989:228) acutely observes, "such a thicket of non-linguisticality at the center of the subject would be an anathema to his entire philosophy." Castoriadis can, on the contrary, fully endorse this point, as he uses it to prove his argument about the monadic core of the psyche. Yet, as I will argue later, one does not need to make such an assumption because even images can communicate, despite the fact that they cannot always be reduced to linguistic descriptions.

22. I am here following Hopper (2003:127), to which I will return in a moment.

23. See Freud (1965:88–89).

24. In my view, this notion of universal archetypes stands at odds with the privileged position that Hillman accords to Greek mythology. According to Carotenuto (1991:272), this is due to the fact that it is in classical mythology we find the archetypal background of the Western psyche.

25. On the concept of social unconscious, see Fromm (2001) and, more recently, Hopper (2003). Debord also used the term *social unconsciousness (inconscient social)* in different moments of his work (for instance, see Debord 1994:33–34:thesis 51).

26. On the convergence between psychoanalysis and historical materialism in the notion of social unconscious, see Zepf (2007).

27. Another difference from Fromm's usage is that it does not imply the notion of social character that is so crucial for Fromm (Fromm 2001). On Fromm's notion of social unconscious see also Brenna (1997) and Zepf (2007).

28. In *New Introductory Lectures on Psychoanalysis*, Freud states that we can "distinguish two kinds of unconscious—one which is easily, under frequently occurring circumstances, transformed into something conscious, and another with which this transformation is difficult and takes place only subject to a considerable expenditure of effort or possibly never at all. . . . We call the unconscious which is only latent, and thus easily becomes conscious, the 'preconscious,' and retain the term 'unconscious' for the other" (Freud 1965:88–89) From this passage it seems that Freud wanted to exclude the preconscious from the unconscious, but other passages seem to point to a different direction (see, for instance, Freud 1923:18).

29. Jung openly states that the unconscious is only a hypothesis (see, for instance, Jung 1990:3, 44).

30. On the universality of the archetypes of the collective unconscious, see Jung (1990:4 in particular).

31. For instance, in collaboration with Benoît Challand I have used the notion of the social unconscious in our work on the myth of the clash of civilizations, where we were not interested in looking for invariants in space and time that unifies the whole of humanity, but rather for what is specific to different societies in the elaboration of the idea that a clash between Islam and the West is taking place (Bottici and Challand 2010). This enabled us to emphasize the spatial and temporal changing nature of a dimension of the unconscious, which is neither individual nor collective, and thus to show that, despite having become a global political myth, the narrative of a clash between civilizations works in very different ways in different contexts.

32. See, for instance, Jung (1990:42–43).

33. On this point, Evans (1996:95–96) observes that whereas for Jung *imagos* have an equally positive and negative effect, in Lacan's work they are weighted firmly toward the negative, being fundamentally deceptive and disruptive elements.

34. Urribarri (2002) in particular insists on this novelty when he speaks about his influence for the development of a "post-Lacanian" notion of the unconscious. I have, however, the impression that Urribarri would have to qualify his claim about the novelty of Castoriadis's approach if he were to also take Jung's notion of active imagination into account.

35. I am grateful to Peter Wagner and Suzi Adams for pointing me to this. In my reading of Castoriadis, I had perhaps first taken the term *monadic* too seriously as indicating something that, like Leibniz's monad, has no windows or doors.

36. On this point, see Wittgenstein's famous argument against the possibility of a private language (Wittgenstein 1975:§258).

37. In this passage Arendt (1982:10) is actually quoting Kant, to whose political philosophy those lectures were devoted.

38. On the reasons why philosophers tend to privilege death, see Arendt (1982) and Critchley (2008).

39. This is a constant theme in Arent's thinking, which is also linked to her remarks about the different notion of temporality presupposed by natality—a theme she attributes to Augustine (Arendt 1996:54–55). But the emphasis on natality is a recurrent theme in her work (see, for instance, Arendt 1982:23, 146–148, Arendt 2005:126–127), which has recently been recovered by Cavarero (2009) and developed in a feminist direction

40. The fact that "mortals" is still often used as a synonym for "human being" is a signal of how entrenched this prejudice is in our culture (Cavarero 2009:55, 75).

41. Besides the already mentioned works of Arendt and Cavarero, see also O'Byrne (2010), who builds on the work of Arendt, Dilthey, Heidegger, and Nancy.

42. It is significant that the only other equivalent that contemporary English has for *mortal* is *earthborn*—a term that equally occults the presence of another in birth for a generic birth from an anonymous "earth" and thus makes of even birth itself a solitary business.

43. See, for instance, the studies done by Michel Odent (1986) and his Primal Health Research Centre on this point.

44. O'Byrne (2010:148, 164) focused on this question mark, by asking what the clone will make of us and of the ontology of birth more in general.

45. In my view, the philosopher who most systematically underlined this point remains Castoriadis, although, as we have seen, he does so from the point of view of a theory of the social imaginary and radical imagination (Castoriadis 1987).

46. I am not sure Rawls would subscribe to this view, but his *Political Liberalism* certainly provides some grounds for this interpretation (see, in particular, Rawls 1996:47–88).

4. A GENEALOGY OF POLITICS

1. See, for instance, Sellin (1978); Rubinstein (1987); and Viroli (1992), but even historically informed political theorists such as Bobbio (1990) and Sternberger (1991) cannot fail to notice this curious fact: despite its Greek origins, the word *politics* is a modern invention.

2. On the distinction between the *polis* and the *oikos*, see Arendt (1958:28–38). It should, however, be noted that the stark opposition between the *oikos* and the *polis* may also be a later interpretation. For instance, according to both Plato and Aristotle, the *polis* derives from the division of labor and thus from the satisfaction of the basic needs of life—a remark that seems to suggest a more fluid relationship between the *oikos* as the primary site for the satisfaction of bodily needs and a superior form of community such as the *polis*. See in particular Plato's *Republic* (368b) and book I of Aristotle's *Politics* (1252b30).

3. Among them, consider two philosophers who will be at the center of the next chapter: Hannah Arendt and Cornelius Castoriadis (see, for instance, Arendt 1958 and Castoriadis 1991).

4. I am grateful to Cinzia Arruzza and Dmitri Nikulin for their helpful insights on this point.

5. As is well known, Aristotle never wrote a book entitled *Ta Politika*. His published works include only dialogues that have all been lost, as we know from testimonies. The texts that currently compose the *corpus aristotelicum* are the notes he used for teaching. In fact, we cannot even say that we possess the texts of his esoteric lessons: the actual shape of the *corpus aristotelicum* derives from the edition of these notes made by Andronicus Rhodius, a later disciple of the Peripatetic who perhaps gave to the *corpus* a division that reflects more the cultural view of the first century BCE than Aristotle's intentions (Adorno 1961b:287).

6. See, for instance, Arendt (1958:7–8).

7. For the medieval uses of the term, see *Patrologia Latina*, the collection of Medieval Latin sources, which gives a lot of entries for *politicus*. By contrast, the *Thesarus Linguae Latinae*, which contains Latin sources until the sixth century CE, gives only a few entries.

8. We will come back to early modern sources a bit later.

9. It is significant to notice that, for instance, somebody deprived of any interest in politics would be called *rerum civilium ignarum*.

10. Sellin (1978); Viroli (1992); and Rubinstein (1987) have already thoroughly treated this matter.

11. Aristotle's *Politics* has been very influential for thinkers such as Marsilius from Padua, Dante Alighieri, and Thomas Aquinas, who opposed political Augustinism.

12. The timing of the birth of modern sovereign states is still controversial among interpreters, but most of them agree in seeing the seventeenth century as a turning point. On the nature and history of modern sovereign states, see Poggi (1990) and Pierson (1996).

13. There is vast agreement among historians of political thought about the link between the birth of the term *politics* and the emergence of the modern state. Besides Viroli (1992); see Bobbio (1990); Sellin (1978); and Rubinstein (1987).

14. See in particular *Discourses* D.I6, D.II8, D.I25, and D.I55. If we consider that other theorists of the reason of states such as Botero already systematically used the word *politica*, it is impossible not to agree with Viroli's interpretation, which argues that Machiavelli is an ambivalent figure of passage (Viroli 1992).

15. For instance, besides the title of his TTP and TP, Spinoza only once uses the expression *politici*, in the phrase "political philosophers" (TP, 1 §2). The TTP VI has *historici politici* as "political historian"; ep. 76 has the adjective twice and ep. 67 once, in the context of the order of the church being political or the idea of a political government/ regime. Finally, ep. 84 only uses the phrase *publica negotia* once. Overall, in Spinoza, the old meaning of *politicus*—knowledge about the things relative to the *polis*—prevails.

16. See, for instance, the introduction to both the English and the Latin editions of the *Leviathan*, published in 1651 and 1668, respectively. Hobbes mainly uses the term *politica* in the old sense of *philosophia civilis*, and, in one of the very few instances where he uses the adjective *politicus* in a sense similar to ours, he says first *"civitas"* and then "that is, so to speak, *corporis politici"*: (Homo enim non modo *corporis naturale* est, sed etiam civitatis, id est (ut ita loquor) *corporis politici* pars).

17. As I have mentioned, historians such as Sellin (1978); Viroli (1992); and Rubinstein (1987) have already done this. It would, however, be interesting to extend their analyses to explore the change from politics to the notion of the political. But we can only mention such a change in this context.

18. For this definition, see, for instance, Weber (1978:1:§17, 4:§1, 2).

19. On the novelties brought about by the modern state, see, for instance, Bobbio (1985) and Poggi (1990).

20. Note that this holds true only for the English language, where the term *politics* denotes both the thing and knowledge about it. On the contrary, in other European languages, such as Italian, French, and German, the corresponding terms (*politics*, *politique*, *Politik*) only denote the thing itself.

21. Strikingly enough, even international relations theorists, imbued with the myth of a Westphalian system of sovereign states that goes back to 1648, tend to neglect the fact that we lived in empires until very recently. Not only was the Westphalian system an experience limited to Europe for a long time, but, as a matter of fact, it is a misleading image because countries like France and England were not sovereign states, but rather imperial ones. As Barkawi (2010:1360) acutely observes, international relations as a discipline "was founded amidst empire, but discovered instead only a world of sovereign states and their collective action problems."

22. On the birth of the social as a separate category, see Donzelot (1984) and Kaufmann and Guilhaumou (2003).

23. See in particular Arendt (1958). Castoriadis (1991) also conceived of Greek democracy as the model for what real politics is and/or should be. We will come back to this in the next chapter.

24. See Rosanvallon (2003:14). The notions of friend and enemy originally developed by Schmitt (1996) have recently been developed by Mouffe (2005) in her agonistic model of democracy. On the broader notion of the "political" as *le politique* in the French context, see also, besides Rosanvallon (2001, 2003), Lefort (1986) and Gauchet (2005:504–557). Another strategy to point to the same insufficiency has been to use *political* to refer to what Weber called *politics* and to reserve the word *politics* for a more attractive activity (see, for instance, Castoriadis's notion of politics, to which we will return toward the end of this chapter).

25. Together with the political and biopolitics, we should at least mention the fact that there has been a proliferation of new terms generated in order to render the novelty brought about by contemporary politics. Beyond the words stemming from the root *polis*, we should at least mention *governmentality* and *governance*, just to name the most fortunate ones. The former is linked to Foucault's notion of power, whereas the World Bank introduced the latter, as we will see later on.

26. There are indeed earlier usages of the word, going as far back as the beginning of the twentieth century. For a careful reconstruction of the history of the term, see Cutro 2005.

27. See, for instance, Agamben (1998); Cutro (2005); Cooper (2008); Esposito (2008); Hardt and Negri (2000, 2009); Lemke (2011); and Rose (2007) for examples of works devoted to this issue.

28. This also explains why, in my view, Foucault is not so consistent in his usage of the terms *biopower* and *biopolitics*, which at times appear to be used by him almost interchangeably. On this point, see Hardt and Negri (2009:57).

29. Note, however, that this chronology is uncertain and changes from one text to another. In Foucault (1990), he seems for instance to place the beginning of this process much earlier.

30. See Agamben (1998:129–160) and Foucault (1997:259).

31. Among the exceptions, as we have already mentioned in chapter 3, are some women philosophers such as Hannah Arendt (see, for instance, Arendt 1996:54–55, 146–148 and 2005:126–127) and Cavarero (2009). On natality, see also O'Byrne (2010).

32. As already mentioned, this is the point developed by Arendt in her reading of Augustine (see, for instance, Arendt 1996:54–55, 146–148, 2005:126–127) and more recently developed by Cavarero (2009).

33. *Genopolitics* is a term that I construct by putting together *genea* (the Greek term for birth) and *gignomai* (the Greek word for coming to life, being born) with *politics*, which as we have seen did not existed in Ancient Greek. This is, properly speaking, an anachronism, but one that I am consciously deploying in order to show the limits of the notion of *thanatopolitics*.

34. Foucault was well aware that the terrain of biopolitics is the economy, as shown by the fact that his course on *The Birth of Biopolitics* is entirely devoted to economic issues (Foucault 2008). More recently, see Cooper (2008) and Hardt and Negri (2000). Interestingly enough, though, Foucault never really focuses on birth as the crucial biopolitical moment.

5. IMAGINAL POLITICS

1. On the history of the notion of body politics, see Adriana Cavarero (2002), who, with her usually subversive style, also proposed a feminist counterhistory of the role of the body in politics. On the metaphor of the state as person, as well as on the difference between this kind of representation of the political community in ancient and modern times, see also Bottici (2009a:26–37, in particular), which I am following here.

2. For a consideration of the notion of representation and a discussion of the elements of continuity and discontinuity in its modern version, see the classic work by Hofmann (1974). Rousseau (1997:book 3), a harsh critic of representation, also emphasizes that political representation is a modern invention.

3. I am rendering here the Italian term *rappresentanza* with the English expression *absolute representation*. I do this because, whereas the Italian language (like German) distinguishes between *rappresentanza* and *rappresentazione*, the English language (like French) has only one word (*representation*). In contrast to *rappresentazione*, the Italian word corresponding to the philosophical notion of re-presenting, the term *rappresentanza*, denotes a form of presenting what is absent that becomes something like an end in itself. This is clearly seen even outside of political theory, in expressions such as "E' solo una questione di rappresentanza," which denotes something that is simply a question of appearances and thus independent of what is supposed to be there (and thus absolute in the etymological sense of *ab-solutus*, untied from, made loose).

4. I should, however, emphasize that while Wark (2004:208) uses the notion of representation as tendentially deceptive and even goes as far as to say that "all representation is false," the theory of the imaginal within which I am using the notion of representation does not make any assumption as to the more or less deceptive nature of representation.

5. I have dealt with the link between sovereignty and the emergence of a political map in Bottici (2009a).

6. See Bauman (1998) and Harvey (1990).

7. See Harvey (1990:248). The author reproduces here a portrait of Queen Elizabeth standing on a map of her territory as representing the power of the dynasty over individuals and the nation.

8. This paradox of the artificiality of the Leviathan is at the center of the debate between Skinner and Runciman on Hobbes's notion of the artificial person. Whereas Skinner argues that it is *a persona ficta*, but not fictitious, Runciman holds the opposite thesis (Skinner 1999; Runciman 2000). In the end the whole debate seems to revolve around the issue of whether an artificial person is by definition fictitious and thus unreal—something that of course depends on the notion of reality one has in mind. Here again emerges the advantage of the notion of the imaginal, which does not presuppose any pregiven notion of reality.

9. Critchley arrives at this conclusion through the notion of a "supreme fiction" and through a detailed discussion of Rousseau (Critchley 2012:21-103). On the centrality of fiction in Rousseau's writings, see Bernstein (1990:80), who succinctly put it in the following way: "only a fiction can accomplish the work of transforming public opinion in a manner that would make a just state possible."

10. While Critchley reads the notion of a supreme fiction together with that of a "faith of the faithless" and thus as a form of political theology, I would rather insist that, whereas fiction is an essential ingredient of politics, theology is not, since not all forms of fictions or of supreme fictions are theological in nature, as I have mentioned before.

11. In his view, the systematic nexus between power and glory is something that modern politics, in its theological-economic nexus, derives from the Middle Ages. But whenever one locates the change, it is hardly deniable that modern politics is, even more so than ancient political forms, an essentially imaginal being.

12. The reference here is obviously to Anderson's *Imagined Communities* (Anderson 1991).

13. Others have developed her intuitions. For instance, on judgment as a model of validity, see Forti (1994:358-372); Beiner and Nedelski (2001); and Ferrara (2008).

14. Arendt (1982:80) goes as far as to say that "the role of imagination for our cognitive faculties is perhaps the greatest discovery Kant made in the *Critique of Pure Reason*."

On Kant's treatment of the concept of imagination, see Arnason (1994); Engell (1981); and Rundell (1994a). On Kant's alleged recoil before imagination, see chapter 2.

15. On the importance of the notion of the "example," see Ferrara (2008). Ferrara, however, criticizes Arendt's analogy between examples and cognitive schemata.

16. Ferrara (2008:49–53) is critical of this analogy between schemes for knowledge and examples for action. Yet, from the point of view of a theory of the imaginal, which suspends the issue of the specific reality of images themselves, the difference is not so crucial because the similarities between these different sorts of images are greater than their differences.

17. In this passage Arendt does not mention the potentially unconscious dimension of images themselves. This is, by contrast, entailed in the notion of the imaginal that we have illustrated in the previous chapter.

18. On the importance of training the imagination to go visiting, see Dish (1996: 141–171).

19. On this point, see Arendt (1968b:237).

20. I am grateful to Elisabeth Suergiu for her research on the syllabus that Arendt used for her New School lectures on *Kant's Political Philosophy* (Arendt 1982).

21. For this definition, see Weber (1978:1:§17, 4:§1, 2) and Weber (2004:32–35).

22. We may remember here that Castoriadis translated Weber's *Economy and Society* into Greek when he was young.

23. Justice for Augustine amounted to God's justice, but the more general point here is that, without the belief in the legitimacy or justice of political power, the latter would not be conceptually any different from the mere use of violence.

24. The importance of the notion of images of the world in Max Weber has recently been emphasized by D'Andrea (2009).

25. Note that in this passage Weber distinguishes between enactment and the value of rational faith (Weber 1978:36), whereas later in the text he unifies enactment and rational grounds for the belief in legitimacy in a single ideal type (Weber 1978:215).

26. In particular, the old narrative that Greek philosophy amounted to an exit from the ancient world of myth has been contested from different philological and historical studies. I have dealt with these in Bottici (2007:20–43).

27. The fact that our word *democracy* has a Greek origin only shows how influential the Greek model of democracy has been for us, but not that the Ancient Greeks invented democracy as such. As archaeologists and scholars of antiquity have shown a long time ago, forms of government analogous to those that we would call democratic can be found among other ancient peoples such as the Sumerians, during the epoch of the early Sumerian city-states (Jacobsen 1943) or even the Medes of the sixth century BCE,

before Darius the Great declared that the best monarchy was better than the best oligarchy or the best democracy (Snell 2001:18).

6. CONTEMPORARY TRANSFORMATIONS BETWEEN
SPECTACLE AND VIRTUALITY

1. On the importance of theater for political philosophy, see Kottman (2007).

2. On the notion of recognition in Hobbes, see Carnevali (2005) and Marcucci (2010).

3. On this genealogy of the concept of governance, see Cochrane, Duffy, and Selby (2003) and Bottici (2006).

4. In the contemporary use, see the classic Rosenau and Czempiel (1992) and Bottici (2001).

5. David Held (1995) has been insisting on this aspect since the 1990s, underlining the structural reasons for the much-debated crisis of democracy.

6. See Held et al. (1999).

7. See Habermas (1998).

8. On this point, see Harvey (1990) and Bauman (1998).

9. On this point, see Strange (1996); and Stubbs and Underhill (1994).

10. Among those that insist on the epochal shift represented by this innovation, see Cerutti (1993, 2007).

11. For instance, on this point, see Eder (2003).

12. The reason why surveys on the role of the media in elections often fail to catch their real impact is that they often simply assess the extent to which media have influenced preferences for one or another official candidate. In fact, the power of the media comes well before the determination of such a preference, in making certain political options appear to be possible while excluding others.

13. In the literature on Rousseau, this is an aspect that is, in my view, not sufficiently underlined. Kohn offers a challenging critique of the contemporary *homo spectator* done in a Rousseauean perspective (see in particular Kohn 2008).

14. Whereas the translator renders the French *spectacle* with "theater," I prefer to use "spectacle" because Rousseau is concerned here with any form of entertainment that can take forms other than the theater, as becomes clear toward the end of the text where he speaks about public festivals.

15. Kohn (2008:477) also insists on the similarity between Rousseau and Debord by observing that the spectacle is for both a vehicle for alienation and socialization.

16. For an account of what they call network capitalism as a reply to 1968, see also Boltanski and Chiappello (2005).

17. In reference to such economic diagnoses, Negri and Hardt have proposed their notion of empire and multitude as a way to accurately describe the biopolitical turn we

are immersed in: the subject of empire is no longer the single worker but the multitude, because we are all constantly producing and thus never outside of the empire (Hardt and Negri 2000, 2004, 2009).

18. On this point, together with Debord (1994), see also the classical Benjamin (2002).

19. This, by contrast, does not come as a surprise if we consider that the definition of reality itself has changed a lot over the centuries. On this point, see below; see also Castoriadis (1987:chapter 4).

20. The exhibition took place in Florence at Palazzo Strozzi between 25 September 2009 and 17 January 2010 and featured works by Olivo Barbieri, Sonja Braas, Adam Broomberg and Oliver Chanarin, Gregory Crewdson, Thomas Demand, Elena Dorfman, Christiane Feser, Andreas Gefeller, Andreas Gursky, Beate Gütschow, Osang Gwon, Tatjana Hallbaum, Ilkka Halso, Robin Hewlett and Ben Kinsley, Rosemary Laing, Aernout Mik, Saskia Olde Wolbers, Sarah Pickering, Moira Ricci, Cindy Sherman, Cody Trepte, Paolo Ventura, and Melanie Wiora.

21. See http://listverse.com/2007/10/19/top-15-manipulated-photographs/ (accessed 14 April 2012).

22. See http://gawker.com/5293988/someone-in-iran-probably-the-government-isnt-good-at-photoshop (accessed 14 april 2012).

23. See http://www.museumofhoaxes.com/hoax/photo_database/image/whatever it takes/ (accessed 14 April 2012).

24. See http://listverse.com/2007/10/19/top-15-manipulated photographs/ (accessed 14 April 2012).

25. See http://thelede.blogs.nytimes.com/2009/11/11/french-embrace-sarkozy-as-zelig-meme/ (retrieved 5 July 2012); I am grateful to Elizabeth Suergiu for pointing this out to me.

26. See http://thelede.blogs.nytimes.com/2009/11/11/french-embrace-sarkozy-as-zelig-meme/ (retrived 5 July 2012); http://fuckyeahsarkozywasthere.tumblr.com/ (retrieved 5 July 2012).

27. I am here developing in a homeopathic direction a suggestion by Kohn (2008:473), who observes that Rousseau's spectacle can serve as a *pharmakon*, that is, both a poison and a cure.

28. See Rousseau (1997a:24). In this regard, Starobinski (1993) emphasizes that Rousseau's strategy consists in finding a remedy in the evil itself. For more on the idea of curing the malady from within, see also Neuhouser (2008). On the ambivalence of Rousseau's treatment of the arts, see also Kelly (1997).

29. According to Starobinski (1988:95), the closed theater is to the festival as opacity to transparency. The dark, gloomy cave of the theater is the site of deception

and melancholy, whereas the open-air public festival is the site of authentic and transparent encounters. However, as Kohn (2008:472) observes, the simple opposition between "indoor/opacity/spectacle" and "outdoor/transparency/festival" breaks down later in the text where Rousseau writes that in winter times there should be indoor balls. These seem, however, to be something like the winter version of the open-air festivals.

30. Notice in this passage that the same dynamic of *amour propre* and the drive for recognition in the other plays a positive role. On the possibly positive role of *amour propre*, see Neuhouser (2008).

31. On this point, see again Neuhouser (2008: in particular, pp. 218–250).

32. Critchley (2012:4, 21–90) makes a similar argument, but he extends it so far as to argue that the social contract itself is a fiction, a fiction that is needed in order to solve the problem of motivation in politics. This is a very original and fascinating reading of Rousseau, but it is inserted in the context of Critchley's more general politico-theological take, which assimilates every form of fiction to that of theology, based on the assumption that political theology is the only way to overcome the lack of motivation that characterizes our current predicament.

7. THE POLITICS OF THE PAST

1. As White (1973:163) observes, the passage where the German historian Leopold von Ranke described the historical method in such terms has been canonical for a long time in the profession.

2. The need for significance is not the need for religion, because something can be significant for a group without answering the ultimate questions of life and death as religion does. See Bottici (2007:44–62, 116–130).

3. Tudor (1972:17) maintains that what renders a myth specifically political is precisely its subject matter. This definition, however, contrasts with the example of the myth of the millennium that he himself analyzes in his work.

4. The term *symbol* originally denoted two halves of a broken object. The term derives from the Greek *syn-ballo*, which means "putting together."

5. Young (1990) introduces the concept of mythology by quoting a passage from Derrida's critique of metaphysics as "white mythology." The mythological aspect here consists of the illusion of the universality of metaphysics that calls itself Reason but is in fact an "Indo-European Mythology," i.e., the *mythos* of a specific idiom.

6. Indeed, it seems as if the white mythologies denounced in the title of Young's book are all those theories that, from Marxism onward, strive toward the idea of a unique "world history," i.e., of history as a totality (Young 1990).

7. The myth of prosperity is particularly important in the mythology of the European Union where at times it even merged with the Greek myth of the heroine Europa raped by the bull (Bottici and Challand 2013:chapter 4).

8. See, for instance, Smith (2000) and Stråth (2000). Even a quasi-supranational polity such as the European Union has its own myths, which at times converge with its founding historical narratives (Bottici and Challand 2012).

9. I am here following Bottici and Challand (2010).

10. On this point, again see Bottici and Challand (2010).

11. *Jahiliyya* is an Arabic term that literally means the "pre-Islamic times" and by extension came to signify an "age of ignorance" (Bottici and Challand 2010:58–59).

For a discussion of Occidentalism, see Bottici and Challand (2010). In this usage of the term, we distance ourselves from Ian Buruma and Avishai Margalit, who mainly look at Occidentalism as a form of dehumanization of the West that began with modernity. See Buruma and Margalit (2004).

12. For an analysis this and similar images in the context of French Islamophobia, see Geisser (2003:23).

13. In this sense, it also differs from Erich Fromm's view of the social unconscious, which defines primarily areas of repression found among the majority of members of a specific class of society. See Fromm (2001).

14. On the universality of archetypes of the collective unconscious, see Jung (1990:4).

15. See, in particular, Abrahamian (2003:529–544).

16. See, e.g., http://news.bbc.co.uk/2/hi/europe/4714540.stm (accessed 14 January 2009).

17. ttp://photos1.blogger.com/blogger/4765/1487/1600/mostots.0.jpg (accessed 15 January 2009).

18. On this point, I am strongly indebted to the research that I conducted on icons of the clash of civilizations with Angela Kuehner during my stay in Frankfurt. Among the products of this collaboration, see Bottici and Kuehner (2011).

19. For a more detailed discussion of Eurocentrism and a critique of the notion of civilization, see Bottici and Challand (2010:chapter 5).

20. It is, therefore, a rather broad meaning, as it primarily refers to a particular way of looking at the geography of the world—that is, the planisphere with Europe at its center. In this sense it differs from a broader cultural or political meaning (Amin 1988; Shoat and Stam 1994).

21. According to Williams, a British military command designation before World War II transformed the old "Near" East into the current Middle East (Williams 1988:333). Since the emergence of systematic geography in Europe, the East had been

divided into Near (the Mediterranean to Mesopotamia), Middle (Persia to Ceylon), and Far (India to China) East. Yet the old meaning still survives in certain sources (Shoat and Stam 1994:2).

8. THE REPOSITIONING OF RELIGION IN THE PUBLIC SPHERE

1. For instance, according to the critics of the concept of secularization, religion has never completely disappeared from the public sphere (Asad 2002). Peter Berger, a former supporter of the secularization thesis, now radically concludes the following: "The world today, with some exceptions to which I will come presently, is as furiously religious as it ever was, and in some places more so than ever. This means that a whole body of literature by historians and social theorists loosely labelled 'secularization theory' is essentially mistaken" (Berger 1999:2).

2. According to Ronald Dworkin, America's religiosity is not new. What differs are the political militancy, aggressiveness, and apparent successes of fundamentalist religion. The fact that Roman Catholic and evangelical priests openly called for John Kerry's defeat or that a group of bishops said that any Catholic voting for him should be excommunicated is an example of such aggressiveness (Dworkin 2006:53).

3. It is still debated as to when this process began. According to Gilles Kepel (1991), the *revanche de Dieu* starts in the 1970s.

4. On the Middle East, see, for instance, Halliday (2005:193–228) and An-Na'im (1999).

5. On this point, see Castoriadis (1987:125).

6. On the definition of autonomy, see Castoriadis (1987:101).

7. We will explore the aporias of the notion of autonomy in the conclusion.

8. On this, see Ferrara (2008:chapter 9).

9. On the contemporary use, see the classic Rosenau and Czempiel (1992) and Bottici (2001).

10. In the 1990s, David Held (1995) insisted on this point, emphasizing the structural reasons for the much-debated crisis of democracy.

11. This is why we have argued that the conservative reproduction of life has become a source of legitimacy for political power as crucial and thus as ideal-typical as the other three identified by Weber.

12. For instance, Kepel (2006) observes that the category of fundamentalism was coined within the Christian world and cannot easily be applied elsewhere.

13. On the imaginary appeal of Islamism, see in particular Challand (2011b), from which I largely draw in what follows.

14. This is the title of a documentary produced by Japanese National Television NHK (NHK 2004).

15. In this and what follows, see in particular Kepel (2006) and Kepel and Milell (2008). For a description of the reinterpretation of certain Islamic notions such as *fard'ayn, jihad,* and *jahiliya,* see Gerges (2005).

16. On the composite nature of Islamist movements, which find their followers among the middle class and the urban poor, see Kepel (2006).

17. The fossilization of political regimes in most of the Arab world reached its peak at the beginning of the new millennium, when, in the face of rapid changes taking place elsewhere, they kept inventing new strategies to justify an anachronistic authoritarianism (Owen 2004:1–22, 131–153, 219–240).

18. On the modernity of Al-Qaeda, see Gray (2003).

19. The anecdote is reconstructed in Buruma and Margalit (2004:13).

20. See, for instance, the Web site http://www.liveprayer.com/index.cfm, which provides a "Live prayer miracle center."

21. A woman suffering from Quincke's syndrome told the media that, exactly at the moment of the pope's death at 9:30 pm on 2 April 2005, she saw the pope blessing her and since then she has been able to breathe normally again (Guizzardi 2005:13).

22. On Islamic banking, see Tripp (2006). On Islam and the market, see Haenni (2005).

23. This is Richard Rorty's famous expression (Rorty 1999).

9. IMAGINING HUMAN RIGHTS

1. For instance, see Bottici (2007) and Bottici and Challand (2011).

2. On human rights and imagination, see Van Peer (1995) or also Nussbaum (1997). On human rights and the imaginary, see Douzinas (2000).

3. This meaning of the term *imaginary* prevails in psychoanalytical approaches to human rights. For instance, Douzinas (2000:319–342) looks at human rights from the point of view of the psychoanalytic concept of the imaginary.

4. See, for instance, the American Declaration of Independence (1776), which states that "all men are created equal and endowed by their creator with inalienable rights," and the French Declaration of the Rights of Man and of the Citizen (1789), which states that "men are born and remain free and equal in rights" (Article 1).

5. In my view, de Gouges's work, as a critique of sexist and racist discrimination, developed while invoking images of humanity, can be seen as a bridge between first-wave feminism, concerned as it was with the attainment of rights, and second- and even third-wave feminism, with their emphasis on identity and representation.

6. Indeed, the same argument could be made by comparing the 1798 Declaration with the 1948 Universal Declaration. One may note here that a long discussion accompanied the drafting of the first article, which states that "All human beings are born

free and equal in dignity and rights" and that the term *human beings* was preferred to *men* precisely because it was feared that the term *men* could be used to exclude women.

7. This is what Ferrara (2008) called the "force of the example": a particular that is nevertheless able to transcend its context of validity. In his work, Ferrara recovers but also develops Arendt's concept of exemplary validity.

8. It is for instance debatable the extent to which the discursive justification of human rights put forth by Habermas and Forst relies on the imaginal. If we understand the discursive justification to be a transcendental device to test the coherence of a certain maxim (similar to Kant's example of the deposit), then the imaginal plays no role. But if the question is understood to be a deliberation over a maxim, assessing what the world would look like if it were applied, then our capacity to form images plays a central role (see in particular Habermas 2001 and Forst 2007).

9. Information under the veil of ignorance thus includes size of the territory, population, and the extent of natural resources or economic development of the peoples they represent (Rawls 1999).

10. Among those who consider the social contract a myth, see La Caze (2002), but also Midgley (2003).

11. Rawls seems to provide some ground for such an interpretation when he says that we should think of being behind a veil of ignorance as like acting a part in a play (Rawls 1996:27).

12. Baccelli (1999:10) implicitly alludes to this when he observes that Rawls's theoretical apparatus is that of an "imaginary universalist."

13. For this criticism, see also Ferrara (2008:123). He observes that the normative basis for this selection cannot be contractarian because Rawls explicitly says that "the political (moral) force [of these rights] extends to all societies, and they are binding on all peoples and societies, including outlaw states" (Rawls 1999:80–81), and the latter do not have representatives in the original position, which includes only reasonable, liberal, and decent peoples.

14. See note 15.

15. Beyond the first chapters of the book, imagination is briefly mentioned in chapter 6, which is specifically devoted to the justification of human rights, whereas it never appears in the crucial chapter 7, on the enforcing of human rights (Ferrara 2008:147–163).

16. For a critique of this view, see Baccelli (2009b: chapter 5). Rather than arguing for the exemplarity of the Western model of human rights, Baccelli, following Rorty, invites us to recognize their built-in ethnocentrism.

17. Arendt uses the vocabulary of imagination understood as an individual faculty, which limits her approach. However, as we have seen, her observations on the political uses related to our capacity to form images can be recovered within a theory of the imaginal.

18. Among those who have insisted on the importance of sentimentality for human rights, see Rorty (1998b). In contrast to Rorty, Van Peer (1995) enters into the details of the forms of sentimentality that are involved in the application of human rights and specifically focuses on literature as a viable way to nourish them.

19. As Lara (2011) points out, Ricoeur (1986) puts forth a similar argument with his idea of semantic innovation.

20. The human capacity to anticipate manifests itself in the most different forms—from dreams, fables, films, and theatre to the great social and philosophical utopias of modernity. This does not imply the belief in an afterlife or in any surrogate for it, since it is possible to ground utopia in even a materialistic conception of history, as Bloch, by reinterpreting Marx's philosophy of history, does (Bloch 1986b:1§17).

21. This does not mean assuming a naive view of human rights. On the contrary, Bloch underlines the link between rights and conflict by speaking of modern rights as *Ansprueche* and *Kampfrechte*. In a book published in the year of the construction of the Berlin Wall, Bloch emphasized the importance of the language of subjective rights as a means to claim one's own dignity and, therefore, potentially subvert the status quo. Coming from a Marxist background, Bloch is well aware of Marx's critique of modern rights as a form of ideology, but the fact that the great masses were actually excluded from the benefit of modern rights in the past does not mean that the language of rights, through which the modern bourgeoisie has conducted its battle, cannot be recovered and used for new forms of emancipation. As it has been observed, the emphasis on the activity of claiming (*Anspruch*) expresses the importance of holding one's head up, of the disposition to fight to realize a world that is perhaps not perfect (as in integral utopias), but at least better than the one we live in (Baccelli 2009b:chapter 6).

22. For a shocking but accurate analysis of Italian detention camps, see Rovelli (2006).

23. *The End of Utopia* is the provocative title of the book by Jacoby (1999) in which he addresses the loss of vitality of the left and radical politics.

24. The right to medical care is recognized by Article 25 of the Universal Declaration of Human Rights (1948) and also recognized by the Italian Constitution, which recognizes the right to free medical care for all individuals and not just citizens (Article 32).

25. In the end, President Giorgio Napolitano was the one who refused to sign it and thus prevented the government from having the last word on the issue.

THE FREEDOM OF EQUALS

1. If not for the fact that he was my granduncle. Although I cannot (yet) speak about his life and writings, it is important to say that the following, more or less abstract, philosophical discussion is my own way of speaking about him.

2. I take this expression from Berti's edition of Bakunin's writings on the notion of freedom (Bakunin 2000).

3. On the first, see for instance Marx's early writings, such as "The Economic and Political Manuscript of 1844" and "On the Jewish Question" (Marx 1978b, 1978c). The second is the view that emerges from his mature writings, at least since *Capital* (Marx 1976). For a general analysis of the problem of freedom in Marx, see Petrucciani (1996).

4. See, for instance, Foucault (1988). On the convergence between post-structuralism and anarchism, see May (1994).

5. On voluntary servitude, a classical text is La Boétie (2005).

6. Note the resemblance to Castoriadis's idea of the imaginary constitution of society (Castoriadis 1987).

7. I have tried to develop a very similar idea through the concept of political myth (Bottici 2007).

8. The concept of recognition has recently been at the center of a lively debate in critical theory. See, for instance, Honneth (1995) and Fraser and Honneth (2003). Bakunin, similar to Honneth, also probably derives the concept of recognition from Hegel.

9. See, for instance, *The Holy Family*, where Marx says that man is not free for the negative force to avoid this or that, but for the positive power to develop his own individuality (Marx and Engels 1975:131). On the distinction between positive and negative freedom, see Berlin (1969) and Bobbio (1995).

10. To begin with, see Foucault (1980).

11. On the origins of the concept and its historical roots in modern moral philosophy, see Schneewind (1998).

12. See, for instance, the following definition of autonomy, which opens a collection of Italian Workerist writings: "Autonomy has no frontiers. It is a way of eluding the imperatives of production, the verticality of institutions, the traps of political representations, the virus of power" (Lotringer and Marazzi 2007:8). More recently, Hardt and Negri developed this concept through Spinoza's notion of the multitude (Hardt and Negri 2004).

13. Proudhon (2001:125–135) pointed this out very clearly when he described the antinomy between the two principles of freedom and authority.

14. In contrast to other scholars who use the term *collectivist* (Miller 2001), I prefer to call it social, because this includes both anarcho-communism, in the line of Kropotkin, and the collectivist variant, which, following Bakunin, leaves some space for the individual enjoyment of property.

15. See, for instance, http://www.anti-state.com/ and http://www.strike-the-root .com/ (accessed on 1 September 2009).

16. On this point, see the critique to utopian socialists and communists in the Manifesto (Marx and Engels 1978:491–499).

17. I am thinking here of the novelty brought about by contemporary fluid capitalism described in chapter 6. For a short but acute presentation of those novelties, see Marazzi (1994).

18. Shukaitis and Graeber offer an interesting explanation of the reasons why Debord is so little quoted in the academic literature; see Shukaitis & Graeber (2007: 21–23).

19. In "Critique of the Gotha Program," we read, for instance, as follows: "Between capitalist and communist society there lies the period of the revolutionary transformation of the one into the other. Corresponding to this is also a political transition period in which the state can be nothing but the revolutionary dictatorship of the proletariat" (Marx 1978a:538). The only other place where it appears is a letter to Weydemeyer in 1852.

20. It is clear from Bakunin's letter of protest that this was the main point of the controversy (Bakunin 1972). On the controversy, see Paul (1980:300–329).

21. In Proudhon's view, there are four main types of government, which correspond to the two main principles of authority and freedom: regimes of authority are both the government of all by one (monarchy) and the government of all by all (what he calls panarchy or communism), whereas regimes of freedom are both the government of all by everybody (democracy) and the government of everyone by everyone, which is anarchy or self-rule (Proudhon 2001:125–133). Proudhon's federalism can indeed be interpreted as a combination of the last two forms of government, what he calls respectively democracy and anarchy. And the same holds for Bakunin's free federation, which we have mentioned earlier.

22. In another brilliant passage, Kornegger (2009 [1975]:495) points out that "feminist capitalism is a contradiction in terms."

23. I cannot enter here into details on the critique of the prevalence of the problem of security in justifications for the existence of the modern state. Let me briefly recall the paradox of such a justification, which, as Agamben (1998) has recently pointed out, consists in the fact that subjects confer to the modern sovereign the right to kill them in order to receive the guarantee of their life.

24. See in particular Hardt and Negri (2000). In contrast to its classical usage, with the term *empire* Hardt and Negri mean a system of authority that has no definitive center, and as such their notion of empire comes very close to the idea of multilayered global governance (Bottici 2006).

25. On this point, see, for instance, Prichard (2010), who provocatively raises the question whether David Held is an anarchist. Indeed, many of the trends in contemporary discourses about globalization, global federation, and federalism are reminiscent of classical anarchist topics.

26. Foucault (1990) first uses the term in part 5 of the first volume of *The History of Sexuality*.

27. I include here both the new (or no) global movement with the Occupy movement, because I think they both illustrate my point very well. Whether they are part of the same movement or movement of movements is a secondary and perhaps also irrelevant question.

28. One of the most interesting examples of such subterranean heredity is the experience of the solidarity-based purchasing groups, which proliferate in the aftermath of the experience of social forums. Such networks are very efficient in providing an alternative model to capitalist consumption, by employing precisely their own networking logic. In other words, they defeat fluid capitalism on its own ground. See, for instance, the Web site of the national network of the Italian GAS at http://www.retegas.org/index.php?module=pagesetter&func=viewpub&tid=2&pid=10 (accessed on 3 September 2009).

29. On the Occupy Wall Street movement, see their official Web site (http://occupywallst.org/).

BIBLIOGRAPHY

Abbagnano, N. 1961. *Dizionario di filosofia*. Turin: UTET.

Abrahamian, E. 2003. The U.S. Media, Huntington and September 11. *Third World Quarterly* 24(3): 529–544.

Ackerman, B. 1994. Political liberalism. *Journal of Philosophy* 91(7): 364–386.

Adorno, F. 1961a. *La filosofia antica. I. la formazione del pensiero filosofico dalle origini a Platone VI–VII Secolo A.C.* Milan: Feltrinelli.

——— 1961b. *La filosofia antica. II. filosofia, cultura, scuole tra Aristotele e Augusto IV–II Secolo A.C.* Milan: Feltrinelli.

Adorno, T. W., and M. Horkheimer. 1997. *Dialectic of Enlightenment*. London: Verso.

Agamben, G. 1998. *Homo Sacer: Sovereign Power and Bare Life*. Stanford: Stanford University Press.

——— 2007. *Il regno e la gloria: Per una genealogia teologica dell'economia e del governo*. Vicenza: Neri Pozza.

Albanese, B. 1983. Persona: Diritto romano. In C. Mortati and G. Santoro-Passarelli, eds., *Enciclopedia del diritto*, pp. 169–181. Milan: Giuffré

Albrow, M. 1996. *The Global Age: State and Society Beyond Modernity*. Cambridge: Polity.

Amin, S. 1988. *L'eurocentrisme: Critique d'une edéologie*. Paris: Anthropos.

Anderson, B. 1991. *Imagined Communities: Reflections on the Origins and Spread of Nationalism*. London: Verso.

An-Na'im, A. 1999. Political Islam in national politics and international relations. In P. L. Berger, ed., *The Desecularisation of the World*, pp. 103–122. Washington, DC: Ethics and Public Policy Center.

Arendt, H. 1958. *The Human Condition*. Chicago: University of Chicago Press.

—— 1964. *Eichman in Jerusalem: A Report on the Banality of Evil*. New York: Penguin.

—— 1968a. *Men in Dark Times*. San Diego: Harvest.

—— 1968b. Truth and politics. In *Between Past and Future*, pp. 223–260. London: Penguin.

—— 1969. Introduction to Walter Benjamin's *Illuminations*. In H. Arendt, ed., H. Zohn, trans., *Illuminations*. New York: Schocken.

—— 1972. Lying in politics. In *Crises of the Republic*. New York: Harvest.

—— 1982. *Lectures on Kant's Political Philosophy*. Brighton: Harvester.

—— 1996. *Love and Saint Augustine*. Chicago: University of Chicago Press.

—— 2005. *The Promise of Politics*. New York: Schocken.

Aristotle. 1964. *On the Soul. Parva Naturalia. On Breath*. Trans. W. S. Hett. Cambridge: Harvard University Press.

Armstrong, D. 1968. *A Materialist Theory of the Mind*. London: Routledge.

Arnason, J. P. 1994. Reason, imagination, interpretation. In G. Robinson and J. Rundell, eds., *Rethinking Imagination: Culture and Creativity*, pp. 155–170. London: Routledge.

Arruzza, C. 2010. *Le relazioni pericolose: Matrimoni e divorzi tra marxismo e femminismo*. Rome: Allegre.

Asad, T. 2002. *Formations of the Secular: Christianity, Islam, Modernity*. Stanford: Stanford University Press.

Baccelli, L. 1999. *Il particolarismo dei diritti*. Rome: Carocci.

—— 2009a. Dieci anni dopo: Il particolarismo dei diritti. In S. Vida, ed., *Diritti Umani: Trasformazioni e Reazioni*, pp. 61–83. Bologna: Bologna University Press.

—— 2009b. *I diritti dei popoli: Universalismo e differenze culturali*. Bari: Laterza.

Bacon, F. 1963. De dignitate et augmentis scientiarum. In *The Works of Francis Bacon*, 1:415–438. Stuttgart: Fromann.

—— 1986. Of the dignity and advancement of learning. In *The Works of Francis Bacon*, 4:275–498. Stuttgart: Fromann.

Bakunin, M. 1872. Letter to La Liberte. In http://www.marxists.org/reference/archive/bakunin/works/1872/la-liberte.htm.

—— 1972. *Stato e Anarchia*. Milan: Feltrinelli.

—— 1974. The political theology of Mazzini. In *Selected Writings*, pp. 214–231. New York: Grove.

—— 1996. *Tre conferenze sull'anarchia*. Rome: Manifestolibri.

—— 2000. *La libertà degli Uguali*. Ed. G. N. Berti. Milan: Eleuthera.

Baptist, G. 2008. Tra ideazione e fatticità: La possibilità della fantasia in Edmund Husserl. In V. Gessa Kurotschka and C. de Luzenberger, eds., *Immaginazione Etica Interculturalità*, pp. 145–157. Milan: Mimesis.

Barkawi, T. 2010. Empire and order in international relations and security studies. In Robert A. Denemark, ed., *The International Studies Encyclopedia*, 3:1360–1379. Chichester: Wiley-Blackwell.

Bauman, Z. 1998. *Globalization: The Human Consequences*. Cambridge: Polity.

Bazzicalupo, L. 2006. *Il governo delle vite: Biopolitica e bioeconomia*. Bari: Laterza.

Beauvoir, S. de. 1953. *The Second Sex*. New York: Knopf.

Beiner, R., and J. Nedelski, eds. 2001. *Judgement, Imagination and Politics: Themes from Kant to Arendt*. Lanham: Rowman and Littlefield.

Benjamin, W. 2002. The work of art in the age of its technological reproducibility. In *Selected Writings*, vol. 3: *1935–1938*. Cambridge: Belknap.

Berardi, F. B. 2011. *The Premonition of Guy Debord*. http://www.generation-online.org/t/tbifodebord.htm.

Berger, P. L., ed. 1999. *The Desecularization of the World*. Washington, DC: Ethics and Public Policy Center.

Berlin, I. 1969. *Four Essays on Liberty*. Oxford: Oxford University Press.

Bernstein, J. 1990. Difficult difference: Rousseau's fiction of identity. In P. Hulme and L. Jordanova, eds., *The Enlightenment Shadows*, pp. 66–84. London: Routledge.

—— 1992. *The Fate of Art: Aesthetic Alienation from Kant to Derrida*. Philadelphia: Pennsylvania State University Press.

Bernstein, R. J. 2010. The specter haunting multiculturalism. *Philosophy and Social Criticism* 36 (3–4): 301–394.

Blaut, J. M. 1993. *The Colonizer's Model of the World: Geographical Diffusionism and Eurocentric History*. New York: Guilford.

Bloch, E. 1986a. *Natural Law and Human Dignity*. Cambridge: MIT Press.

—— 1986b. *The Principle of Hope*. Cambridge: MIT Press.

Block, N. 1981. *Imagery*. Cambridge: MIT Press.

Blumenberg, H. 1983. *The Legitimacy of Modern Age*. Cambridge: MIT Press.

—— 1985. *Work on Myth*. Cambridge: MIT Press.

Bobbio, N. 1985. *Stato, governo, società: Per una teoria generale della politica*. Turin: Einaudi.

—— 1990. Diritto. In N. Bobbio, N. Matteucci, and G. Pasquino, eds., *Dizionario di politica*, , pp. 312–316, 800–809. Turin: UTET.

—— 1995. *Eguaglianza e libertà*. Turin: Einaudi.

Boggs, C. 2000. *The End of Politics: Corporate and the Decline of the Public Sphere*. New York: Guilford.

Boltanski, L. 1999. *The Distant Suffering: Morality, Media and Politics*. Cambridge: Cambridge University Press.

Boltanski, L., and E. Chiappello. 2005. *The New Spirit of Capitalism*. London: Verso.

Bottici, C. 2001. Globalizzazione, sovranità, anarchia. In D. D'Andrea and E. Pulcini, eds., *Filosofie della Globalizzazione*, pp. 169–196. 2d ed. Pisa: ETS.

—— 2006. War and conflict in a globalising world: Governance or empire? *Romanian Journal of Political Science* 6(1): 3–23.

—— 2007. *A Philosophy of Political Myth*. Cambridge: Cambridge University Press.

—— 2009a. *Men and States: Rethinking The Domestic Analogy in a Global Age*. Hampshire: Palgrave Macmillan.

—— 2009b. The politics of imagination and the public role of religion. *Philosophy and Social Criticism* 35(8): 1–22.

—— 2011a. From imagination to the imaginary and beyond: Towards a theory of imaginal politics. In C. Bottici and B. Challand, eds., *The Politics of Imagination*, pp. 16–38. London: Routledge/Birkbeck Law Press.

—— 2011b. Imaginal politics. *Thesis Eleven* 106:72.

—— 2012. Another Enlightenment: Spinoza on myth and imagination. *Constellations* 19(4): 1–19.

Bottici, C., and B. Challand. 2006. Rethinking political myth: The clash of civilisations as a self-fulfilling prophecy. *European Journal of Social Theory* 9(3): 315–336.

—— 2010. *The Myth of the Clash of Civilisations*. London: Routledge.

——, eds. 2011. *The Politics of Imagination*. London: Routledge/Birkbeck Law Press.

—— 2013. *Imagining Europe: Myth, Memory, and Identity*. Cambridge, Cambridge University Press.

Bottici, C., and A. Kuehner. 2011. Der Mythos des "clash of civilizations" zwischen politischer Philosophie und Psychoanalyse, coauthored with Angela Kuehner. In R. Haubl and M. Leuzinger-Bohleber, eds., *Psychoanalyse: Leise Stimme des Unbewussten. Festschrift zum 50 Jährigen Bestehen des Sigmund-Freud-Instituts*. Gottingen: Vandenhoeck and Ruprecht.

Breeur, R. 2006. Du verre dans l'âme: L'imaginaire et sa pathologie selon Sartre. In C. Fleury, ed., *Imagination, Imaginaire, Imaginal*. Paris: PUF.

Brenna, B. 1997. Erich Fromm: From social unconscious to class consciousness. *Public* 4:5–18.

Buck-Morss, S. 2003. *Thinking Past Terror: Islam and Critical Theory on the Left*. London: Verso.

—— 2011. Visual studies and global imagination. In C. Bottici and B. Challand, eds., *The Politics of Imagination*, pp. 214–233. London: Routledge/Birkbeck Law Press.

Buruma, I., and A. Margalit. 2004. *Occidentalism: The West in the Eyes of Its Enemies*. New York: Penguin.

Busino, G., ed. 1989. *Autonomie et Autotransformation de la Société: La Philosophie Militante de Cornelius Castoriadis*. Geneva: Droz.

Butler, J., E. Laclau, and S. Žižek. 2000. *Contingency, Hegemony, Universality*. London: Verso.

Camassa, G. 1986. Phantasia da Platone ai neoplatonici. In M. Fattori and M. Bianchi, eds., *Phantasia-Imaginatio*, pp. 23–55. Rome: Ateneo.

Campitelli, A. 1983. Persona: Diritto intermedio. In C. Mortati and G. Santoro Passerelli, eds., *Enciclopedia del diritto*, pp. 181–193. Milan: Giuffrè.

Carnevali, B. 2005. Potere e riconoscimento: Il modello Hobbesiano. *Iride* 46:313–335.

Carotenuto, A. 1991. *Trattato di psicologia della personalità e delle differenze individuali*. Milan: Raffaello Cortina.

Castoriadis, C. 1976. The Hungarian source. *Telos* 76(29): 4–22.

—— 1987. *The Imaginary Institution of Society*. Cambridge: Polity.

—— 1991. Power, politics, autonomy. In *Philosophy, Politics, Autonomy: Essays in Political Philosophy*, pp. 143–174. Oxford: Oxford University Press.

—— 1997a. *Fait et à Faire: Les Carrefour du Labyrinthe 5*. Paris: Seuil.

—— 1997b. Institution of society and religion. In D. A. Curtis, ed. and trans., *World in Fragments: Writings on Politics, Society, Psychoanalysis, and the Imagination*, pp. 311–330. Stanford: Stanford University Press.

—— 1997c. The discovery of the imagination. In D. A. Curtis, ed. and trans., *World in Fragments: Writings on Politics, Society, Psychoanalysis, and the Imagination*, pp. 246–272. Stanford: Stanford University Press.

—— 1997d. Radical imagination and the social instituting imaginary. In D. A. Curtis, ed., *The Castoriadis Reader*, pp. 321–337. Oxford: Blackwell.

Cattanei, E. 2008. Melanconia, deliberazione e *phantasia*: Stati patologici e fisiologici dell'immaginazione deliberativa in Aristotele. In V. Gessa Kurotschka and C. de Luzenberger, eds., *Immaginazione Etica Interculturalità*, pp. 39–52. Milan: Mimesis.

Cavarero, A. 2002. *Stately Bodies: Literature, Philosophy, and the Question of Gender*. Ann Arbor: University of Michigan Press.

—— 2009. *Nonostante Platone: Figure femminili nella filosofia antica*. Verona: Ombre Corte.

Cerutti, F. 1993. Ethics and politics in the Nuclear Age. The end of deterrence? *Praxis International* 12(4): 387–404.

—— 2007. *Global Challenges for Leviathan: A Political Philosophy of Nuclear Weapons and Global Warming*. Plymouth: Lexington.

Challand, B. 2011a. Religion and the struggle for people's imagination: the case of contemporary Islamism. In C. Bottici and B. Challand, eds., *The Politics of Imagination*. London: Routledge/Birkbeck Law Press.

—— 2011b. The counter-power of civil society and the emergence of a new political imaginary in the Arab World. *Constellations* 18(3): 271–283.

Chanter, T. 2006. *Gender: Key Concepts in Philosophy*. New York: Continuum.

Chiodi, G. M. 2010. *Speculum symbolicum: Mondo immaginale e simbolica politica*. Naples: Scripta Web.

Cochrane, F., R. Duffy, and J. Selby, eds. 2003. *Global Governance, Conflict, and Resistance*. Basingstoke: Palgrave Macmillan.

Cocking, J. M. 1984. Bacon's view of imagination. In M. Fattori, ed., *Francis Bacon: Terminologia e fortuna nel XVII secolo*. Rome: Lessico Intellettuale Europeo.

—— 1991. *Imagination. A Study in the History of Ideas*. London: Routledge.

Cooper, M. 2008. *Life as a Surplus: Biotechnology and Capitalism*. Seattle: University of Washington Press.

Corbin, H. 1979. *Corp spirituel et terre céleste*. Paris: Buchet-Chastel.

Corradi, L. 2013. Black, red, pink and green. Breaking boundaries, building bridges. In J. Blumenfeld, C. Bottici, and S. Critchley, eds., *The Anarchist Turn*, chapter 7. London: Pluto.

Cotta, M. 1983. Rappresentanza politica. In N. Bobbio, N. Matteucci, G., and Pasquino, eds., *Dizionario di politica*, pp. 954-959. Turin: UTET.

Cotta, S. 1983. Persona: Filosofia del diritto. In C. Mortati and G. Santoro Passerelli, eds., *Enciclopedia del diritto*, pp. 159-169. Milan: Giuffrè.

Coulter, J. 1999. Discourse and mind. *Human Studies* 22:163-181.

Courtine, J-F. 1992a. Realitas. In G. Gabriel, K. Gründer, and J. Ritter, eds., *Historisches Wörterbuch der Philosophie*, 7:178-185. Darmstadt: Wissenschaftliche Buchgesellschaft.

—— 1992b. Realitätidealität. In G. Gabriel, K. Gründer, and J. Ritter, eds., *Historisches Wörterbuch der Philosophie*, 7:185-193. Darmstadt: Wissenschaftliche Buchgesellschaft.

Critchley, S. 2008. *The Book of Dead Philosophers*. New York: Vintage.

—— 2012. *The Faith of the Faithless: Experiments in Political Theology*. London: Verso.

Croce, B. 1913. *Breviario di estetica: Quattro lezioni*. Bari: Laterza.

Cumming, R. 1992. Role playing. Sartre's transformation of Husserl's phenomenology. In C. Howells, ed., *Cambridge Companion to Sartre*, pp. 39-66. Cambridge: Cambridge University Press.

Cutro, A. 2005. *Biopolitica. Storia e attualità di un concetto*. Verona: Ombre Corte.

D'Andrea, D. 2009. Tra adattamento e rifiuto: Verso una teoria delle immagini del mondo. *Quaderni di Teoria Sociale* 9(17): 49.

Debord, G. 1994. *The Society of the Spectacle*. New York: Zone.

Deleuze, G. 2006. *Nietzsche and Philosophy*. New York: Columbia University Press.

De Kerckhove, D. 1990. *La civilisation video-chretienne*. Paris: Retz.

Dennett, D. 1986. *Content and Consciousness*. London: Routledge.

Dews, P. 2002. Imagination and the symbolic: Castoriadis and Lacan. *Constellations* 9(4): 516-521.

Dicey, A. V. 1959. *Introduction to the Study of the Law of the Constitution*. London: Macmillan.

Dillon, J. 1986. Plotinus on the transcendental imagination. In J. P. Mackey, ed., *Religious Imagination*, pp. 55–64. Edinburgh: Edinburgh University Press.

Disch, S. 1996. *Hannah Arendt and the Limits of Philosophy*. Ithaca: Cornell University Press.

Donzelot, J. 1984. *L'invention du social: Essai sur le déclin del passions politiques*. Paris: Fayard.

Doran, M. 2002. Somebody else's civil war. *Foreign Affairs* 81(1): 22–42.

Douzinas, C. 2000. *The End of Human Rights*. Oxford: Hart.

Douzinas, C., and L. Nead. 1999. *Law and Image*. Chicago: University of Chicago Press.

Dworkin, R. 2006. *Is Democracy Possible Here?* Princeton: Princeton University Press.

Eder, K. 2003. Social movements and democratisation. In G. Delanty and F. Isin, eds., *Handbook of Historical Sociology*, pp. 276–287. London: Sage.

Eisenstadt, S. N., ed. 2002. *Multiple Modernities*. New Brunswick: Transaction.

Engell, J. 1981. *The Creative Imagination: Enlightenment to Romanticism*. Cambridge: Harvard University Press.

Esposito, R. 1998. *Communitas: Origine e destino della comunità*. Turin: Einaudi.

—— 2008. *Bios: Biopolitics and Philosophy*. Minneapolis: University of Minnesota Press.

Evans, D. 1996. *An Introductory Dictionary of Lacanian Psychoanalysis*. London: Routledge.

Fattori, M., and M. Bianchi, eds. 1986. *Phantasia-imaginatio*. Rome: Ateneo.

Ferrara, A. 2008. *The Force of the Example: Explorations in the Paradigm of Judgment*. New York: Columbia University Press.

Ferraris, M. 1996. *L'immaginazione*. Bologna: Il Mulino.

Fichte, J. G. 1982. *The Science of Knowledge*. Ed. and trans. Peter Heath and John Lachs. Cambridge: Cambridge University Press.

Finlayson, J.G. 2010. Bare life and politics in Agamben's reading of Aristotle. *Review of Politics* 72(1): 1–71.

Fleury, C., ed. 2006. *Imagination, Imaginaire, Imaginal*. Paris: PUF.

Flynn, T. 1992. Sartre and the poetics of history. In C. Howells, ed., *Cambridge Companion to Sartre*, pp. 213–260. Cambridge: Cambridge University Press.

Flood, C. 1996. *Political Myth: A Theoretical Introduction*. New York: Garland.

Forst, R. 2007. *Das Recht auf Rechtfertigung*. Frankfurt: Suhrkamp.

Forti, S. 1994. *Vita dell amente e tempo della polis: Hannah Arendt tra filosofia e politica*. Milan: Franco Angeli.

Foucault, M. 1980. *Power-Knowledge*. New York: Harvester.

—— 1988. *Technologies of the Self: A Seminar with Michel Foucault*. Ed. L. H. Martin, H. Gutman, and P. Hutton. Amherst: University of Massachusetts Press.

—— 1990. *The History of Sexuality: An Introduction*. New York: Vintage.

——— 1997. Society must be defended. In *Lectures at the Collège de France, 1975–1976*. New York: Picador.

——— 2008. *The Birth of Biopolitics: Lectures at the Collège de France, 1978–79*. New York: Palgrave Macmillan.

Fraser, N., and A. Honneth. 2003. *Redistribution or Recognition? A Political-Philosophical Exchange*. London: Verso.

Frazzi, F. 2004. "Dai dirottamenti all'11 settembre: Terrorismo e supereroi in vent'anni di fumetti." MA thesis. Bologna: Università di Bologna.

Freud, S. 1923. The ego and the id. In J. Strachey, with A. Freud, eds., *The Standard Edition of the Complete Psychological Works of Sigmund Freud*, 19:1–66. London: Hogarth.

——— 1937. *Interpretation of Dreams*. London: Allen and Unwin.

——— 1950. *Totem and Taboo*. New York: Norton.

——— 1959. *Group Psychology and the Analysis of the Ego*. New York: Norton.

——— 1965. *Introductory Lectures on Psychoanalysis*. New York: Norton.

——— 1989. *Jokes and Their Relation to the Unconscious*. New York: Norton.

Freudenthal, J. 1863. *Ueber den Begriff des Wortes Phantasia bei Aristoteles*. Göttingen: Universitaet-Buchdruckerei.

Friese, H. 2001. Imagination: history of the concept. In N. J. Smelser and P. B. Baltes, eds., *International Encyclopedia of the Social and Behavioural Sciences*, 11:7197–7201. Amsterdam: Elsevier.

Fromm, E. 2001. *Beyond the Chains of Illusion: My Encounter with Marx and Freud*. New York: Continuum.

Fukuyama, F. 1992. *The End of History and the Last Man*. New York: Free Press.

Gadamer, H. G. 1988. *Truth and Method*. London: Sheed and Ward.

Gauchet, M. 2002. Redefining the unconscious. *Thesis Eleven* 71:4–23.

——— 2005. *La condition politique*. Paris: Gallimard.

Galilei, G. 1996. Il saggiatore. In *Opere*, vol. 1. Turin: UTET.

Galli, C. 1988. *Modernità: Categorie e profili critici*. Bologna: Il Mulino.

Gehlen, A. 1988. *Man, His Nature and Place in the World*. New York: Columbia University Press.

Geisser, V. 2003. *La nouvelle islamophobie*. Paris: La Découverte.

Gerges, F. A. 2005. *The Far Enemy: Why Jihad Went Global*. New York: Cambridge University Press.

Ghiron, V. 2001. *La teoria dell'immaginazione di Edmund Husserl. Fantasia e coscienza figurale nella fenomenologia descrittiva*. Venice: Marsilio.

——— 2002. Percezione ed immaginazione nella fenomenologia descrittiva di Edmund Husserl. In R. Lanfredini, ed., *Forma e contenuto: Aspetti di teoria della conoscenza, della mente e della morale*, pp. 113–131. Milan: LED.

Goodman, P. 2009. Freedom and autonomy. In R. Graham, ed., *Anarchism. A Documentary History of Libertarian Ideas*, 2:329–331. Montreal: Black and Rose.

Graeber, D. 2002. The new anarchists. *New Left Review* 13:61–73.

Gramsci, A. 1996. *Prison Notebooks*. New York: Columbia University Press.

Gray, J. 2003. *Al-Qaeda and What It Means to Be Modern*. London: Faber and Faber.

Guenancia, P. 2006. La critique cartésienne des critiques de l'imagination. In C. Fleury, ed., *Imagination, Imaginaire, Imaginal*, pp. 43–76. Paris: PUF.

Guizzardi, G., ed. 1986. *La narrazione del carisma*. Turin: Eri.

—— 2005. Esserci anche dopo. *Religioni e Società*, 53:12–21.

Gutman, S. A., S. M. Parrish, J. Rufting, and P. H. Rufting Jr. 1995. *Konkordanz zu den Gesammelten Werke von Sigmund Freud*, vol. 2. Waterloo: North Waterloo Academic.

Habermas, J. 1987. *The Philosophical Discourse of Modernity: Twelve Lectures*. Cambridge: Polity.

—— 1992. *Postmetaphysical Thinking: Philosophical Essays*. Cambridge: MIT Press.

—— 1998. *The Inclusion of the Other: Studies in Political Theory*. Cambridge: MIT Press.

—— 2001. Remarks on legitimation through human rights. In *The Postnational Constellation*, pp. 113–130. Cambridge: MIT Press.

—— 2006. Religion in the public sphere. *European Journal of Philosophy* 14(1): 1–25.

Haenni, P. 2005. *L'Islam de marché: l'autre révolution conservatrice*. Paris: Seuil.

Halliday, F. 2005. *Middle East in International Relations: Politics and Ideology*. Cambridge: Cambridge University Press.

Hardt, M., and A Negri. 2000. *Empire*. Harvard: Harvard University Press.

—— 2004. *Multitude: War and Democracy in the Age of Empire*. New York: Penguin.

—— 2009. *Commonwealth*. Harvard: Harvard University Press.

Harvey, D. 1990. *The Condition of Postmodernity: An Inquiry Into the Origins of Cultural Change*. Hoboken: Wiley-Blackwell.

Hays, C. 2009. *Plaid Kilts and Black Jackets: Social Imaginary and the Construction of Community*. Saarbrücken: Lambert Academic.

Heidegger, M. 1997. *Kant and the Problem of Metaphysics*. Bloomington: Indiana University Press.

Hegel, G. W. F. 1875. *Aesthetics*, vol. 1. Trans. T. M. Knox. Oxford: Clarendon.

—— 1975. *Philosophy of Mind*, part 3 of the *Encyclopedia of the Philosophical Sciences*. Trans. William Wallace. Oxford: Clarendon.

Held, D. 1995. *Democracy and the Global Order: From the Modern State to Cosmopolitan Governance*. Cambridge: Polity.

Held, D., A. Mcgrew, D. Goldblatt, and J. Perraton. 1999. *Global Transformations*. Cambridge: Polity.

Hillman, J. 1971. *Psychology: Monotheistic or Polytheistic?* Putnam: Spring.

—— 1972. *The Myth of Analysis: Three Essays in Archetypal Psychology*. Evanston, IL: Northwestern University Press.

—— 2005. *Healing Fiction*. Putnam: Spring.

Hofmann, H. 1974. *Repräsentation*. Berlin: Dunker and Humblot.

Hoffmann, F. et al. 1992. Realismus. In G. Gabriel, K. Gründer, and J. Ritter, eds., *Historisches Wörterbuch der Philosophie*, 7:148–170. Darmstadt: Wissenschaftliche Buchgesellschaft.

Honneth, A. 1995. *The Struggle for Recognition: The Moral Grammar of Social Conflict*. Cambridge: Polity.

Hopper, E. 2003. *The Social Unconscious: Selected Papers*. London: Jessica Kingsley.

Howells, C. ed. 1992. *Cambridge Companion to Sartre*. Cambridge: Cambridge University Press.

Huntington, S. 1996. *The Clash of Civilizations and the Remaking of World Order*. New York: Simon and Schuster.

Husserl, E. 1976. Idee zu einer reinen Phänomen.ologie und phänomenologischen Philosophie. In J. N. Findlay, trans., *Husserliana*, vol 3. The Hague: Nijhoff.

—— 1980. Phantasie, Bildbewusstsein, Eriunnerung. Zur Phänomenologie der anschaulichen Vergegenwärtigungen. Texte aus dem Nachlass (1898–1925). In J. N. Findlay, trans., *Husserliana*, vol. 23. The Hague: Nijhoff.

—— 1984 [1901]. Logische Untersuchungen. In J. N. Findlay, trans., *Husserliana*, vol. 19. London: Routledge.

Jacobsen, T. 1943. Primitive democracy in Ancient Mesopotamia. *Journal of Near Eastern Studies* 2(3): 159–72.

Jacoby, R. 2000. *The End of Utopia: Politics and Culture in an Age of Apathy*. New York: Basic Books.

Jenny, L. 1990. The unrepresentable enemy. *Art and Text* 35:35–112.

Jonas, H. 1973. Zwische Nichts und Ewigkeit: Zur Lehre vom Menachen. In G. Bien, ed., *Die Grundlegung der Politischen Philosophie bei Aristoteles*. Freiburg: Karl Alber.

Jung, C. G. 1936. Traumsymbole des Individuationsprozess. In *Grundwerke*, vol. 12. Meilen: Walter.

—— 1962. *Psychological Types: Or the Psychology of Individuation*. Trans. H. Goodwin Baynes. New York: Pantheon.

—— 1990. *The Archetypes and the Collective Unconscious*. Trans. R. F. C. Hull. Princeton: Princeton University Press.

Juris, J. S. 2009. Anarchism; or, The cultural logic of networking. In *Contemporary Anarchist Studies: An Introductory Anthology of Anarchy in the Academy*. London: Routledge.

Kant, I. 1991. An answer to the question: What is Enlightenment? In *Kant Political Writings*, pp. 54–60. Cambridge: Cambridge University Press.

—— 1997. *Critique of Practical Reason*. Cambridge: Cambridge University Press.

—— 1998 [1781]. *Critique of Pure Reason*. In P. Guyer and A. W. Wood, trans., *The Cambridge Edition of the Works of Immanuel Kant*. Cambridge: Cambridge University Press.

—— 2000. *Critique of the Power of Judgment*. In P. Guyer and A. W. Wood, trans., *The Cambridge Edition of the Works of Immanuel Kant*. Cambridge: Cambridge University Press.

Katz, E., and D. Dayan. 1992. *Media Events*. Cambridge: Cambridge University Press.

Kaufmann, L., and J. Guilhaumou. 2003. *L'invention de la Société: Nominalisme Politique et Science Sociale au XVII Siècle*. Paris: Ecole des Hautes Etudens en Sciences Sociales.

Kearney, R. 1988. *The Wake of Imagination: Toward a Postmodern Culture*. London: Routledge.

Kelly, C. 1997. Rousseau and the case against (and for) the Arts. In C. Orwin and N. Tarcov, eds., *The Legacy of Rousseau*. Chicago: University of Chicago Press.

Kepel, G. 1991. *Revanche de dieu: Chrétiens, Juifs et Musulmans a la reconquête du monde*. Paris: Seuil.

—— 2006. *Jihad: The Trial of Political Islam*. London: I. B. Tauris.

Kepel, G., and J.-P. Milell, eds. 2008. *Al Qaeda in Its Own Words*. Cambridge: Belknap.

Kerényi, K., and C. G. Jung. 1963. *Essays on a Science of Mythology*. Princeton: Princeton University Press.

Kind, A. 2001. Putting the image back in imagination. *Philosophy and Phenomenological Research* 62(1): 85–109.

Kohn, M. 2008. Homo spectator: Public space in the age of the spectacle. *Philosophy and Social Criticism* 34(5): 467–486.

Kornegger, P. 2009 [1975]. Anarchism: The feminist connection. In R. Graham, ed., *Anarchism. A Documentary History of Libertarian Ideas*. Montreal: Black Rose.

Kosslyn, S., W. Thompson, and G. Ganis. 2006. *The Case for Mental Imagery*. Oxford: Oxford University Press.

Kottman, P. 2007. *A Politics of the Scene*. Stanford: Stanford University Press.

Kulvicki, J. 2006. *On Images: Their Structure and Content*. Oxford: Clarendon.

Kurotschka, V. G., and C. de Luzenberger. 2008. *Immaginazione etica ed interculturalità*. Milan: Mimesis.

La Boétie, E. de. 2005. On voluntary servitude. In R. Graham, ed., *Anarchism: A Documentary History of Libertarian Ideas*, 2:329–331. Montreal: Black and Rose.

Lacan, J. 1999. *Écrits*. Paris: Seuil.

La Caze, M. 2002. *The Analytic Imaginary*. Ithaca: Cornell University Press.

Laplanche, J., and J. B. Pontalis. 1992. *Vocabulaire de la psychanalyse*. Paris: PUF.

Lara, M. P. 1998. *Moral Textures: Feminist Narratives in the Public Sphere*. Cambridge: Polity.

—— 2007. *Narrating Evil: A Postmetaphysical Theory of Reflective Judgement.* New York: Columbia University Press.

—— 2011. Feminist imagination: The aesthetic role of critique and representation. In C. Bottici and B. Challand, eds., *The Politics of Imagination*, pp. 195–213. New York: Routledge.

Lazzarato, M. 1997. *Lavoro immateriale: Forme di vita e produzione di soggettività.* Verona: Ombre Corte.

—— 2011. From biopower to biopolitics. http://www.generation-online.org/c/fcbio politics.htm (accessed 17 January 2011).

Lefort, C. 1986. *Essais sur le politique.* Paris: Seuil.

Lemke, T. 2011. *Bio-Politics. An Advanced Introduction.* New York: New York University Press.

Lentin, A. 2005. Replacing "race," historicizing "culture" in multiculturalism. *Patterns of Predjudice* 38(4): 379–396.

Levi, P. 2005. *Se questo è un uomo.* Turin: Einaudi.

Lévi-Strauss, C. 1969. *The Raw and the Cooked.* New York: Harper and Row.

—— 1973. *From Honey to Ashes.* New York: Harper and Row.

—— 1978. *The Origin of Table Manners.* New York: Harper and Row.

—— 1981. *The Naked Man.* New York: Harper and Row.

Lindekilde, L. E. 2008. "Contested caricatures: Dynamics of Muslim Claims-Making During the Muhammad Caricatures Controversy." PhD thesis, Florence: European University Institute.

Live Prayer. The first global prayer meeting. http://www.liveprayer.com/index.cfm (accessed 26 September 2008).

Lotringer, S., and C. Marazzi, C. 2007. *Autonomia: Post-Political Politics.* Los Angeles: Semiotext(e).

Mack, A. 2011. The image: Seeing more and seeing less than is there. *Social Research* 78(4): 1263–1275.

MacKinnon, C. 2000. *Are Women Human? And Other International Dialogues.* Cambridge: Belknap.

Maguire, M. 2006. *The Conversion of Imagination: From Pascal Through Rousseau to Tocqueville.* Cambridge: Harvard University Press.

Malatesta, E. 2001. *L'anarchia.* Rome: Datanews. English trans. http://theanarchistli brary.org/HTML/Errico_Malatesta__Anarchy.html.

Mannheim, K. 1966. *Ideology and Utopia.* London: Routledge.

Marazzi, C. 1994. *Il posto dei calzini: La svolta linguistica dell'economia ed I suoi effetti sulla politica.* Turin: Bollati Boringhieri.

Marcucci, N. 2010. Lo specchio del Levitano: Il potere di riconoscere tra antropologia e rappresentanza. In L. Bernini, M. Farnesi, and N. Marcucci, eds., *La sovranità scomposta: Sull'attualità del Leviatano*, pp. 55–87. Milan: Mimesis.

Marcuse, H. 1974. *Eros and Civilization: A Philosophical Inquiry Into Freud*. Boston: Beacon.

—— 1991. *One-Dimensional Man: Studies in the Ideology of Advanced Industrial Society*. Boston: Beacon.

Marx, K. 1969. The eighteenth Brumaire of Lois Bonaparte. In *Karl Marx and Friederich Engels: Selected Works in Three Volumes*, 1:394–488. Moscow: Progress.

—— 1976. *Capital*, vol. 1. London: Penguin.

—— 1978a. Critique of the Gotha Program. In R. C. Tucker, ed., *Marx-Engels Reader*, pp. 525–541. New York: Norton.

—— 1978b. On the Jewish question. In R. C. Tucker, ed., *Marx-Engels Reader*, pp. 26–52. New York: Norton.

—— 1978c. The economic and philosophical manuscripts of 1844. In R. C. Tucker, ed., *Marx-Engels Reader*, pp. 66–125. New York: Norton.

—— 1978d. The Grundrisse. In R. C. Tucker, ed., *Marx-Engels Reader*, pp. 221–468. New York: Norton.

Marx, K., and F. Engels. 1975. The holy family; or, Critique of critical criticism: Against Bruno Bauer and company. In *Karl Marx and Frederick Engels Collected Works*, 5:1–540. London: Lawrence and Wishart.

—— 1976. The German ideology. In *Karl Marx and Frederick Engels Collected Works*, 4:1–211. London: Lawrence and Wishart.

—— 1978. Manifesto of the communist party. In R. C. Tucker, ed., *Marx-Engels Reader*, pp. 469–500. New York: Norton.

May, T. 1994. *The Political Philosophy of Poststructuralist Anarchism*. University Park: Pennsylvania State University Press.

Maza, S. 2005. *The Myth of the French Bourgeoisie: An Essay on the Social Imaginary, 1750–1850*. Cambridge: Harvard University Press.

McDonough, T. 2011. Unrepresentable enemies. *Afterall* 28:42–55.

McGowan, J. 2011. L'immaginazione in Hannah Arendt. *Iride* 62:81–101.

Mead, G. H. 1967. *Mind, Self, and Society*. Chicago: University of Chicago Press.

Meyer, T. 2002. *Media Democracy: How the Media Colonize Politics*. Oxford: Polity.

Midgley, M. 2003. *The Myths We Live By*. London: Routledge.

Miller, D. 2001. Anarchy. In S. M. Lipset, ed., *Political Philosophy. Theories Thinkers Concepts*. Washington, DC: CQ.

—— 2003. *Political Philosophy: A Very Short Introduction*. Oxford: Oxford University Press.

Mitchell, W. J. T. 2005. *What Do Pictures Want? The Lives and Loves of Images*. Chicago: Chicago University Press.

Mirzoeff, N. 1998. *The Visual Culture Reader*. 2d ed. London: Routledge.

Mouffe, C. 2005. *On the Political*. London: Routledge.

Muller, C. 1986. Fantasie et imagination sont-ils synonymes? In M. Fattori and M. Bianchi, eds., *Phantasia-Imaginatio*. Rome: Ateneo.

Newman, B. 1999. *The Mass Marketing of Politics: Democracy in an Age of Manufactured Images*. London: Sage.

Neuhouser, F. 2008. *Rousseau's Theodicy of Self-Love: Evil, Rationality, and the Drive for Recognition*. Oxford: Oxford University Press.

NHK. 2004. Jihad via the media. Documentary. National Japanese Television.

Nietzsche, F. 1982. *Daybreak*. Cambridge: Cambridge University Press.

Nikulin, D. 2002. *Matter, Imagination, and Geometry: Ontology, Natural Philosophy and Mathematics in Plotinus, Proclus, and Descartes*. Aldershot: Ashgate.

Norris, P., and R. Inglehart. 2004. *Sacred and Secular. Religion and Politics Worldwide*. Cambridge: Cambridge University Press.

Novalis. 1965. S *Schriften: Zweiter Band: Das Philosophische Werk I*. In P. Kluckhohn and R. Samuel, eds., *Die Werke Friedrich von Hardenbergs*, vol. 2. Darmstadt: Wissenschaftliche Buchgesellschaft.

Nussbaum, M. 1978. *Aristotle's De Motu Animalium: Text with Translation, Commentary, and Interpretive Essays*. Princeton: Princeton University Press.

—— 1995. *Poetic Justice: The Literary Imagination and Public Life*. Boston: Beacon.

—— 1997. *Cultivating Humanity*. Cambridge: Harvard University Press.

Nussbaum, M., and A. O. Rorty, eds. 1992. *Essays on Aristotle's De Anima*. Oxford: Clarendon.

O'Byrne, A. 2010. *Natality and Finitude*. Bloomington: Indiana University Press.

Odent, M. 1986. *Primal Health*. London: Century Hutchinson.

Ortner, S. B. 1996. *Making Gender. The Politics of Erotic Culture*. Boston: Beacon.

Owen, D. 2010. Genealogy. In Mark Bevir, ed., *Encyclopedia of Political Theory*, 2: 549–551. London: Sage.

Owen, R. 2004. *State, Power, and Politics in the Making of the Modern Middle East*. New York: Routledge.

Pace, E. 2007. *Introduzione alla Sociologia delle Religioni*. Rome: Carocci.

Pascal, B. 1963. *Ouvres Complètes*. Paris: Seuil.

Paul, T. 1980. *Karl Marx and the Anarchists*. London: Paul and Kegan.

Pedrini, B. 2001a. *Versi Liberi e Ribelli*. Carrara: Anarchiche Baffardello.

—— 2001b. *Noi Fummo i Ribelli, Noi Fummo i Predoni: Schegge Autobiografiche di Uomini Contro*. Carrara: Anarchiche Baffardello.

Petrucciani, S. 1996. Il problema della libertà in Marx. *Filosofia e Questioni* 2(1): 119-131.

Pierson, C. 1996. *The Modern State*. London: Routledge.

Piro, F. 2008. Immaginazione e profezia. Riflessioni su uno strano legame. In V. Gessa Kurotschka, V. Gessa Kurotschka, and C. de Luzenberger, eds., *Immaginazione Etica Interculturalità*, pp. 251-273. Milan: Mimesis.

Plato. 1989. *The Collected Dialogues*. Trans. E. Hamilton and H. Cairns. Princeton: Princeton University Press.

—— 1992. *Protagoras*. Trans. S. Lombardo and K. Bell. Indianapolis: Hackett.

Poggi, G. 1990. *The State: Its Nature, Development, and Prospects*. Cambridge: Polity.

Popper, K. 1978. Three worlds. *The Tanner Lectures on Human Values*. Ann Arbor: University of Michigan.

Prichard, A. 2010. David Held is an anarchist: Discuss. *Millennium Journal of International Studies* 39(2): 439-459.

Proudhon, P. J. 2001. *Critica della proprietà e dello stato*. Milan: Eleuthera.

Pulcini, E. 2012, *The Individual Without Passions: Modern Individualsim and the Loss of the Social Bond*. Plymouth: Lexington.

Rawls, J. 1973. *A Theory of Justice*. Oxford: Oxford University Press.

—— 1996. *Political Liberalism*. New York: Columbia University Press.

—— 1999. *The Law of Peoples: With "The Idea of a Public Reason Revisited."* Cambridge: Harvard University Press.

Ricoeur P. 1986, L'imagination dans le discourse et dans l'action. In *Du texte à l'action*. Paris: Seuil.

—— 1992. *Oneself as Another*. Chicago: Chicago University Press.

Roberstson, R. 1992. *Globalization: Social Theory and Global Culture*. London: Routledge.

Robinson, G., and J. Rundell, eds. 1994. *Rethinking Imagination: Culture and Creativity*. London: Routledge.

Rousseau, J. J. 1997. *The Social Contract, in The Social Contract and Other Later Political Writings*, pp. 39-152. Cambridge: Cambridge University Press.

Rorty, R. 1998a. Feminism and pragmatism. In *Truth and Progress. Philosophical Papers*, 3:202-227. Cambridge: Cambridge University Press.

—— 1998b. Human rights, rationality and sentimentality. In *Truth and Progress. Philosophical Papers*, 3:167-185. Cambridge: Cambridge University Press.

—— 1999. Religion as a conversation-stopper. In *Philosophy and Social Hope*. London: Penguin.

Rosanvallon, P. 2001. Towards a philosophical history of the political. In D. Castigkione and I. Hampsher-Monk, eds., *The History of Political Thought in National Context*. Cambridge: Cambridge University Press.

—— 2003. *Pur une histoire conceptuelle du politique*. Paris: Seuil.

Rose, N. 2007. *The Politics of Life Itself: Biomedicine, Power, and Subjectivity in the Twenty-First Century*. Princeton: Princeton University Press.

Rosenau, J. N., and E. O. Czempiel, eds. 1992. *Governance Without Government: Order and Change in World Politics*. Cambridge: Cambridge University Press.

Rousseau, J. J. 1960. *Politics and the Arts. Letter to d'Alembert on the Theatre*. Ithaca: Cornell University Press.

—— 1997a. Discourse on the sciences and arts (first discourse). In *The Discourses and Other Early Political Writings*, pp. 1–28. Cambridge: Cambridge University Press.

—— 1997b. Preface to Narcissus. In *The Discourses and Other Early Political Writings*, pp. 92–106. Cambridge: Cambridge University Press.

—— 2009. Considerations on the government of Poland and on its projected reformation. In *The Social Contract and Other Later Political Writings*, pp. 177–260. Cambridge: Cambridge University Press.

Rovelli, M. 2006. *Lager italiani*. Milan: BUR.

Roy, O. 2010. *Holy Ignorance: When Religion and Culture Part Ways*. Columbia: Columbia University Press.

—— 2011. The new markets of religion. http://www.resetdoc.org/story/00000021515 (accessed 18 September 2011).

Rubinstein, N. 1987. The history of the word *politicus* in early modern Europe. In A. Pagden, ed., *The Languages of Political Theory in Early-Modern Europe*, pp. 41–57. Cambridge: Cambridge University Press.

Runciman, D. 2000. Debate: What kind of person is Hobbes's state? A reply to Skinner. *Journal of Political Philosophy* 8:268–278.

Rundell, J. 1994a. Creativity and judgment: Kant on reason and imagination. In G. Robinson and J. Rundell, eds., *Rethinking Imagination: Culture and Creativity*, pp. 87–117. London: Routledge.

—— 1994b. Introduction. In G. Robinson and J. Rundell, eds., *Rethinking Imagination: Culture and Creativity*, pp. 1–11. London: Routledge.

Said, E. 1978. *Orientalism*. London: Routledge.

Sargent, L., ed. 1981. *Women and Revolution: A Discussion of the Unhappy Marriage of Marxism and Feminism*. Boston: South End.

Sartre, J-P. 1940. *L'imaginaire*. Paris: Gallimard.

Schild, W. 1990. Person-Rechtperson: Rechtpersönlichkeit. In J. Ritter, ed., *Historisches Wörterbuch der Philosophie*, pp. 322–335. Darmstadt: Wissenshaftliche Buchgesellschaft.

Schlegel, F. S., and A. W. Schlegel. 1992. *Athenäum: Eine Zeitschrift von A. W. Schlegel und F. S. Schlegel*. Darmstadt: Wissenschaftliche Buchgesellschaft.

Schmitt, C. 1996. *The Concept of the Political*. Chicago: University of Chicago Press.

—— 2005. *Political Theology: Four Chapters on the Concept of Sovereignty*. Chicago: University of Chicago Press.

Schneewind, J. B. 1998. *The Invention of Autonomy*. Cambridge: Cambridge University Press.

Schofield, M. 1978. Aristotle on the imagination. In G. E. R. Lloyd and G. E. L. Owen, eds., *Proceedings of the Seventh Symposium Aristotelicum*. Cambridge: Cambridge University Press.

Sellin, V. 1978. Politik. In O. Brunner, W. Conze, and R. Koselleck, eds., *Geschichtliche Grundbegriffe*, 4:789-874. Stuttgart: Klett-Cotta.

Semmerling, T. J. 2006. *Evil Arabs in American Popular Films*. Austin: University of Texas Press.

Sepper, D. L. 1989. Descartes and the eclipse of the imagination, 1618-1630. *Journal of the History of Philosophy* 27:379-403.

Shaheen, J. 2001. *Reel Bad Arabs: How Hollywood Vilifies a People*. New York: Olive Branch.

Shoat, E., and R. Stam. 1994. *Unthinking Eurocentrism: Multiculturalism and the Media*. London: Routledge.

Shukaitis, S., and D. Graeber. 2007. *Constituent Imagination: Militant Investigations, Collective Theorisation*. Oakland: AK.

Simpson, J. A., and E. S. C. Weiner, eds. 1989. *The Oxford English Dictionary*. Oxford: Clarendon.

Singer, J. P. 2002. *Imagery in Psychotherapy*. Washington, DC: American Psychological Association.

Skinner, Q. 1999. Hobbes and the artificial person of the state. *Journal of Political Philosophy* 7:1-29.

Smith, K. E. 2005. Re-imagining Castoriadis's psychic monad. *Thesis Eleven* 83:5-14.

Snell, D. C. 2001. *Flight and Freedom in the Ancient Near East*. Boston: Brill.

Starobinski, J. 1988. *Jean-Jacques Rousseau: Transparency and Obstruction*. Chicago: University of Chicago Press.

—— 1993. *Blessing in Disguise; or, The Morality of Evil*. Cambridge: Harvard University Press.

Stavrakakis, Y. 2002. Creativity and its limits: Encounters with social constructionism and the political in Castoriadis and Lacan. *Constellations* 9(2): 522-539.

Steele, M. 2005. *Hiding from History: Politics and Public Imagination*. Ithaca: Cornell University Press.

Sternberger, D. 1991. Il vocabolo politica e il concetto del politico. In *Immagini Enigmatiche dell'Uomo. Saggi di Filosofia e Politica*. Bologna: Il Mulino.

Stirner, M. 1990. *L'unico e la sua proprietà*. Milan: Mursia.

Strange, S. 1996. *The Retreat of the State: The Diffusion of Power in the World Economy*. Cambridge: Cambridge University Press.

Stråth, Bo. 2000. *Myth and Memory in the Construction of Community: Historical Patterns in Europe and Beyond*. New York: Peter Lang.

Stubbs, R., and R. D. Underhill. 1994. *Political Economy and the Changing Global Order*. London: Macmillan.

Sullivan, A. 2001. This is a religious war. *New York Times Magazine*, 7 October, http://www.nytimes.com/2001/10/07/magazine/this-is-a-religious-war.html.

Tarizzo, D. 2009. *Introduzione a Lacan*. Bari: Laterza.

Taylor, C. 1989. *Sources of the Self. The Making of Modern Identity*. Cambridge: Cambridge University Press.

—— 1992. *Multiculturalism and the Politics of Recognition*. Princeton: Princeton University Press.

—— 1995. *Philosophical Arguments*. Cambridge: Harvard University Press.

—— 2004. *Modern Social Imaginaries*. Durham: Duke University Press.

—— 2007. *A Secular Age*. Cambridge: Belknap.

Tripp, C. 2006. *Islam and the Moral Economy: The Challenge of Capitalism*. Cambridge: Cambridge University Press.

Tudor, H. 1972. *Political Myth*. London: Macmillan.

Tye, M. 2000. *The Imagery Debate*. Cambridge: MIT Press.

Urribarri, F. 2002. Castoriadis: The radical imagination and the post-Lacanian unconscious. *Thesis Eleven* 71:40–51.

Van Peer, W. 1995. Literature, imagination, and human rights. *Philosophy and Literature* 19(2): 276–291.

Vattimo, A. 1999a. Estetica. In *Enciclopedia di Filosofia*, pp. 340–345. Milan: Garzanti.

—— 1999b. Immaginazione. In *Enciclopedia di Filosofia*, pp. 528–530. Milan: Garzanti.

Vercellone, C. 2007. From formal subsumption to general intellect: Elements for a Marxist reading of the thesis of cognitive capitalism. *Historical Materialism* 15:13–36.

Vico, G. 1999. *Principi di Scienza Nuova*: Milan: Mondadori.

Viroli, M. 1992. The evolution in the concept of politics. *Political Theory* 20(3): 473–495.

Vlastos, G. 1965. Degrees of reality in Plato. In R. Bambrough, ed., *New Essays on Plato and Aristotle*. London: Routledge.

Volonté, P. 1997. *Husserl's Phänomenologie der Imagination: Zur Funktion der Phantasie bei der Konstitution von Erkenntnis*. Freiburg: Alber.

Von Savigny, E. 1991. Common behavior of many a kind. In R. L. Arrington and H. J. Glock, eds., *Wittgenstein's Philosophical Investigations: Text and Context*, pp. 105–115. London: Routledge.

Wark, M. 2004. *Hacker Manifesto*. Harvard: Harvard University Press.

Watson, G. 1988. *Phantasia in Classical Thought*. Galway: Galway University Press.

Weber, M. 1978. *Economy and Society*. Berkeley: University of California Press.

—— 2004. *The Vocation Lecture: Science as Vocation, Politics as Vocation*. Indianapolis: Hackett.

White, H. 1973. *Metahistory: The Historical Imagination in Nineteenth-Century Europe*. Baltimore: Johns Hopkins University Press.

—— 1987. *The Content of the Form: Narrative Discourse and Historical Representation*. Baltimore: Johns Hopkins University Press.

Whitebook, J. 1989. Intersubjectivity and the monadic core of the psyche: Habermas and Castoriadis on the unconscious. In G. Busino, ed., *Autonomie et Autotransformation de la Société: La Philosophie Militante de Cornelius Castoriadis*, pp. 225–245. Geneva: Droz.

Williams, R. 1988. *Keywords: A Vocabulary of Culture and Society*. London: Fontana.

Wittgenstein, L. 1922. *Tractatus Logico-Philosophicus*. London: Routledge.

—— 1975. *Philosophical Investigations*. Oxford: Blackwell.

Wunenburger, J. J. 2001. *Imaginaire du politique*. Paris: Ellipses.

—— 2006. La créativité imaginative, le paradigme autopoïétique (E. Kant, G. Bachelard, H. Corbin). In C. Fleury, ed., *Imagination, Imaginaire, Imaginal*, pp. 153–182. Paris: PUF.

Young, R 1990. *White Mythologies. Writing History and the West*. London: Routledge.

Zavala, I. M. 1992. *Colonialism and Culture: Hispanic Modernisms and the Social Imaginary*. Bloomington. Indiana University Press.

Zepf, S. 2007. The relationship between the unconscious and consciousness: A comparison of psychoanalysis and historical materialism. *Psychoanalysis, Culture and Society* 12:105–123.

Žižek, S. 1999a. *Enjoy Your Symptom! Jacques Lacan in Hollywood and Out*. New York: Routledge.

—— 1999b. *The Ticklish Subject: The Absent Centre of Political Ontology*. London: Verso.

—— 2006. *How to Read Lacan*. London: Granta.

Zwicker, J. E. 2006. *Practices of the Sentimental Imagination: Melodrama, the Novel, and the Social Imaginary in Nineteenth-Century Japan*. Cambridge: Harvard University Press.

INDEX

GPSR Authorized Representative: Easy Access System Europe, Mustamäe tee
50, 10621 Tallinn, Estonia, gpsr.requests@easproject.com